# On Performatics

ISSUE EDITORS: RICHARD GOUGH & GRZEGORZ ZIÓŁKOWSKI

1 Editorial: On Performatics
RICHARD GOUGH
& GRZEGORZ ZIÓŁKOWSKI

8 Towards an Anthropology of Performance(s)
LESZEK KOLANKIEWICZ

26 The Performative Matrix: *Alladeen* and Disorientalism
JON MCKENZIE

39 My Performatics
TOMASZ KUBIKOWSKI

47 The Ceramic Age: Things Hidden Since the Foundation of Performance Studies
ALAN READ

60 Song from Beyond the Dark
DARIUSZ KOSIŃSKI

80 Surrogate Stages: Theatre, Performance and the Challenge of New Media
CHRISTOPHER BALME

93 A Debate between Włodzimierz Staniewski and Leszek Kolankiewicz, led by Grzegorz Ziółkowski

111 The Key to All Locks: Conversation between Wojciech Dudzik, Dariusz Kosiński, Tomasz Kubikowski, Małgorzata Leyko and Dobrochna Ratajczakowa

123 Back of Beyond
RICHARD GOUGH

139 Raft and Mooring
DARIUSZ KOSIŃSKI

149 Notes on Contributors

**DEFINITIONS**

7 LYNETTE HUNTER
25 PAUL ALLAIN
25 RUDI LAERMANS
37 MARIA M. DELGADO
& CARIDAD SVICH
46 ENZO COZZI
59 FREDDIE ROKEM
76 JOHANNES BIRRINGER
92 FLORIAN FEIGL
110 KAROLINE GRITZNER
121 PAUL RAE
137 DAN WATT
138 PETER HULTON
146 ANA VUJANOVIĆ
147 STEPHEN BOTTOMS

# Forthcoming Issues

## Congregation
Vol.13 No.3

Congregation brings together writings about performance and religious practice – suggesting in its title a space in which voices gather. The question that Congregation asks is a simple one – how might looking at religion through the lens of performance, that is, through practice rather than belief, illuminate and better inform some of the ways we think about religion? At a time when religion has once again entered the public arena as a divisive and contentious subject, Congregation addresses the religious imagination – exploring how religious practice informs artistic practice. The issue covers a broad territory and many religious traditions, artistic and scholarly approaches, levels of engagement with religious practice and reflections on art, artists, pasts and futures.

## on Appearance
Vol.13 No.4

Beginning from the conviction that appearance matters – and matters as the very 'stuff' and substance of the kind of things we call performance – this issue examines the materiality of appearance as a key component of theatrical and social events. Exploring the role appearance plays in a range of cultural forms – from body art to live TV, shamanic invocation to video installation, magic show to 'non-professional' performance – *On Appearance* charts the construction, circulation and contestation of some of the imagined possibilities, lived realities, political identifications, and performative opportunities opened up by thinking through the logic of appearance. As well as examining the correlation between modes of appearance and practices of disappearance, and investigating their inscription in the recuperative dynamics of power, *On Appearance* explicates the ways in which appearance matters in affecting and positively producing the conditions, forms and relations structuring what Jacques Rancière calls 'the distribution of the sensible': the political organisation of sense-making activities within the intelligible framework of the visible.

# Submissions

*Performance Research* welcomes responses to the ideas and issues it raises. Submissions and proposals do not have to relate to issue themes. We actively seek submission in any area of performance research, practice and scholarship from artists, scholars, curators and critics. As well as substantial essays, interview, reviews and documentation we welcome proposals using visual, graphic and photographic forms, including photo essays and original artwork which extend possibilities for the visual page. We are also interested in proposals for collaborations between artists and critics. *Performance Research* welcomes submissions in other languages and encourages work which challenges boundaries between disciplines and media. Further information on submissions and the work of the journal is available at: http://www.performance-research.net or by e-mail from: performance-research@aber.ac.uk

All editorial enquiries should be directed to the journal administrator: Sandra Laureri, *Performance Research*, Centre for Performance Research, The Foundry – Penglais Campus, Aberystwyth, Ceredigion, SY23 3AJ, UK. Tel: +44(0)1970 628716; Fax: +44(0)1970 622132.

e-mail: performance-research@aber.ac.uk

www: http://performance-research.net

ISSN 1352-8165

Copyright © 2008 Taylor & Francis. All rights reserved. No part of this publication may be reproduced, stored, transmitted, or disseminated, in any form, or by any means, without prior written permission from Taylor & Francis Limited, to whom all requests to reproduce copyright material should be directed, in writing. Taylor & Francis Limited grants authorization for individuals to photocopy copyright material for private research use, on the sole basis that requests for such use are referred directly to the requestor's local Reproduction Rights Organization (RRO). The copyright fee is $25 exclusive of any charge or fee levied. In order to contact your local RRO, please contact: International Federation of Reproduction Rights Organizations (IFRRO), rue du Prince Royal, 87, B-1050 Brussels, Belgium; email: IPPRO@skynet.be; Copyright Clearance Center Inc., 222 Rosewood Drive, Danvers, MA 01923, USA; email: info@copyright.com; Copyright Licensing Agency, 90 Tottenham Court Road, London, W1P 0LP, UK; email: cla@cla.co.uk. This authorization does not extend to any other kind of copying, by any means, in any form, and for any purpose other than private research use.

Typeset at The Design Stage, Cardiff Bay, Wales, UK and printed in the UK on acid-free paper by Bell & Bain, Glasgow.

Abstracting & Indexing services: *Performance Research* is currently noted in *Arts and Humanities Citation Index*, *Current Contents/Arts & Humanities* and *ISI Alerting Services*.

# Editorial
## On Performatics

RICHARD GOUGH & GRZEGORZ ZIÓŁKOWSKI

In December 2006 the Grotowski Centre in Wrocław, Poland, hosted an international conference entitled *Performance Studies and Beyond*. The event celebrated the translation and publication of Richard Schechner's textbook *Performance Studies: An Introduction*, but the conference hosts and conveners were keen to think beyond the North American schools of performance studies and seek relevance and application for the term (and field) within the advanced and sophisticated modes of theatre studies in Poland.

The conference was organized by the Centre directors Jarosław Fret and Grzegorz Ziółkowski together with Tomasz Kubikowski from Warsaw Theatre Academy with help from Adam Mickiewicz Institute. It not only created a space for dialogue on approaches to theatre and research, which were part of the Grotowski Centre's mission from its very beginning (to examine in theory and in practice intersections between theatre and cultural research)[1] but also marked the Centre's transformation into an Institute. In fact, the conference was the final public event co-organized by the Grotowski Centre before it became Instytut im. Jerzego Grotowskiego.[2] The significance of the transformation is an acknowledged policy shift to initiating and stimulating growth in a young generation of artists with an emphasis on being an active and *living* site/place functioning with purpose and vitality in contemporary Polish culture. The interdependence of conducting research and sharing it through transmission processes and artistic projects guided the curation of the event and paralleled the way of thinking promoted by the guests gathered at the conference.

The translator of Schechner's book, *Performance Studies*, Tomasz Kubikowski, proposed the term *Performatyka* for the broad field of performance studies and this was adopted for the title of the book and for the greater project behind the conference: to introduce, translate, adopt and mutate the field of study and speculate upon its development. The Polish title of the conference was *Performatyka: perspektywy rozwojowe*, which can be translated as *Performance Studies: perspectives for development*.

However, in thinking about a journal issue arising from and responding to the conference (and not wanting it to be merely a publication of proceedings), we wondered whether it was more provocative if the literal translation were retained and *Performatyka* were rendered back into English as *Performatics*. What might this term suggest? Does it have the potential to function widely and denote a field of study that might otherwise be captured by an Anglo-American definition (and possibly restrictive terms of reference)? Performance Studies, as a term, is often lost in translation, diffused and confused. What relevance and currency could *Performatics* have? Might it supply an adjective of performance (as an alternative to the over-used and often mis-used performative)?

We hoped this issue of *Performance Research*

[1] Full title: Ośrodek Badań Twórczości Jerzego Grotowskiego i Poszukiwań Teatralno-Kulturowych ['Centre for Studies of Jerzy Grotowski's Work and for Theatrical and Cultural Research'].

[2] The transition from Centre to Institute was formally completed on 28 December 2006. The statute of the renamed institution stressed the need for providing more space for education and artistic activities within the programme of the institution.

could function as an extension of the conference's debates and findings. We especially wanted the journal's pages to help balance the voices of Polish and non-Polish speakers, as, at the conference, Polish theatre scholars and practitioners listened to the representatives of theatre and performance studies from abroad and, even though reflections and counter-opinions were shared and doubts and reservations expressed, the conference was mainly a one-way street. Now, the collaboration on this issue of the journal creates the chance to address and redress this.

Producing an issue of *Performance Research* on the theme *Performatics* also creates the opportunity to make up for the unfortunate absence from the conference of representatives of the Institute of Polish Culture (at Warsaw University) whose contribution to developing and nurturing in Poland a way of looking at theatre as a phenomenon embedded in culture has been particularly significant. It is within the milieu of the Institute of Polish Culture that the milestone textbook *Antropologia widowisk* ['Anthropology of Performances'] was edited and published in 2005. This volume compiles fragments of classical texts by researchers of such diverse disciplines as anthropology, philosophy, sociology and psychology, as well as literature and theatre studies from Poland and abroad in order to create a poly-vocal 'whole' that helps (young) people to understand, or at least to be more aware of, the rapid changes that contemporary culture is undergoing as a result of mediatization and globalization processes. This perspective (approach and methodology) has resonance with Performance Studies - harmonies and dissonance.

We are therefore especially pleased to open this issue with a text by Leszek Kolankiewicz, the director of the Institute of Polish Culture, and for his permission to translate and publish his introduction to the aforementioned volume. The title of his article *Towards an Anthropology of Performance(s)* not only echoes the seminal publication of Jerzy Grotowski, *Towards a Poor Theatre* (Kolankiewicz collaborated closely with Grotowski in the late 1970s and early 1980s), but also stresses interdisciplinarity and extends boundaries. In this way Kolankiewicz's performance anthropology resembles Performance Studies - as he himself acknowledges, while positing that Performance Studies focuses on behavioural patterns and generalizations rather than on differences and types of human actions (such as rituals, games, ceremonies, carnivals) with their innumerable variants - which the Warsaw 'anthropology of performances' does (Pałach 2006: 253).

However, Grotowski's presence in Kolankiewicz's article cannot be reduced to the title only. The Polish director's insistence on an incessant search for what is essential in human beings leaves a question mark hanging in Kolankiewicz's deliberations. The mythical character of trickster that represents what in humans is ever-changing - that which belongs to the realm of social adaptation and remains the subject of the game of history - is counterbalanced, by Kolankiewicz, with another archetypal character rooted in, among others, apocryphal texts from Christian traditions: the 'Standing One', associated with never-changing elements in humans, their essence, core - and the aim of Grotowski's alchemical quest. Therefore, an 'anthropology of performances', as envisaged by Kolankiewicz and his colleagues, seems to owe as much to Victor Turner as to Jerzy Grotowski and on the deeper level tries to reconcile them.

From the perspective of Polish theatre studies we then shift to the ever-broadening field of North American performance studies. Foregrounding 'problems' arising from speaking in English and the global role of English as a language in many disciplines - and mindful that his lecture was being simultaneously interpreted into Polish - Jon McKenzie proposes a 'performative matrix' that he believes will become more evident in years to come. Starting from The Builders Association / motoroti production *Alladeen*,[3] he enquires about the

---

[3] This is another example of the multimedia and intermedial work described by Christopher Balme and which further explores the phenomenon of call centres in India (http://www.thebuildersassociation.org/).

relationship between globalization and large-scale multi-media theatre, and then proceeds to focus on economic and cultural globalization, glocalization and strategies for 'localizing globalization'. Then through a reflection on the original concept of the performative matrix (coined by the Critical Art Ensemble) he turns to anti, normative and resistant globalization. McKenzie appositely brought to the conference and brings to this discussion his broad view of performance and the inter-layering of performance paradigms from business and economics: organizational, technological and governmental (which have relevance and significance for new Polish realities). The text of this lecture advances issues that readers may well be familiar with from his book *Perform or Else*, but here, through insightful analysis of the production *Alladeen* and the implications surrounding globalization/glocalization, the project is advanced.

As mentioned earlier, the conference was co-organized by Tomasz Kubikowski, the translator of the Polish edition of Richard Schechner's *Performance Studies: An Introduction* (2006) and - more recently - an editor of a Polish adaptation of Marvin Carlson's *Performance: a Critical Introduction* (2007). Kubikowski is also an author of an inspiring book *Reguła Nibelunga* ['The Principle of the Nibelung'] (2004) in which he views theatre in the light of recent research into consciousness. In his text *My Performatics*, which is a reworked version of his Wrocław speech, he allows us a brief glimpse of his many questions and considerations and along the way also manages to throw light onto the dramatic achievements of Shakespeare.

At the centre of his analysis Kubikowski poses a question about the relationship between performative human behaviour and the performative character of our consciousness. Referring to philosopher John Searle, neurobiologist Gerald Edelman, neurologist António Damásio and cognitivist Daniel Dennett, Kubikowski states that the attitude the mind adopts in front of the world is not of a cognitive nature but of a dramatic one. As Małgorzata Szpakowska writes in her review of Kubikowski's book: 'the mind does not contemplate reality but enters into interactions with it, and from this clash draws conclusions, sometimes adding a layer of words' (Szpakowska 2007: 161).

Alan Read takes a long view and places performance studies on a grander timeline than it is usually accustomed to. In thinking about 'yesterday' he jumps backwards 40,000 years to the Stone Age and then works forward towards today via the Ceramic Age. Skilfully grafting homespun analects of his children at play, with developments in critical theory, philosophy and ethics, Read spins the tail of Performatics and appeals to the voluminous void that lurks beneath the stage of theatre as a space of subterfuge and subversion with the potential to disturb and trouble studies of performance.

We decided also to include here the debate between the iconoclastic artist Włodzimierz Staniewski - the leader of Gardzienice Theatre Association (and an equally distinguished scholar) - and Leszek Kolankiewicz, a debate moderated by Grzegorz Ziółkowski during the conference that the Grotowski Centre co-organized in November 2004, two years prior to the *Performatyka* meeting. We recommend reading this stimulating material alongside Dariusz Kosiński's text on Theatre ZAR's *Gospels of Childhood*, as both articles focus on theatre undertakings - the process and productions of Gardzienice and ZAR. Both companies exceed achievement merely within the aesthetic field and express an artistic ethos in which the performances are seemingly only a tip of an iceberg where the bigger part - research, including field expeditions to the borders of European and Christian dominions (as well as training encompassing voice, body, breath and rhythm) - remains hidden or at least less visible, while being no less important.

But what Jarosław Fret, the director of ZAR, who worked in Gardzienice for a short period, learned from Staniewski cannot be reduced only to an understanding of art as a transformative practice. Fret's work with ancient polyphonic musical structures, found amongst such diverse cultures as Georgian, Bulgarian, Sardinian and Corsican, resembles Staniewski's earlier findings inasmuch as the younger artist sees the indispensability of creating a special and particular environment for his work, grounding it in personal experiences and memories and by doing so bringing the spirit of Polish romanticism back to life. Both Gardzienice and ZAR are process- not product-oriented, both base their work on deep research into musical universes, translated into transformative practices, both try to help us to hear not just to listen. And, last but not least, both attempt to discover what the song can do with the singers rather than what the singers can do with the song.

The essential difference between Staniewski and Fret is that the former focuses more and more on ancient Greece with Dionysius as a central character, while the latter questions our Christian heritage and roots, and this, inevitably, brings him closer to Grotowski. But on the deeper level Staniewski's and Fret's paths meet, since in their artistic practices they research performance *displacement* (namely, performance's place in a complex net of practices no less important than performance itself) and use performance as research into humankind's concordance with the earth. Therefore in both these texts we find a similar dialogic operation at play, with Kolankiewicz and Kubikowski presenting their scholarly positions and with Staniewski and Fret (in Kosiński's understanding of it) advocating for their artistic choices.

Christopher Balme provocatively enquires into the relationship between performance and new media and the questions that arise from innovative formations, alliances and mergers across forms - ranging from the resonant image of Proust listening to 'live' concerts in his cork-lined room via the theatrophone to the work of Rimini Protokoll and their city tour of Berlin (via mobile phone and call centre) Call Cutta (to which at the conference Heiner Goebbels also made reference). At another end of the performance spectrum from Theatr ZAR's physical and choral presence, Balme's article focuses on how new technologies, both visual and acoustic, mediate the theatrical experience and indicates this as a significant and dominant area of contemporary practice (if not of the mainstream itself or of theatre studies). Through the precise optic of German Theatre Studies, which evidently embraces some of the territorial claims of Performance Studies (or rather recognizes no such borders between theatre and performance), Balme cogently argues that these developments between performance and new technologies have major disciplinary implications.

Four months after the conference a gathering of Polish scholars and researchers was convened to consider the aftermath, impact and implications of the event (together with the book launch). This included Wojciech Dudzik, Dariusz Kosiński, Tomasz Kubikowski, Małgorzata Leyko and Dobrochna Ratajczakowa. The conversation *The Key to All Locks*, translated here for *Performance Research*, was hosted by *Dialog* (a monthly journal) and appeared in its July-August 2007 issue supplementing translations of Marvin Carlson's and Jon McKenzie's Wrocław papers.[4] By doing so, the Warsaw journal affirmed its special position in bringing to Polish readers new thought and research into theatre and performativity. Dariusz Kosiński, who led the dialogue and wrote the review (*Raft and Mooring* included later), rightly accentuated Alan Read's statement expressed in Wrocław that what *performatyka* will become in Poland depends on what Polish praxis does with it. For English readers this transcript of the conversation may provide a mix of hesitation, reluctance, hope and anxiety expressed by Polish scholars in the face of the new phenomena storming the gates. Dobrochna Ratajczakowa's warm welcoming words have a particular resonance:

> In the past a disastrous thing occurred in Polish theatre studies: we neglected phenomenology, which would have opened various doors - to

4 Two more speeches, by Phillip Zarrilli and Christopher Balme, were published in *Dialog*'s December 2007 issue.

structuralism, semiotics, communication theory. That is why we should not reject Performance Studies, as it may constitute a real opportunity for our research.

Ratajczakowa's statements have, to use a Polish expression, a 'second bottom', that is, a hidden meaning, as they are in fact an expression of belief in the strength of Polish culture (and also in the power of the academic milieu) which aims to and is able to digest and adapt to its needs, foreign, or even alien, solutions and findings.

Richard Gough staged a peformative lecture interleaving texts with images and structuring the presentation around the exposition and explication of a selection of books - a library of longing. The edited transcript reproduced here functions as a collector's confessional, weaving autobiographical doubt with institutional aspiration, hopes for developments between the academy and the profession with fears about an incipient and corrosive de-lamination of theory and practice. The patchwork of texts and images are re-worked here as artists pages in an attempt to evoke the 'live' and resist (avoid) the conventional academic presentation.

Our selection of material arising from the conference concludes with a review by Dariusz Kosiński of both the translated work of Richard Schechner (*Performatyka: wstęp*) and the conference itself. This appeared several months after the event in *Didaskalia*. Although this may appear to be a reflection within a reflection (*mise en abîme / droste effect*), we feel it is a useful conclusion to convey to readers of this journal the reception of the conference (and book) within the Polish context. Partly due to wishing to redress the balance of Polish voices (texts) within the conversations about performatics/performatyka, we have not included all the papers and presentations that were made at the Wrocław conference (also some of these pre-existed or have now been published elsewhere), but we publish below the full conference schedule (poster) so readers can see the range of distinguished guests who were present and so other material relating to this theme can be searched. We would however, like to thank the other conference contributors whose papers could not be included here but who inspired us through their presentations and remarks at the conference: Marvin Carlson, Heiner Goebbels, Patrice Pavis, Janelle Reinelt, Richard Schechner and Phillip Zarrilli, and all the assembled delegates.

In addition to the material springing from the conference proceedings together with the substantial sections from Polish scholars and practitioners that were gathered after the event and in response to it, we felt it necessary to expand the debate further and to speculate upon what currency (if any) performatics might have as a term. We are therefore especially pleased to have received a range of 'definitions' for performatics - provocations, interpretations, misapprehensions; some playful, some outraged, many illuminating and all engaging with the problematic of performatics with perspicacity. We are greatly indebted to this diverse group of scholars and practitioners, whose texts are distributed throughout these pages, who responded to the invitation partially reproduced on page 7.

The final line inviting a consideration of the term *Performatics* 'its potential, efficacy and limitations and more generally the current state of ideas and practices in the field of contemporary performance research' may also be addressed to you, the reader of these pages. We hope that, with the material gathered at the conference together with Polish scholars expressing a whole array of reactions to Performance Studies and Performatics, the debates may continue.

**Richard Gough and Grzegorz Ziółkowski**

REFERENCES

Pałach, Joanna (2006) 'Interesują nas ośrodki społecznego wrzenia' ['We are interested in the centres of social turmoil'] in conversation with Leszek Kolankiewicz, *Dialog* 5-6.

Szpakowska, Małgorzata (2007) 'Teatr i mózg' ['Theatre and Brain'] *Dialog* 7-8.

COLLABORATION AND ACKNOWLEDGEMENTS

This issue of Performance Research arises from a major collaboration between the Centre for Performance Research and the Grotowski Institute, which will see co-curated research programmes, performance presentations in both Wales and Poland and a series of key Polish theatre scholarship translated into English (2008-12). We would like to thank all members of staff from both organizations who have worked on this journal issue both directly and indirectly, but most especially we should like to thank Cathy Piquemal (Research and Publications Officer at CPR) for her industrious and unflagging efforts to oversee the translation and production of all the material.

www.grotowski-institute.art.pl

www.thecpr.org.uk

• Poster and conference programme of *Performatyka: perspektywy rozwojowe . Performance Studies and Beyond*

## A Call for Definitions  *Extracts from a letter of invitation sent in December 2007*

*The thirteenth volume of Performance Research will include a special edition inspired by, arising from and responding to the Performance Studies: and Beyond conference at the Grotowski Centre in December 2006; 13:2 On Performatics will reflect on the impact and efficacy of this term in Poland, today and for the future, and will offer a critical historical perspective together with speculation on its potential currency beyond.*

*I would like to invite you to contribute a short entry to our forthcoming issue of Performance Research On Performatics. In addition to articles, artist pages, dialogues and interviews arising from the conference, we want to include and distribute throughout the issue short entries from practitioners, theorists and activists currently working in the field of contemporary performance arts and research that reflect upon or respond to the term Performatics. The entries may include polemic and manifesto as well as analysis and reflection. They may take the form of dictionary-style entries, letters to readers, images or sets of instructions. I would be delighted if you would contribute a short piece of between 150 and 500 words (no more than a page) on a working definition for or a provocation about Performatics.*

*As Ric Allsopp wrote in the invitation to entries for the Performance Research issue 11:2, "Lexicon": 'the Journal has been putting forward terms as provocations for debate and conversation since 1996. We are interested in discussions of the way words, vocabularies and discourses are changing, through attending to terms that are contested or in flux, and that in their current usage signify some of the preoccupations of the artistic, political and intellectual cultures of which they are a key part'.*

*I very much hope that you will help us to consider this term Performatics, its potential, efficacy and limitations and more generally the current state of ideas and practices in the field of contemporary performance research.*

## Performatics: Making a noun out of an adjective

Performatics: implies 'the science of performance', or knowledge about performance. So far, so good. But there's a sense of distancing, of metadiscursive layers, about the word that's worrying. Feels like the informatics of performance. Performativity, or the rhetoric of performance, insists already on the connection between the performed/performance and the body in its long life of contexts, in its duration.

Performatics: the science of making through form(s), or knowledge about making through form(s). Fine, but forms, shapes, are nothing without material, so the emphasis has to be on 'through' rather than 'form', so it's the science of making through if it's a science at all, 'peractics'? not only a science but a production, sliding into operatics, with its hyperbole and excess.

Performatics: hysterical performance analysis, over the top, exaggerated, schizophrenic, traumatic. The wounded study of performance: wounding, gaps, unclosed rips in the fabric, like looking into the sky at night and seeing the impossible distance in denial.

Performatics: performance that is like itself like dramatics or cinematics are like drama and like cinema but not quite the thing itself, liking or perhaps not liking it performance becomes performatic.

Performatics: performance that has become its own extension into the axiom(atic), the dark sub-roof attic area of Greek suffixes and prefixes and fixes on culture that make it all fit, the automatic, dogmatic, this is how we know, this is how you know, this is how everyone should know.

Performatics: the temple of performance, fanatical structures precluding ecstasy, stuck in the ecstatic/static, emblematic process, symptomatic of the stasis but not the presence of stillness.

Performatics: to seek always for the charisma, the enigma, the stigma and soma, the demos under cractic rule always eluding the descriptive, the script that guts it of the body.

Performatics in English is tied to the machine, but in other languages it's more fluid, and why should English exercise a phatic imperialism.

But it's still making a noun out of an adjective, displacing the description of the thing into the thing itself.

Will it breathe there?
Will i breathe there?

**LYNETTE HUNTER**

# Towards an Anthropology of Performance(s)

LESZEK KOLANKIEWICZ

1

The metaphor of the world as theatre, repeated over the centuries by orators and writers, has become a topos - a common motif - in European literature, under the name *theatrum mundi*. Writers developed a liking for it during the baroque period in particular, at a time when drama and theatre were in full bloom. From this period originates perhaps its most famous, even trite, formulation - the Latin inscription from the emblem of London's Globe Theatre (built in 1599 for the company in which Shakespeare had a stake and for whom he was also the principal playwright): *Totus mundus agit histrionem*. The whole world acts a comedy.

According to Ernst Robert Curtius, the author of this motto must have been inspired by a recent reissue (1595) of *Polycraticus* by the medieval humanist, John of Salisbury: *totus mundus iuxta Petronium exerceat histrionem* (1990: 140-1). In fact, as can be seen, the phrases differ only slightly: the verb *exercere* (to perform) replacing *agere* (to act, to play), and the source is given 'after Petronius'. Only a little earlier (1588), Petronius's adage had been cited by Montaigne after Justus Lipsius, a philologist and contemporary of Petronius - although with a different but more or less equivalent adjective (*universus* instead of *totus*): *Mundus universus exercet histrionem* (Montaigne 1991: 1143).

The author of *The Essays* employed this topos within his moral philosophy. Montaigne correctly interpreted the Latin word *histrio*, which means 'actor', although sometimes with pejorative connotations, implying a second-rate actor, a clown, a fool, or - metaphorically - any kind of 'poseur'. And he stated that the majority of human activities and occupations - from undertaking a simple craft, through taking office, to wearing a crown - by their very nature are characterized by histrionics. The roles we are given always need to be performed in the proper way. But one should not forget that these are only roles, imposed and assumed, which constitute something like a separate, foreign person - they are only masks, not the true essence of a human being. And one should not allow one's duties to transform oneself internally, or, as Montaigne puts it, to 'puff up' or 'inflate' one's soul (1991: 1144). (In modern times, in *The Marriage*, Gombrowicz comes to call this acquisition of significance 'inflation' - and depth psychology defines it as inflation of the ego). A decent man does not avoid the responsibilities of his office, but also - the moralist warned, sneeringly - neither does he puff up and inflate himself right down to his guts and liver, striving to 'uphold his office even on the lavatory seat' (Montaigne 1991: 1144). Here we can almost hear the Shakespearian definition, from *Macbeth*, of life as a poor player that struts and frets his hour upon the stage and then is heard no more. It is known that Shakespeare read Montaigne and that *The Essays* was supposedly the book upon which another character, Hamlet, meditated. Coming from the mouth of the defeated Macbeth, the topos loses its moralistic overtones and takes the shape of a tragic recognition. But this recognition, as distinct from *anagnorisis* in Greek tragedy, does not lead to *katharsis*, because – as Jan Kott suggested – it is a recognition of the absurdity of the world and the absurdity of the human condition. (The author of *Shakespeare Our Contemporary* read *Macbeth*, along with *King Lear*, as if these tragedies were already an interpretation of existentialism, and similar to Beckett's plays).

Even Shakespeare's comedies left a bitter taste. 'All the world's a stage, / And all the men and women merely players.' That is how, in *As You Like It*, a kind of short essay begins in which Jaques, anticipating Hamlet, develops and explains the metaphor of the universal theatre as an expression of the absurdity of existence. Perhaps in this way, in this comedy – of 1599 or the first half of 1600 – Shakespeare provided his interpretation of the motto of the new Globe Theatre.

Ultimately we do not know exactly what Petronius Arbiter's adage – the source of the motto – looked like. Nevertheless, it harmonizes with the image of daily life in Nero's Rome, as portrayed in the *Satyricon*, which was attributed to Petronius. The *nouveau riche* lifestyle of freedmen, people without tradition and restraints, who become rich through profiteering, might be considered a good example of the posturing of the 'poseur'. According to Erich Auerbach, Petronius's novel 'marks the ultimate limit to which realism attained in antiquity' and almost immediately brings up associations with Thackeray's *Vanity Fair* or Balzac's *The Human Comedy* (Auerbach 1957: 26); except that making a fortune and spending it, as an image of the changeability of human existence, was not depicted here within a social and economical background [Auerbach writes 'within its economic and political context'] as in the nineteenth-century novel, but in accordance with the mythical imagination of the times (1957: 26-7). Shortly before, in Octavian Augustus's times, Ovid had expressed an old philosophical thought about the perpetual and unavoidable transformation of everything – even the gods – by drawing on mythical sources in his *Metamorphoses*. And from the myth of blind Fortune at the helm of human life came a dynamic interpretation of the fate of humanity: beings subject to ceaseless changes, the unfavourable consequences of which might be avoided, according to the Romans, by ritus – rites carried out with superstitious scrupulousness at every turn. (Fellini, in his free adaptation of Petronius's romance, deprived the various twists of fate and the sequence of events in general of their everyday logic, in such a way that the actions of the characters in his film became dark rituals, as if they were acting out a myth with an obsolete meaning – as in the theatre of cruelty depicted in Artaud's writings.) Formalistic, obsessive ritualism on the one hand and morals left in tatters by *cabotinage* on the other may have prompted this line of thought regarding the theatricality of human life.

This perspective was repeatedly formulated in Rome by the Neo-Stoics, in the time of the Principate. It appears in the *Moral Letters to Lucilius* by Seneca – philosopher and advisor to Nero – and in Epictetus of Hierapolis's *Handbook (of Stoic Ethics)*, as recorded by his disciple, Flavius Arrian. A man is an actor in a performance that he did not create, in which he enacts a part that he did not choose: one's role is short, another's long; one is a monarch, another a beggar – all that is needed, according to Epictetus, is to perform the given role to the best of one's abilities. The Stoics may have derived this comparison of a man to an actor from the Cynics, for whom the figure of the 'mime of life' – *humanae vitae mimus*, in a later phrase of Seneca's – became a recurrent stylistic trope. Supposedly, at the hour of his death – this scene from Suetonius will return on several occasions in Pascal Quignard's writings – Octavian Augustus repeatedly asked if he had acted the farce of his life (*mimum vitae*) well, and requested a last ovation from those gathered around his deathbed.

One could trace the history of the theatrical metaphor in its various formulations both backwards and forwards from this point (Curtius 1990: 139-42). Backwards - to Plato, who in *Philebus* put words about the tragedy and comedy of life into the mouth of Socrates; forwards - to the Fathers of the Church: Clement of Alexandria, who will speak about the theatre of the whole universe, or Saint Augustine, who will call life the comedy of the human species. John of Salisbury will say the same - that human life on earth is a comedy - adding that the spectator in this theatre of life is God. When, later, Luther referred to history as *Spiel Gottes* - 'God's play' - he deemed God something more than a mere spectator to this play. In fact, this bold phrase had its own history already: one can hear an echo of the words of Bishop Synesius of Cyrene, and of Plato (late, in the *Laws*) - *theou paignion* (God's plaything) and a toy or puppet in the hands of the gods, respectively.

The theatrical metaphor was revitalized during the Renaissance, principally by Erasmus of Rotterdam. It recurs later in literature, particularly drama, and more and more frequently within the theatre itself. *Le monde est un théâtre, et les hommes acteurs* - the world is a theatre, and the people actors - Ronsard wrote this on the occasion of a carnival ball in 1564, several decades before Shakespeare; and he added, almost out of necessity, that Fortune manages the stage of human life and that the heavens are the spectators in this theatre. In the literature of the Spanish Golden Age, the theatrical metaphor will be used so often that there and then it will become a topos. When Don Quixote (in the second part of Cervantes's novel from 1615) compares the life of this world to a comedy and its people to actors, Sancho Panza does not deny that the comparison is splendid, but he adds that it is not new at all, that he has heard it numerous times before (Cervantes 1998: 537-8). It was familiar from the sermons of the time, which attacked the deepening decadence of Spanish society (later compared by Montesquieu to that of the Romans) that appears in the picaresque novel of Mateo Alemán and in Lope de Vega's comedies.

But the most famous - and perhaps semantically richest - formulation of the theatrical metaphor will appear in Calderón's play of 1635, *Life is a Dream*, and in his philosophical and theological auto of the same year, or slightly earlier, *The Great Theatre of the World*.

The world is a great theatre, of everything in Creation, where people - transformed into actors - play their roles. Life is as brief as a part in a performance - from the entrance to the exit: from the cradle to the coffin. Man is born, plays his part - always too short - and dies. But on the universal stage no one chooses their role: rich or poor, king or peasant - a task is given (along with costumes and props) from which there is no escape, and which must be performed well, without prior knowledge of the script, without a single rehearsal. But roles are not important: after the performance is completed everyone returns their costumes, becoming equal in death. Life is just a play, the world is a place of delusion - according to Calderón. If his *auto sacramental* can still speak to audiences today, after existentialism and the theatre of the absurd, it is thanks to its concept of the world as a bleak playground.

The play *Life is a Dream* deepens this vision. Life is a dream in which a king dreams himself a king, a beggar dreams himself a beggar, even a martyr only dreams his martyrdom; and these dreams are dreamed - another level of the metaphor - by shadows imprisoned in the world. It is these dreams upon which *el gran teatro del mundo*, in which Fortune plots her cruel tragedies, is built. Life is madness, illusion, nothingness.

Previously only Shakespeare had drawn such deep significance from the theatrical metaphor. In *Macbeth* he called life a tale told by an idiot, full of sound and fury, signifying nothing, and in *The Tempest* he described people as the stuff of dreams, elusive visions, shadows of a performance that will disappear into nothingness. With *The Tempest* (1611), Shakespeare departed from the theatre. (In

*Everything and Nothing* Borges will add, in the spirit of our time, that Shakespeare, too, who dreamed so many people in his works, was himself only God's dream, and no one was in him ("*Nadie hubo en él*", Borges 1974: 181). This is already a far cry from the flat, moralistic interpretations of this metaphor - moving towards cosmogony and ontology. It brings associations with the Orient: Islam and - farther and earlier - Hinduism. In *The Qur'ān*, a phrase recurs that the life of this world is an illusory pleasure or a vain decoration - only play, or a game.[1] The Sanskrit notion of *līlā* signifies any kind of game or play, and in the context of cosmogony - the games of the gods. The cosmic performance of Śiva, the one who is called Nataraja, the king of dancers, and whose lineage can even be traced back to pre-Aryan thought, is such a game. Hence it is no coincidence that he is exceptionally revered in the South of India, where the world of [cultural] performances is so exuberant and varied: Teyyam and Mudiyettu ritual performances, Kudiyattam temple theatre, Krishnanattam theatre, Kathakali theatre - we could name many more. In Hindu doctrine *līlā* is always paired with the celebrated *māyā*, this notion signifying the particularly illusory or fictitious nature of the world.

Incidentally, the Latin noun *illusio* is derived from the verb *illudere*: 'to play, to make fun of someone, to deceive'. *Illusio* belongs to the same family of words as the nouns denoting 'play' and 'game' (*lusio, lusus, ludus - ludi* in the plural: 'performances, games, celebrations') and, metonymically, 'theatre art' - all from the verb *ludere*: 'to play at something, to dance, to have fun, to pretend, to mimic, to perform something, to play a part, to play jokes on someone, to deceive'. Hence, the rough equivalent of the notion of *līlā* would be ludus, and that of *māyā* - *illusio* or *fictio*. The Sanskrit word *māyā* went through a similar semantic evolution as did *fictio*: from 'creation' or 'shaping' to 'delusion, fantasy, appearance, hallucination, magic trick' and, in the end, 'artistic fiction'.

The Hindu notion of *māyā* went through similar changes. Firstly, during the Vedic period, it simply denoted power, the creative potency of the gods. With time, in the Vedantic doctrines, it began to signify their capacity to create an illusory, fictitious reality. The art of conjuring up a performance: when witnessed it appears to be real, then it disappears into nothingness.

Īśvara, the Lord, or personal deity - most often the dancing and miming god Śiva - creates the world like a conjurer, an illusionist. Here, there are no rational or moral preconceptions. There is no pre-written play to be performed, no directing of events. The creations happen spontaneously, as in a dance improvisation. But with his frantic, dizzying dance - described by the South Indian name *ānandatāṇḍava*: 'a terrifying dance of joy' - Śiva first creates the world then sustains its existence, only in order to destroy it in the end. The *ānandatāṇḍava* is a cosmogonic pantomime, a magic trick, a creator's game.

In the *Mahābhārata* - the great Indian epos, often considered the fifth veda - it is said that the creator plays with his creations like a toddler with a toy. Śiva performs the *ānandatāṇḍava* within a burning circle, symbolizing the world and the cyclical nature of existence. He has four arms, which symbolize his power over the four elements from which matter is shaped and over the four corners of the world. In one hand he holds a little drum in the shape of an hourglass, whose inwardly directed spheres symbolize a penis and a vagina at the critical moment before their disconnection - the end of the world and of time. For the world exists in an everlasting cycle of creation and destruction, and the blind fate that rules it corresponds to the play of Śiva and his wife Pārvatī, the personification of its energy as cosmic power. According to the Vedantic doctrine of Śaṅkara, the only purpose and sense behind this creation is this *līlā*, the play of the creator with himself.

The cosmic dance of Śiva is a wonderful spectacle of the divine theatre of cruelty. But it is not only an inhuman and empty game; it also constitutes a necessary sacrifice. The dancing Śiva crushes a prone dwarf with his foot, the

---

[1] See *Al-Qur'ān: A Contemporary Translation*, trans. Ahmed Ali, (Princeton, NJ: Princeton University Press, 2001): 'Know that the life of this world/is only a frolic and mummery, an ornamentation' (Al-Hadid), sura 57, verse 20, p. 471; 'As for the life of this world,/it is nothing but a merchandise of vanity' (*Al-'Imrān*), sura 3, verse 185, p. 70; 'As for the life of this world,/it is nothing but a frolic and frivolity', (*Al-An'ām*), sura 6, verse 32, p. 117; 'The life of this world is only a sport and a play', (*Al-'Ankabut*), sura 29, verse 64, p. 342; 'Verily the life of this world/is no more than a sport and frivolity', (*Muhammad*), sura 47, verse 36, p. 438. As an alternative set of translations, we have also provided the following, more homogenous renderings, as a potential option for the author and editors, from *The Holy Qur'ān: Text, Translation and Commentary*, trans. A. Yusuf Ali, (Brentwood, Maryland: Amana Corp., 1983): 'Know ye (all), that/ The life of this world/Is but play and amusement...', (*Hadid*), sura 57, verse 20, pp. 1503-4; 'For the life of this world/Is but goods and chattels/Of deception' (*Al-i-'Imrān*), sura 3, verse 185, p. 172; 'What is the life of this world/But play and amusement?', (*An'ām*), sura 6, verse 32, p. 297; 'What is the life of this world/ But amusement and play?', ('*Ankabut*), sura 29, verse 64, p. 1047; 'The life of this world/Is but play and amusement', (*Muhammad*), sura 47, verse 36, p. 1387. Trans.

personification of an idle human soul which - having been imprisoned in the world - has forgotten its destiny. Śiva's dance is ambivalent, just like the god himself; he annihilates the world and human beings but at the same time restores the memory of liberation.

Perhaps the metaphor of *theatrum mundi* is always streaked with ambivalence. In actual fact, in order to make this claim, and to view the entire, visible world as the effect of a magic trick - as illusion and nothingness - one does not need to refer to Vedantic treatises, Vedic hymns or the *Mahābhārata*. Similar conceptions can be found in the works of Shakespeare and Calderón and later, in the second part of Goethe's play about Faustus, in which Mephistopheles, as a mystagogue, introduces the alchemist to the art of conjuring the images of other beings. He then tells Faustus of the Mothers. Their domain is emptiness, beyond the whole world of Creation, beyond space and time. From pure forms, from schema - in a play with neither beginning nor end - their 'Eternal Mind' forms and continuously transforms the images of Creation. Images that are perceptible only here, in this world, and which, there, in the domain of the Mothers, disperse as incense smoke (Goethe 1994: 166-8).

In order for this eternal play to continue, occurring on its own and for its own sake, a movement is needed to which Hans-Georg Gadamer will refer as a to-and-fro movement not tied to any specific goal, renewing itself in constant repetition - neither tied to the subject nor to the carrier - the source of all games and all action (2004:103-5). This is also the case for culture, understood in the dynamic sense - as a human or arch-human game or play, a drama. Aristotle says in the *Poetics* that the Dorians described action as *dran* and the Athenians as *prattein* - from the former was supposedly derived the word for 'drama' (*drama*), from the latter, the name for action (*praksis*). The anthropology of performance(s) perceives culture as a dramatic practice.

2

In the last century, the metaphor of the world as theatre recurred so often within the humanities - and eventually in such significant formulations - that by the end of the 1960s a German sociologist, Sir Ralf Dahrendorf, deemed it one of the foremost means of explaining social phenomena. It had become embedded within his field in the 1930s - along with the introduction and broad application of the concept of the social role.

Representatives of various disciplines of knowledge had contributed to this situation. At the end of the nineteenth and beginning of the twentieth centuries, psychology and sociology crossed paths in these endeavours. In contemporary psychology, the self-contained nature of the psyche had been put into question; in sociology, the self-containedness of society. The American psychologist and philosopher William James, advocate and popularizer of pragmatism, noticed that the sense of individual identity was not something isolated and constant but was rather a social self - the product of interactions, of a never-ending, participatory process in which people imagine how they are assessed by others and what might be the expectations of those whose opinion they value. In turn, the German sociologist and theorist of culture Georg Simmel, who formulated the theory of interactionism, became interested not so much in society taken as a whole - unchangeable and schematic - but in social life in all its spontaneity, in the ebb and flow of its intensity, in the dynamic impact of individuals on one another, in the mutual exchange which takes place in all human relationships. Finally, the American sociologist and social psychologist Charles H. Cooley, originator of the concept of primal groups - small, non-formalized social groups such as a family, neighbourhood or peer group - contended that in such groups, living amongst the people closest to them, individuals develop their psychic identities as 'looking-glass selves': reflected, since they refer their own images to the images of them which they ascribe to other people, to whom they are tied by direct relations. In this way, from different angles, these three researchers approached the idea of a 'social role'.

Robert E. Park, the American urban sociologist and founder of the Chicago School, was probably the first to employ this concept in his 1926 article 'Behind Our Masks'. According to his conception, social groups adopt characteristics of the wider society thanks to multiple interactions, in which accommodative processes contribute to the formation of 'Social Organization', and assimilative processes to the formation of culture and its corresponding 'Social Personality'. This personality is associated with the various roles performed by an individual within different groups and different situations and manifests itself in their behaviour or manner, which is adjusted to the prestige and status assigned to each of these roles by society.

In the 1930s and 1940s, further conceptions of 'social role' were constructed and developed by Mead, Znaniecki, Linton and Parsons.

The American social psychologist and philosopher George Herbert Mead, one of the originators of social pragmatism, claimed that individuals do not experience themselves in a direct and immediate manner but that their experience occurs through the internalization of the external viewpoints of other individuals, and hence through the assimilation of group perspectives. This complex process of taking roles bears some resemblance to play, although it is more like a specific game since it involves submission to the rules established by the group as a whole.

Florian Znaniecki, who treated sociology as a science of interaction - of the establishment of contact and co-operation amongst individuals, between individuals and groups and also between groups themselves - developed an analogy to the theatre, and probably his theory of social roles constitutes the most valuable part of his sociological work. According to this theory, social roles, defined as the system of normative relations between an individual and a given social circle, establish the social function of individuals and condition their social selves. In this conception, the personality of an individual is a dynamic synthesis of all of their social roles. (In Poland, Znaniecki's theory was developed further during the 1960s by his student, Jan Szczepański. He remarked that the process of realization of a social role, understood as a relatively constant and coherent system of behaviours consisting of reactions to the behaviour of other people and following a fixed pattern, is dependent on the biological and psychological features of an individual, their personal pattern - a combination of the ideal ways of behaving that functions as the script for a role - on the definition of their role within a group, on the structure and organization of the group, and also on the degree of identification of an individual with the group.)

The American anthropologist of culture Ralph Linton believed that role is a dynamic aspect of status: the cultural patterns of attitudes, values and behaviours connected with the given status and realized in order to confirm entitlement to a particular status. Finally, the American sociologist Talcott Parsons, a leading functionalist, defined role as the link joining an individual - understood as a psychological existent - to the social structure. (He simply called the individuals who act within society 'actors'.)

Later Robert K. Merton, a student of Parsons, remarked that a 'role set', rather than one role, is connected to status: a varied set of social roles that constitute a response to the different expectations of partners regarding the owner of a particular status. These partners, with whom a given individual maintains social relations, were named 'role senders' by Ragnar Rommetveit. Thus, the terminology of the social role evolved alongside these theoretical developments, testifying to its consolidation within the realms of sociology.

This short survey presents the process of absorption and development of the theatrical metaphor by the social sciences. It eventually consolidates its position there in the 1940s. Znaniecki's book, *The Social Role of the Man of Knowledge*, appears in 1940 and Linton's *Concepts of Role and Status* in 1947. When in the mid-1960s Znaniecki's handbook *Social Relations and Social Roles* is posthumously published, containing the most elaborate formulations of his conception of the social role, a co-authored volume, *Role Theory: Concepts and Research*, also appears, whose appended bibliography already contains approximately 1,500 entries.

At the beginning of the 1960s, this rise in quantity leads to a shift in quality. This occurs due to the appearance in 1959 of the extended version of a book by Erving Goffman, *The Presentation of Self in Everyday Life*. Incidentally, this book became a bestseller in the United States, selling over half a million copies – an unprecedented figure – perhaps because the author chose to write it in an accessible way, giving the impression that it was also aimed at the general public. (It is worth mentioning here that Eric Berne's book, *Games People Play: The Psychology of Human Relationships*, published five years later, also became a bestseller. This publication came from another field – depth psychology – although it provides a similar perspective.) The work of Goffman – a student of Herbert Blumer, who developed the theory of symbolic interactionism – will not simply be yet another formulation of the 'social role', but it will introduce what the author calls a 'dramaturgical perspective' to an unprecedented degree within the social sciences, encompassing the whole realm of the sociology of everyday life. And here, precisely, is the point at which a new perspective on the anthropology of performance(s) will open.

This was no longer only about the notion of a 'social role'. With time, it came to be defined as an elementary structure mediating between the individual and society, as the individual's system of interpersonal behaviours when acting within small groups. According to the 'microsociologist' Jacek Szmatka – who synthesized different conceptions of social role at the beginning of the eighties – every small group, however it is structured, creates particular configurations of instrumental roles, which assist those of its activities connected with performing tasks, and of expressive roles, which support internal integration. The point of focus in this theory therefore shifts towards the system, and it is on this side that the social role is located.

Things are conceived differently in Goffman's book (2005). He was not at all interested in roles as elements of a structure or in the entire social system in general. The revolutionary aspect of his vision lay in a shift in the centre of gravity, from the system towards the spontaneous – the unrestrained and unguided – flux of the social world, which he perceived as a multitude of more or less spontaneous interactions. (Thus it was not by chance that this vision was – in some respects, accurately – called a Heraclitusian sociology.) Goffman focused all his efforts on the observation of everyday life and on searching for some regularities within its unstable matter, for an order that is constantly formulated anew. When people meet face-to-face, their behaviour transforms under the gaze that is exchanged between them, into something that Goffman described as a 'performance'. This common English word, which has so many meanings, will go on to have a brilliant career in the humanities. Goffman understood it as the actions of an individual participating in interactions, whose purpose is to create a particular impression on the other participants within these interactions. For the 'I' is only an impression derived by others, a specific 'stage effect', as Goffman calls it – the 'I' is the result of a 'scene' and of a character who has just performed in it, an 'I' as it is ascribed to a person by others, and with which he is inclined to identify. If another identity should lie beneath, as with a mask, then it is only the identity of the performer, the 'I' of an actor caught up in multiple roles, of a worn-out creator of impressions who directs the performance of his 'I'.

Goffman's man in interaction is closely related to the man 'thrown into a situation', as described by the existentialists. It is not far from Genet, or Gombrowicz. In Gombrowicz's *The Marriage*, in the key scene between Henryk and Władzio, Henryk starts to doubt if it is really he who feels or thinks, whether it is he himself who makes decisions - whether he exists at all, in himself. And he is haunted by the suspicion that things are not decided by him, but that decisions are made between himself and others, that what is interpersonal determines and constitutes a human being. The forces that emerge between people - so powerful as to be almost magical, even absolute - can inflate a human being or toss him around like a piece of straw, but they always take him within their possession. People create one another, examining themselves in others as in a mirror, adjusting to each other - condemned to a life of acting, of endlessly playing themselves, for others and for themselves. Gombrowicz named the dominant and determining power of the interpersonal a 'Form'; he wrote this word with a capital letter, as one writes the word 'God'. This peculiar absolute is created between people in every moment, from the very beginning - in the celebrations that they enact, in an incessant, interpersonal, people's mass, as the Drunkard (an arch-Polish Mephistopheles) says in *The Marriage*. For Gombrowicz, Form is artificial and spontaneous all at once: by succumbing to it and by deferring to others within one's interactions, man participates in a celebration of culture for which he is never sufficiently mature, and he allows the collective force which is at work within it and through it to take control over him. A man always remains inauthentic (Gombrowicz 2000).

However, Goffman did not seem to be concerned with the tragedy of inauthenticity. His descriptions and analyses, so similar to those of Gombrowicz, Genet and the existentialists, retain the qualities of descriptions of behaviour, and of sociological analysis. Sociological, because Goffman's interest does not lie - as in the Polish title of his book - in 'man in the theatre of everyday life' but in life itself, comprised of situations in which people attempt to accomplish their performative tasks. He thus does not investigate - as he puts it in his subsequent book, *Interaction Ritual: Essays in Face-to-Face Behavior* - men and their moments, but moments, as they are, and their men (Goffman 2005: 3). And he investigates what it is within these moments, situations or episodes that transforms them into interaction rituals. By performing interaction rituals, people, whether they like it or not, become celebrants of everyday life, or - as Gombrowicz would put it - 'natural actors'. From Goffman's perspective they might be more like conjurors, busying themselves in order to create and sustain the impression of the reliability of their own 'I'. They are also - and have to be - skilled players, cunning tacticians and cautious strategists.

When, at the beginning of the 1980s, Clifford Geertz was reviewing modern configurations of social and cultural thought, he classed Goffman, in an insightful move, as one of the leading representatives of a group that makes use of game analogies . Three dominant approaches are distinguished by Geertz - one that employs the analogy to games, one that is based on analogies to drama and theatre and one that makes use of analogies to text (Geertz 1993: 19-35). In truth, these are not clearly denoted - they overlap; different researchers and theoreticians oscillate between various analogies, sometimes even within the same study. Such is the case with Goffman as well. Because although he resorted to the theatrical metaphor in his analysis of everyday life, developing it extensively, in the face-to-face situations that he investigated, he was less concerned with how these interactions progressed and more with the behaviour of the participants, which proceeded according to a conventionalized, rule-oriented game of expression and impression, of making and receiving impressions - as an intricate and manneristic game of communication, whose participants force their way through it however they can, as in a spy novel: disguising themselves, deceiving one another, using tricks and conspiring in order to realize a winning strategy.

According to Goffman, in everyday life everyone always plays for the same stakes: to create and maintain a credible (to others and to oneself) picture of the 'I' - someone who is, as they say, 'all right', who feels comfortable in their own skin. Some situations take on the form of interaction rituals, which are about collaborating within a 'team' of performers, just as in the celebration of a rite; others take the form of strategic interactions in which a competitive aspect is more evident, as in playing the market. All in all, there is always some agonistic element at work. From this perspective, interactions boil down to a ritualized game of profits, a game in which the participants are restricted by conventionalized and overwhelming rules of behaviour or acting.

Approaching this sociological vision, but from the other side, is Eric Berne's psychological conception - so similar that it could well be considered another outstanding example of the same configuration. According to this American psychiatrist, almost all interactions are transactions in which the purpose is to gain measurable profits: social, psychological and existential; and almost all interactions - from rituals to games - are highly structured. The most complex, and the darkest, games are always dishonest, based on leading the partners on, on ambushing them in order to reap the rewards. Games are ambivalent: on the one hand they structure people's time and guarantee them a certain equilibrium, on the other they ruin lives and turn them into tragic nightmares.

To the characters in Gombrowicz's *The Marriage*, which is so reminiscent of *Hamlet* (although not named after the protagonist), it seems that the only escape from these situations that they find themselves thrown into - it is not known from where or by whom - is to perform various forms of ceremony. Who will be the first to lift a spoon to their mouth, who will kneel before whom, who will preside over whose marriage: the pressure of Form on these people is overwhelming. Thus, in accordance with the formal logic of the situation, Henryk's surge for liberation aims to be realized precisely in this: that he, 'inflated' by the anointment of others, will preside over and officiate at his own marriage. The triumph of Form over will is complete when, as the result of a peripeteia, Henryk is to organize a funeral instead of a marriage - as in a nightmare - and to condemn himself to imprisonment. The game of Form - the cultural drama - appears here as both play and a sacrificial ritual, at the same time.

3
Geertz proposed the anthropologist Victor W. Turner as the leading representative of this modern configuration of social and cultural thought that makes use of the analogy to drama and theatre. Just as Goffman had opened up perspectives on the anthropology of performance in sociology, Turner did so in the field of the anthropology of culture.

Turner became famous for his 1957 study, *Schism and Continuity in an African Society*, which was the outcome of his fieldwork amongst the Ndembu tribe. This work was immediately deemed an important continuation of the work of Max Gluckman and was counted among the greatest achievements of the Manchester school. (In his account of British social anthropology, Adam Kuper considered Turner a member of this school, although the latter published *The Ritual Process* in 1969 and *From Ritual to Theatre: The Human Seriousness of Play* in 1982 - the year before his death - in the United States and had already spent more than ten years there by the time of Kuper's survey (Kuper 1996). One of Turner's last pieces was an article with the characteristic title 'Are There Universals of Performance in Myth, Ritual and Drama?'; after his death a further book, *The Anthropology of Performance*, appeared (1986). Even a quick glance at Turner's work reveals that he was not only the author of an original theory, which in the field of anthropology was called the 'processual approach', but also a pioneer of the anthropology of performance as a new investigative approach.

Richard Schechner, the American neo-avant-garde theatre director, theatre theorist and anthropologist who consistently formulates his ideas under the aegis of the theory and study of performance, has a different approach: initially, in 1977, he published *Essays on Performance Theory*, and recently, in 2002, his work consolidated itself into an academic handbook – *Performance Studies: An Introduction*. Even in the mid-1980s – when he published *Between Theater and Anthropology* – Schechner was still inclined towards the anthropology of performance as a peculiarly theatrical perspective on cultural anthropology; later, however, he spoke in favour of distinguishing performance studies as a separate area of research.

This was probably partly due to the fact that in the international nomenclature 'anthropology of theatre' emerged alongside the somewhat different notion of 'theatre anthropology', making things rather complicated. At the end of the 1970s and the beginning of the 1980s, two neo-avant-garde theatre artists, Jerzy Grotowski and Eugenio Barba, initiated research projects that arose from the interplay between research in the domains of theatre and anthropology: Grotowski commencing a trans-cultural project, Theatre of Sources, in 1978; Barba establishing the International School of Theatre Anthropology (ISTA) in 1979. In the practice of this school, theatre anthropology effectively entails the comparative study of performance techniques – in theatre and dance – and attempts to discover trans-cultural rules on which these techniques are based. It is an anthropological discipline because the pre-expressive basis revealed through this method is defined as common to all theatre cultures. Grotowski in turn – commencing from the aforementioned Theatre of Sources project, through Objective Drama and on to Ritual Arts – focused on investigating ritual from a performative perspective in his work with subsequent international groups but, as he formulated it, beyond differentiation into the various genres of performing arts. This research was incorporated within an institutional frame when, in 1997 – two years before his death – Grotowski received the *Chaire d'Anthropologie théâtrale*, the chair of theatrical anthropology, established especially for him at the Collège de France. He considered ritual to be a general, parent field of and for performative actions, particularly those which held the significant advantage of active, direct cognition and self-cognition.

Thus, even though this research in the domain of theatre anthropology (comparative theatre studies) and the working hypotheses of ritual arts (theatrical anthropology) have contributed to a large degree to the development of the anthropology of performance(s), neither one nor the other matches it exactly. In order to illustrate these differences it is worth returning to Turner's conception.

In his case it all started from a fairly typical ethnological question: how, in the Ndembu tribe, which is a matrilineal community, do men solve the structural problems between brothers-in-law? Since a man is forced to give his sister to the household of her husband, and since it is accepted that his nephew will become his heir, he always ends up trying to take the child from his brother-in-law. In this community this is a source of perpetual conflict, resulting in the gradual destabilization of the society. Turner investigated countless cases of such antagonism in detail, as well as the problem-solving methods established by the various communities. He noticed that when a conflict escalates and the entire social group is faced with the threat of a crisis, they usually resort to a kind of 'tried and tested' performance in which both sides of the conflict are engaged as actors. The efficacy of this remedy is based on collective participation in – and the repeatability of – actions, on re-enacting – but also reliving – always the same ritual structures. Turner named this common route within the social process 'social drama', and derived its scheme from Aristotle's definition of action as the object of mimetic performance in tragedy. (This approach was criticized by his teachers, Raymond Firth and Max Gluckman, and later by Clifford Geertz, who accused Turner's conception of a simplified uniformity: of gathering evidence to prove an already familiar thesis which suggests that the more things change, the more they remain the same. On the other hand, Mary Douglas contrasted his approach with the structuralism of Claude Lévi-Strauss, arguing that Turner's scheme stresses the emotional content of symbols, which are not only re-enacted but also re-lived during performances, thus distinguishing his conception from the arbitrariness posited by structuralist schema and filling it with the contents of real, life dramas.) Turner was indeed interested in the dynamics of social actions within the fluctuating 'matter' of life, in their potential to result in change - from this he creatively developed the notion of *rites de passage*, rites of passage, formulated within ethnography by Arnold van Gennep.

By focusing on rites - and on performances in general - Turner accentuated the collective and organized character of social actions, demonstrating at the same time how the course of the entire, multi-shaped social process progresses according to the rhythm of distinct actions. By referring to Schechner's scheme of an '8' lying on its side (Schechner 1977: 144), which portrays the complex reciprocal interaction between social and aesthetic drama or - in a broader sense - any kind of so-called cultural performance, he showed how the suggestive rhythms of drama penetrate life, temporarily restoring a shaken homeostasis or structural order. Since, as Turner would have it, life consists of conflicts and is a conflict in itself, the dramas re-enacted in cultural performances are well-suited to performing the function of meta-social commentaries, that is - according to Geertz - stories that societies tell themselves about themselves.

Turner's approach was revolutionary: the theatrical metaphor was applied here to the entire spectrum of social life, but - as distinct from Goffman's view - it completely lost its moralist significance. Here, drama and theatre - and cultural performances in general - are the most efficient tools for aiding the regeneration of society, for they accumulate and ignite collective experiences, and by toning down and resolving conflicts they shape social energy. Thanks to them society sees itself as a dynamic whole.

In time Turner broadened his perspective: from ethnographical and ethnological to anthropological. He discovered and indicated the tension between the 'persona' and the 'individual' within individuals taking actions, which, in the field of performance, is expressed by the difference between liminality - a change of status that is key to the scenarios of *rites de passage*, accomplished by the symbolic crossing of a threshold (*limen*) - and liminoid, the inner transformation of the spectator, which is the purpose of a theatrical performance. He traced and described the antagonisms within communities: between society - as a state and as a structure - and *communitas* (participation, community, bond, communing, a feeling of connection, social awareness) - as anti-structure and 'phase'. Finally - at the highest level of generalization, and from a paleoanthropological perspective - in terms of defining our species, he recognized that the range of human actions occurs between two contradictory dynamisms: one that ethologists call ritualization and one that he himself named playfulness; the former is hindering and sublimating, the latter is ludic and subversive - both are culture-forming. This perspective thus escapes the one-sidedness of which the great conceptions of Freud, the discoverer of obsessions and repetition compulsion, and of Huizinga, the eulogist of man as a ludic creature, were accused.

So later, when in *The Future of Ritual* (1993) Schechner came to broaden the definition of ritual - as any kind of dynamic performative system consisting of actions that can be considered as 'restored behaviour' - he emphasized this interdependency between ritual and play at every turn. Schechner's perspective is typical of performance studies. Performativity is a feature of numerous human actions that are performed / carried out in the presence of other people. In fact, every time we deal with a person acting within a group, performativity - to a greater or lesser degree - is evident. Culture is driven by performativity; through performativity the dynamic aspect of culture emerges. Thus, investigating the performative dimension of culture is an investigation of every kind of social situation in which there is direct communication - where recipients of communications are present during the communicative act and react to it immediately and directly.

If we recall the classic definition of Sir Edward B. Tylor - which is repeated by Lévi-Strauss - according to which culture is constituted by knowledge, beliefs, art, morality, law, customs and all the other skills and habits that are acquired by a person as a member of a society (Tylor 1871: 1), we can say that the anthropology of performance(s) would probably not encompass this whole complex of phenomena. All kinds of performative action remain within its field of view: from everyday life to the art of the theatre, from play to ritual. But it focuses its attention on cultural performances. Understood as cultural institutions whose purpose is symbolically to perform (formulate, enact and relive) meta-social commentaries, cultural performances are an important aspect of the functioning of society, because - due to the fact that they are programmed in time and space, that they are organized in ritual, ludic and aesthetic terms and demand immediate and collective participation - they make society focus on actively maintaining and redefining traditions, and on reflecting on social bonds and communication: a reflection that takes place within a form of communication that allows these bonds to be renewed on each occasion.

For the most part, the anthropology of performance(s) perceives a social memory within culture, which is stored in dramatic structures and dynamic regularities of learned and repeated behaviour. Here culture is investigated as a whole through what is most intense in social life, the centre of the festive turmoil - through performances and their dramatic action. In these - and beginning from these - man is revealed in all his being as the subject of anthropological reflection.

In the 1930s, the leading representative of the French school of sociology, Marcel Mauss, sketched in two short papers - one dedicated to techniques of the body (delivered in 1934, published in 1936), the other focusing on the notion of a person and the notion of 'I' (published in 1938) - the outline of an anthropological theory of using the body and of individual identity. The bodily techniques applied and acknowledged by society - any effective actions that are sanctioned by tradition - are taught to individuals through presentation and repetition. In demonstrating and emphasizing the role of social authority in this field - he even wrote of 'taming' and 'drill' - Mauss refuted the idea of the unmediated, 'natural' body, which he considered the primary human tool, and he defined the various ways of using it precisely as functional practices, which involved the characteristic domination of social models over the biological. Later Barba will refer to Mauss's conception in his comparative research of extra-daily body techniques applied in theatre and dance in different performative traditions, as will Grotowski, in searching for the so-called 'objective' ritual techniques that might open the door to cognitive mystic or gnostic acts, and that derive mainly from the practices of ethno-dramatic cults or danced religions. Both one and the other are *opus contra naturam*, action against nature; art in its most elementary form.

Simultaneously with Mauss, in the study *Sex and Temperament in Three Primitive Societies* (1935) the American anthropologist Margaret Mead questioned the link between a person's sex and the features of personality connected to a man's or woman's status. In the New Guinean communities that she investigated - Arapesh and Mundugumor - there was no distinction whatsoever between men and women; in the

Tchambuli community there was, but with the attribution of features such as a war-like spirit, imperiousness and sexual initiative to women, and submissiveness, sensitivity and a certain 'actor's charm' to men. Based on this research, Mead recognized that the difference between the masculine and feminine features of personality is artificial; for her it is only a social illusion, an arbitrary classification that draws individuals into its net as soon as a boy is admonished for being a cry-baby or a girl cautioned not to become a rascal. Gender theorists will in future refer to these cases, and to other conceptions such as that of Mary Douglas, who in her book *Purity and Danger: An Analysis of Concept of Pollution and Taboo* (1966) demonstrated how a society establishes various taboos regarding the allegedly 'natural' body, and how it brings cultural order by arbitrarily interpreting the differences between what is masculine and what is feminine. According to Judith Butler, gender is a performance - a result of the credibility attributed by a social audience to an actor taking part in ritual social dramas; it is not determined by biological sex but rather is, in itself, inauthentic.

Mauss also briefly reminded us how late the category of 'I' was established: the work of Neo-Stoics and Roman lawyers, of Christian thought and finally of Kant and Fichte. Simultaneously, he pointed out that the older, and frequently used notion of a person (*persona*) as a character (*le personnage*) pertains to the social structure and includes name, status and social roles as well as a person's predecessors and their 'mask' - that is to say, particular rituals. *Persona*, understood in this way, is a cycle of events of a ritual nature. As early as 1909, in a book which was to maintain its importance throughout the twentieth century, van Gennep reconstructed a dramatic schema according to which - during *rites de passage* - a society leads an individual through a complete transformation of identity. On the other hand psychoanalysis, which significantly contributed to the breaking of the concept of the monolithic 'I' in psychology, presented *psyche* as a stage on which a drama takes place, where autonomous factors - *Es*, the Id, and *Über-Ich*, the Super-Ego - enter into conflict with the conscious *Ich*, the Ego. According to Carl Gustav Jung, disciple of Freud and dissident within the psychoanalytical movement, the *psyche* [*psukhē*] is comprised of something like numerous different characters, which incidentally are of different genders: the persona, which mediates between a person's 'I' and the external world represents the same gender, whereas the *anima* (for men) or *animus* (for women), represents the opposite gender and mediates between the 'I' and the world of the collective unconscious. From this perspective the *psyche* is seen as a process, a Faustian drama of cognition and alchemical transformation.

Jacques Lacan, originator of the French branch of psychoanalysis, conceived - perhaps like no one else - of the illusory aspect of the subject. In his theory, the subject as an entity is established more according to the imaginary and symbolic order than to that of reality - on some kind of different stage, which is only a mirror image, an illusion. All this subject's cravings are the cravings of the Other, and in this sense the subject is a subject of the Other. But the Other, being a symbolic order - of language, law and culture - is in fact a lack. Admittedly, the subject plots its mythical fantasies of assassinating the Father (God) and castrating the phallic Mother, but only in order to camouflage the fundamental and mysterious fact that the alterity of the Other is in fact a lack. Each subject, each symbol, each ritual comes into being - paradoxically - only because, always and from the very beginning, the Other confirms in it its own absence.

The anthropology of performance(s) investigates what happens precisely on the stage of culture, focusing on the alluring performance of the symbolic order - undiscouraged by the lack or absence that this spectacle was thought to conceal. It recognizes, and manages to comprehend and evaluate the power of illusion.

## 4

Today action is usually associated with cinema. An action movie is not defined in terms of its genre, it spans films of various types: spy movies, gangster movies, crime movies and particularly within the latter category - cop movies. In action movies the most important feature is the action itself - which results from the rapid actions of the characters; it is fast-moving, with sudden twists. Assassination attempts, chases, fights. But nothing deserves the name 'action movie' more than the thriller. The main element of its structure is indeed the action: it is filled with extraordinary, not necessarily motivated events, abundant in threads and twists, and - as a result - it also keeps the audience in suspense. Everything is subordinated to these dynamics: threads that seem to be secondary and to slow down the course of the action in the end appear to contribute to the development of the plot; the protagonist and the other characters are characterized almost exclusively by their actions, in which they demonstrate their cunning, dexterity, reflexes and bravery; any wider presentation of the historical and social background is lacking; and the geographical backdrop - with sudden changes of action, shifting from place to place - is sometimes reminiscent of a series of postcards. The thriller - or novel of a similar type - might well be crime-oriented with the action developing alongside the investigation, which aims to unravel the mystery of the crime; it might be a 'spy story' with conspiratorial motives and attempts at detection; it might be also a - spy or terrorist - thriller with unexpected dangers, a character facing destructive powers alone and a thrilling, never-ending build-up of suspense. But thriller is a broad expression: in other languages it testifies to its genealogy, to its distant original, which was the *novela picaresca* with its adventurous plot (in German *Schelmenroman*) and - the archetypical trickster (*Schelm*) - as the main character; its contemporary incarnation being an intelligence agent.

*The Bourne Identity* by Robert Ludlum, the first part of a best-selling trilogy on the Bourne character, was classified, as were its film adaptations - the original, with Richard Chamberlain, and the latest with Matt Damon - as an 'action thriller'. The thrills that the reader or spectator is to experience are down to a typical 'sensational' plot, allied with a non-typical way of constructing the action.

Bourne is constantly confronted with a mysterious threat, fights for his life, kills - and perseveres in his search. The reader only discovers who Bourne really is in the last few pages - he literally remembers on the last one. But this construction is in agreement with the principles of the art - it is typical of spy and terrorist thrillers, which are indeed often characterized by this structure. But the idea which makes this novel a thriller is unconventional. The title character of *The Bourne Identity*, suffering from post-traumatic amnesia and chased by unidentified murderers, must - in order to restore his memory, to go back to the past - join the action as it progresses. Anamnesis is not achieved here by introspection, as in a psychoanalyst's office, but - quite literally - won back in the world. Recognition is completed only in the course of direct actions, through active participation in the action; thus the man striving for recognition resembles a warrior.

But behind the thought that self-recognition is action, and action self-recognition, the presence of which in the action thriller genre might at first seem surprising, there looms the shape of its immortal literary original. In *King Oedipus*, the main character, as he takes up the investigation to find his father's assassin, does not know that he will find what he is after within himself, when he discovers the truth about who he really is. In *The Bourne Identity*, the main character, searching for the truth about himself, forced to run away from murderers, discovers in himself a killer of terrorists. Sophocles's tragedy, which in fact is a crime mystery, has been considered - ever since Francisque Sarcey - to be the prototypical crime novel. The crime novel adopted the structure of *King Oedipus* (although not the full dimension of its action, as this takes place - as Humphrey D. F. Kitto reminds us - at the same time on a higher, parallel level) and, by multiplying it in countless versions, made this structure into a schema, one easily digestible for an undemanding public. The pleasure of reading a thriller such as *The Bourne Identity*, and also of reading a detective novel (for example, *The Murder of Roger Ackroyd* by Agatha Christie and Umberto Eco's subsequent analysis of it in his Harvard lectures (1998)) is based on all the operations of replacement, shift and turning around, for which the scheme outlined in *King Oedipus* is a prototype. (Lévi-Strauss will further demonstrate that this scheme may be recognized even in a work that belongs to a genre even more distant from tragedy, that is to say in the vaudeville piece *An Italian Straw Hat*, by Eugène Labiche (1988:198-204)).

And schematic about *The Bourne Identity* is the following: the sensational character and the course of events in which fate forces Bourne to participate may obscure the analysis - conducted unobtrusively and without too much ambition - of this man who was suddenly derailed from his normal course. Ever since the injury, Bourne does not feel like himself. This persistent, tiresome distance - towards himself and towards the world - is a source of feelings of alienation. In an unfamiliar and hostile world the character behaves like an alert tracker. He studies objects, he studies others, and he studies his own reactions. His attention is always - as it has to be - directed simultaneously, and with great intensity, towards both the outer and the inner worlds. Because both are a mystery for him, both fill him with fear. Bourne is the sort of man about whom one could say 'he was thrown into a situation'. Forced to take action, he does what the circumstances demand of him, but he does not know why he is doing it and for what purpose. One might call it an experience of uncertainty and impermanence and, perhaps, the absurdity of existence.

Of course, we should not overstate this. The ongoing concerns of the character result rather from criminal threats, from his feelings of abandonment, from his agent's mission. The alarming chaos of events - in accordance with the principles of the genre - finds a straightforward explanation in the structure of the operation, which was premeditated by secret intelligence bureaus. At the end of the day, Bourne is neither Gregor Samsa nor Joseph K., nor Henryk from *The Marriage*.

In his 1972 book *What Do You Do After You Say Hello? The Psychology of Human Destiny*, Eric Berne points out how and why each human being puts in motion a certain script within their life, rooted in children's illusions and encoded within the unconscious: by structuring their time, filling it with rituals, entertainment and games, which reward them with benefits and pleasure, they - unwittingly - move further along the action of this script. Little Red Riding Hood (which was earlier analysed by, amongst others, the neo-psychoanalyst Erich Fromm in his 1951 book *Forgotten Language: An Introduction to the Understanding of Dreams, Fairytales and Myths*) is one such script, and an example used by Berne; there are other fairytales and myths. A fundamentally different interpretation of various fairytales and myths, from the perspective of gender studies, was proposed by Clarissa Pinkola Estés in the book *Women Who Run with the Wolves*, who found in this material the archetype of a Wild Woman. Elsewhere, Jung's disciple, Joseph Campbell, browsing through myths and fairytales was looking for what he called, after Joyce, a 'monomyth' - the singular myth of the hero, recounted in various ways in every culture and epoch. Inspired by the ideas of van Gennep and Jung, in his book *The Hero with a Thousand Faces* (1948), he proposed that the structure of action of a monomythical plot involves the sequence of transitions of a cultural hero over the course of his heroic journey, within which he is subject to two liminal changes. Firstly, in order for him to participate in his new role in social life, and then in order to connect with heaven and the underworld, to find a vertical axis.

It is difficult to judge whether the life of a woman may progress according to the scenarios outlined in the tale of Little Red Riding Hood, or in the myths and fairytales of the Wild Woman; whether the life of a man may progress according to the myth of Oedipus, from which Freud discerned not only the fate of the characters from *Hamlet* and *The Brothers Karamazov*, but also the experience of every male individual; or, generally, whether the lives of men and women may progress according to the monomythical scheme of the adventures of a cultural hero. In any case this is not a fundamental issue. It forms the line of a certain action, in which regularities may be distinguished, and which perhaps deserves to be called a drama.

In *theatrum mundi* a person is an actor, to whom the task falls to play different characters.

Initially, the character who emerges from the lower regions as a blind, demonic force, an obsession or compulsion, the power of destiny, according to Freud. And from there the curse of the oracle strikes us, according to which we all are Oedipus, beings that know who we are but do not know the mystery of our origin. For Freud a person's whole life is an unconscious repetition of childhood events, and the childhood events only the repetition of original patterns.

Within society, a person is forced to become a character, which is given as a social role. Social roles partly stem from our so-called vocations, but mostly they are an inevitable product of social interactions, which is why an individual often perceives them as being enforced: either as a 'mug' fitted to them by others (Gombrowicz 2000), or as a discipline which they impose upon themselves. The development of a character from the performance of social roles occurs over the course of a long-lasting, multi-phased and imperceptible process - almost reminiscent of vegetative processes - which we can regard in short, in accordance with general opinion, as the process of creating a human being as such, since within social roles lie hidden techniques of materializing values that are acknowledged by a given society - and first of all, a skilful means of dealing with biological drives.

Both of these characters are performed by individuals throughout their lives, and thanks to this long-term association, they merge with them. However, they are not inseparable since they exist as schema: one in the biological code, the other within social patterns. In other, less individualized societies than ours, they were placed upon individuals as the mask of an ancestor.

Cultural performances use still further characters - theatrical ones, for instance - behind which there always lies a ritual prototype - the ghosts of the dead. Recalling and embodying these characters is fundamental for collective celebrations of memory. What would a society be without them - and without the performances in which they return?

Myths speak of yet another character, that of the archetype, which exists within the vertical axis of Mystery rituals. It is said that it remains as a deposit in the higher regions, inaccessible to death. It is likely that this character too - or perhaps this is the first - is a product of culture, a higher order of existence. But maybe it stems from culture in a similar way to how a social role - as the ritualization of an aggressive drive - spontaneously grows out of a biological being. According to the Mystical religions, this mythical character is the first true form of man. In Neo-Pythagoreanism, Neo-Platonism, Gnosticism and Hermeticism this figure was called the Standing One. Simon Magus of Samaria, the Faustian prototype, taught of the one who stands high above in uncreated power, the one who stands low in streams of matter, created in the image, and who will stand high above next to this uncreated power when he - having returned - finally becomes an image. (The appellation *hestos* appears in Greek records, a participle of the verb *histanai*, which in the passive voice means 'to be caused to stand, to appear to last, to stop, to be stood upright, to raise oneself up, to ascend'.) In the figure of the Standing One we can discern a reference to the topos of *kinesis akinetos*, a motionless motion, which was applied by philosophers from Plato to Proclus. A man is revealed to be the Standing One in different worlds and times: here, within streams of matter - through action as it develops - and there, in the mythical beginning. In human experience this archetype flashes, paradoxically, only during periods of exceptionally intense action. This action is either prompted, as in ritual, or is sweeping, as in the cataclysm of war. Then the one who is still, in motion - as in Miron Białoszewski's *A Memoir of the Warsaw Uprising* (1991) - squatting in the midst of all-encompassing flight, recalls yet another archetypical figure: an infant or a foetus lying in the womb.

Two mythologems describe human fate. The mythologem of the Trickster depicts humans as cultural heroes, creators and ingenious innovators, immersed in the current of life and capable of changing its course. And the mythologem of the Standing One - capable of freezing time, of nullifying it. In this image the mobility of anthropological inquiry finally comes to a standstill, as within it cultural differences and historical changeability cease.

Translated by Adela Karsznia and Duncan Jamieson

REFERENCE LIST

Ali, Ahmed (2001) *Al-Qur'a̅n: A Contemporary Translation* Princeton, NJ: Princeton University Press.

Auerbach, Erich (1957) *Mimesis: The Representation of Reality in Western Literature*, trans. Willard R. Trask, New York: Doubleday Anchor Books.

Białoszewski, Miron (1991) *A Memoir of the Warsaw Uprising*, trans. and ed. Madeline Levine, Evanston: Northwestern University Press.

Borges, Jorge Luis, (1974) *Obras Completas*, vol. 2, Buenos Aires: Emecé Editores.

Cervantes, Miguel de (1998) *Don Quixote de la Mancha*, trans. Charles Jarvis, Oxford: Oxford University Press.

Curtius, Ernst Robert (1990) *European Literature and the Latin Middle Ages* Princeton: Princeton University Press.

Eco, Umberto (1998) *Six Walks in the Fictional Woods* Cambridge MA: Harvard University Press.

Gadamer, Hans-Georg (2004) *Truth and Method* London: Continuum.

Geertz, Clifford (1993) 'Blurred Genres: The Refiguration of Social Thought', *Local Knowledge: Further Essays in Interpretive Anthropology*, London: Fontana Press.

Goethe, Johann Wolfgang von (1994) *Faust*, trans. Louis MacNeice, London: Continuum.

Goffman, Erving (2005) *Interaction Ritual: Essays in Face-to-Face Behavior*, New Jersey: Aldine Transaction.

Gombrowicz, Witold (1969) *The Marriage*, trans. Louis Iribarne, New York: Grove Press.

Kuper, Adam (1996) *Anthropology and Anthropologists: The Modern British School*, 3rd revised edition, London and New York: Routledge.

Lévi-Strauss, Claude (1988) *The Jealous Potter*, trans. Benedicte Chorier Chicago: University of Chicago Press.

Montaigne, Michel de (1991) *The Complete Essays*, trans. M. A. Screech London: Penguin Classics.

Schechner, Richard (1977) *Essays on Performance Theory*, New York: Drama Book Specialist.

Schechner, Richard (1977) 'Selective Inattention', *Essays on Performance Theory*, New York: Drama Book Specialists, pp. 140-56.

Tylor, Edward B (1871) *Primitive Culture*, Volume 1, London: John Murray.

## Performatyka

Wrocław is 'the meeting place'. Or so the city's slogan announces as I arrive at the airport almost a year on from the 'Performatyka' event. I wonder what Grotowski would have made of such a marketing ploy? For he had another concept of meeting, a word central to his paratheatrical activities that took place in and around this burgeoning city. He was looking for some human essence, for an open encounter between people. Meeting was even the title of one of the paratheatrical programmes – *Spotkanie*. What are we searching for now? Cheap beer, a stag party location? The word may be the same, but a lot has changed in our sense of it and around it. Wrocław – Breslau – Vratislav. Performance – Performatics – Performatyka. But in Poland it's all spectacle – *spektakl*. No wonder Grotowski decided to walk away from the theatre.

Yet as we come together for a Workcenter of Jerzy Grotowski and Thomas Richards conference in the *Apocalypsis* room, where Grotowski left theatre behind and where theatre performance turned into a meeting ground, they are still trying to bury words that are dead and mint new ones. In the Polish translation of *Performance Studies*, even names start to change as they are declined – Barbarze, Peggy, Dianie, the dedication reads – and we're not even on page 1. And if we compare, we see different photographs replacing those too expensive to reproduce in Poland, and those that mean little to the Poles replaced by those that connect more to Polish experiences – including one of mine of Gardzienice Theatre Association (now renamed the Staniewski Centre for Theatre Practices: Gardzienice) in the Ukraine.

Translation is of course not just words. Words change their meaning with time and decline (in Polish), when even names alter. Meetings can become slogans, emptied of their human potential. Yet ironically it is the city that now brands itself with such marketing that also funds international meetings such as 'Performance Studies: and Beyond' and the one I now attend. And ironically, these happen at the very heart of the free market economy, in the Rynek, the market square home of Grotowski.

*Performatyka* – take off your (old) spectacles, wear it on a (new) badge. Is this the future guise of theatre studies in Poland?

**PAUL ALLAIN**

## The Reality of 'Doing Reality'

A performative statement does what it says. If one says 'I promise that I will be in time for dinner this evening', one makes or does a promise. Performative statements thus highlight the reality-creating character of language and, more generally, of discourse.

A theatre or a dance performance does not need to make use of language in order to be performative. Signs of whatever kind can be used in such a way that they have a genuine 'reality effect'. That discursively created and sustained reality is usually observed or framed as a fictitious one. A fictional reality is a reality within Reality, and thus 'not really real'. Yet, the used movements, props or whatever signifiers are real. They (are) matter, even if their materiality disappears in their function of being mere carriers of meaning, transparent messengers without a body.

Performativity equals 'doing reality', creating a reality effect by means of signs or discourse. The performing arts change into performance art when the materiality of this performativity is not negated or repressed but pointed out. When the reality of 'doing reality' matters.

**RUDI LAERMANS**

# The Performative Matrix: *Alladeen* and Disorientalism

JON MCKENZIE

*Lecture given at the Grotowski Centre, Wrocław, Poland, 8 December 2006. Earlier versions of this talk were delivered at Northwestern University, Evanston, Illinois, in August 2006 and at the Volksbühne, Berlin, in February 2005.*

I wish to thank Tomasz Kubikowski and Grzegorz Ziółkowski for inviting me to speak today, and I am honoured to be here at the Grotowski Centre.

The concepts of performance I will discuss today are drawn mainly from my book *Perform or Else*. I realize I am speaking to an audience for whom the English term 'performance' may be new, especially in the multiple senses in which I will be using it, and that translating all of these senses into Polish is very challenging. Indeed, the connections I make may seem arbitrary, but given the global role that English has come to play in such areas as business, science and culture, I believe the matrix I will describe today will become more and more evident in the future, for better and for worse.

I will begin by discussing a multimedia theatre piece called *Alladeen*, which toured worldwide from 2003 to 2005, playing in Chicago in April 2003. *Alladeen* is a collaboration between the US performance company The Builder's Association and the British media art company motiroti. The question I will entertain today is this: *what is the relation of large-scale, multimedia theatre, on the one hand, and globalization, on the other? Alladeen* is a global performance from the very outset: as a collaboration between a US performance group and a British media arts group, it is also a performance about globalization. It focuses on the phenomenon of Indian call centres—specifically, groups of workers in India who handle telephone calls for US businesses, often pretending to be Americans and certainly behaving as if they're conversant with American life and popular culture.

*Alladeen* is very loosely based on the rags-to-riches story of Aladdin, a poor Arab boy who finds an oil lamp, is granted wishes by the genie who lives inside, and then eventually becomes a king. This story is apparently an Orientalist construct, as it first appeared in France in the eighteenth century, and no original Arabic text has been found. The Aladdin narrative, however, plays mostly an allegorical role in the *Alladeen* performance. As the story is mined primarily for the theme of making a wish. In 'Call Span', *Alladeen*'s fictionalized call centre, Indian workers help American callers 'fulfill their wishes' - such as driving to Las Vegas or dealing with a faltering love affair - while also negotiating their own globalized desires - to get rich, to travel, to find a connection with someone else, even if on the other side of the world from India.

The performance is structured into three parts, plus a prologue, and its actions take place in three cities on different continents. The prologue is a short scene on a New York City street. A street defined by a storefront, a bus stop and reflections of passing vehicles - but all of this is achieved not by traditional set and props but by a large-scale computer projection composed right before our eyes. The prologue opens with an empty stage and the words "New York' projected across a large screen, approximately 8 feet tall and 30 feet wide. The words are replaced by rectilinear shapes that move in from left, right, top and bottom, shapes that quickly compose the interior of a music store, with racks of CDs and listening stations. Electronic music accompanies the entrance of a silhouetted customer, who is soon enclosed by more shapes, which compose the store's exterior walls and windows and then album posters and the store's logo and sign: Virgin MegaStore. Reflections of passing cars zip by as the sidewalk takes shape via projections of a mailbox, fire hydrant and hot dog stand, as well as bus stop and 'walk/don't walk' signs.

A young South Asian woman enters stage left, carrying a cup of coffee as she walks quickly while talking on a mobile phone headset. The entire scene's dialogue consists of a series of fast-paced, one-sided phone conversations. Played by Tanya Selvaratnam, the young woman stops centre stage and describes to a close friend her night out singing karaoke in a Chinatown bar – 'I'm a genie in a bottle, baby' – and the two plan to sing karaoke on an upcoming trip to Las Vegas, where the friend has booked a room at the Aladdin Hotel. The young woman then hangs up to call a car rental service, but immediately has difficulty communicating with Monica, the rental agent. Exasperated, she says, 'Don't you speak English? You know, I can't understand a word you're saying. Where are you from?' She quickly hangs up to take an incoming call from her old roommate from Hong Kong, to whom she describes her Las Vegas plans in Chinese, interspersed with English terms, such as 'really good package deal'. As silhouettes of pedestrians pass by or stand awaiting a bus, the young woman again hangs up to take another call, this one from her first friend calling back. She's soon interrupted, however, as a noisy city bus rolls up, entirely filling the projection screen. After the bus pulls away, the young woman exits stage left, describing her attempt to rent a car: 'I don't know where they get these operators from. It's like they don't speak English!'

*Alladeen*'s opening prologue thus confronts us with signature traits of contemporary globalization: a British music store on a New York City street, wireless phone technology,

• © *The Builders Association and motiroti. Photo by Simone Lynne*

multilingual talk of karaoke, Chinatown, London and Las Vegas, as well as the disorienting experience of international call centres. The last act of *Alladeen* also takes place in the West, a London nightclub, and it also emphasizes the effects of globalization. In a final scene, Rizwan Mirza plays a call centre worker whose success takes him to London. There, from a karaoke bar, he makes a late night call to his boss in India, who answers in the morning there. Not only do we see the mixing of leisure and labour activities, we also sense the temporal jolt of the globalized, 24/7 workday.

Sandwiched between the New York and London scenes, the main action of *Alladeen* is set in Bangalore, India. Act 1 takes place in a training session of a call centre where Indian characters sit studying American culture and practicing American English under the watchful eyes and listening ears of an American trainer and an Indian manager. Projected behind them is video of an actual training session, which the Builders and motiroti shot on location in a Bangalore call centre. Throughout this act, the words and gestures of the video-taped workers and on-stage actors sync-up and feedback with each other, creating uncanny effects for the audience. For instance, in one scene, Jasmine Simhalan plays a call centre trainee practicing the names of US cities, which she reads off a list: 'Santa Fe, New Mexico. Albany, New York. Raleigh, North Carolina.' Simultaneously, the audience sees and hears on screen an actual male trainee reading the same list. At one point, the trainers – on-stage and on-screen – reiterate the pronunciation of 'Bismarck, North Dakota', emphasizing where the stress falls in 'Bismarck', with a quick twist of the torso. With comic effect, the on-stage trainee obliges by also twisting her torso when again saying 'Bismarck'.

This scene captures one of the defining themes

acting and recorded training, as well as the content of that training, namely, the learning of American English by Indian call-centre workers. Because its main focus deals with Indian call centres increasingly used by US firms, *Alladeen* engages a number practices associated with economic globalization, in particular, 'outsourcing' or the hiring of an external firm to perform tasks formally done by internal employees. However, because one can outsource locally within one's own country, it is more precise to say that *Alladeen* engages both outsourcing *and* 'off-shoring', the practice of moving jobs to other countries in order to reduce labour costs.

Now although *Alladeen* expressly addresses outsourcing – its own promotional materials stresses this – I want to focus on a related practice of economic globalization, one that explicitly involves cultural globalization. That practice is 'glocalization'. Not globalization but glocalization. Glo*cal*ization is a term often used to describe how goods and services are sold globally through highly localized and culturally-sensitive marketing strategies. A common example is McDonalds's replacement of Ronald

• © The Builders Association and motiroti. Photo by Simone Lynne

of *Alladeen*: the disorienting and uncanny play of proximity and distance, presence and absence, familiarity and strangeness, self and other. While the prologue concentrates on the intimate planning of a romantic vacation undertaken on a busy Manhattan street, Act 1 juxtaposes both live

McDonald in France with the French comics hero Asterix – and more relevant here – McDonalds's marketing in India of a vegetarian 'Maharaja Mac' in place of its all-beef Big Mac. Glo*cal*ization, then, is a strategy for localizing glo*bal*ization.

In *Alladeen*, however, we face a contorted version of glocalization. Through the Bangalore call centre, we have US companies marketing their services to US customers – only, those services are delivered by Indian workers. And because they are providing services rather than manufacturing goods, these workers must perform 'as Americans'. The optimal goal is for Indians to assist American callers without the Americans noticing any significant cultural difference. That's why the workers are trained in American English: to iron out both their native accents and the colloquialisms of school-learned British English.

Obviously, there is more to glocalization than pronunciation. Just as important to successful glocalization are shared cultural references that create a sense of commonality. In this same scene, another character, Saritri, gives a presentation about the popular American TV show, *Friends*, focusing on the personalities of each character. Her cross-cultural descriptions of Joey, Rachel, Monica, Phoebe and Chandler got laughs from my American theatre audience: as the *Friends* characters were translated on stage into an Indian frame of cultural reference, they became defamiliarized.

So far, then, *Alladeen* has – sometimes comically, sometimes critically – staged the uncanny cultural experience of glocalization, in this case a strange mix of East and West that both grants wishes and disorients the wishers, that both reinforces the feeling of belonging and disrupts any settled notion of place or home. But I want to consider *Alladeen* in a way that reaches beyond its own effective staging of the experience of glocalization. I want to suggest that *Alladeen* also – and unwittingly – points us to emerging forces of global power and knowledge that can be called 'the performative matrix'.

The term 'performative matrix' was coined in the early 1990s by Critical Art Ensemble, a collective of artists, activists and theorists that is also known by the initials CAE. In *The Electronic Disturbance*, their 1994 manifesto, CAE argued that in the 1960s groups such as The Living Theater had succeeded in breaking down the barrier between theatre and life, effectively creating what CAE termed a 'performative matrix' that included both the stage and street, both art and life, both aesthetics and politics. The performative matrix, in short, is an expansive site or situation of action, one that displaces performance outside the institution of theatre. In many ways, their first notion of performative matrix corresponds to the field of cultural performance, that broad spectrum of activities described by Richard Schechner as including theatre, performance art, ritual and practices of everyday life.

However, Critical Art Ensemble also argued that this expanded performance space had lost its radical potential. Picking up the flag of the historical avant garde, they threw down a series of polemical gauntlets. Taking aim at activists, they proclaimed: *the streets are dead capital.* And turning to solo performance artists, they said: *the personal is not political.* CAE made these provocations as a way to further expand and radicalize the performative matrix. Theorizing a second notion of the performative matrix, they extended it beyond art and life and into the virtual space of electronic networks.

I will now articulate a third notion of the performative matrix, one that builds on these first two while also gathering together a number of concepts from my own research. Following a suggestion by Ricardo Dominguez, a former member of CAE and co-founder of the hacktivist group Electronic Disturbance Theatre, I believe my research 'opens up the performative matrix'. How so? Today I will argue that my research opens up the performative matrix in two distinct, yet interconnected ways.

First, my research has not been limited to the field of cultural performance but extends to other areas of performance production and research: organizational, technological, governmental and financial. In short, I analyse many different *paradigms of performance*, not just cultural performance. For instance, in the US – and increasingly around the world – workers and managers, and indeed entire departments and organizations, are said to 'perform'. These performances are routinely measured through formal 'performance reviews' and assessed through 'performance evaluations'. Throughout most of the 1990s, the entire US government was evaluated annually through a programme called the National Performance Review, and such evaluations continue under the Bush administration. More broadly, a distinct form of organizational theory and practice has arisen around performance since the Second World War; called 'performance management', it has displaced the scientific management associated with Frederick Taylor. This is the paradigm I call 'organizational performance', and its discourses and practices obviously differ greatly from those found in cultural performance. More importantly, unlike cultural performance, whose dominant value - at least in the US - is the social efficacy of performances, that is, their potential to effect social change or critique, organizational performances are guided by the value of efficiency, by their capacity to maximize outputs and minimize inputs.

Another performance paradigm I study is *technological performance*, the performance crafted by engineers, computer scientists and other applied scientists and technicians. Here we find performances enacted not by artists or workers, not by humans at all, really, but by technologies. Plastics and alloys perform, as do sports cars and stereos, as well as communication networks and municipal infrastructures. Highly detailed 'performance specs' or technical specifications can be found on nearly all consumer products and on much more advanced 'high performance' products and systems. For instance, around the world, there is a network of 'high-performance computer centres', which not only provide highly competitive access to high-performance supercomputers but also conduct benchmarking or performance tests on other advanced computer systems. Unlike cultural or organizational performance, technological performance is not evaluated by social efficacy or organizational efficiency but by technical *effectiveness*, by the ability to meet highly specified criteria such as speed, endurance and reliability - but there are literally thousands and thousands of other possible criteria.

I want to suggest that my own opening up of the performance matrix proceeds in two distinct but interrelated ways. First, along an axis of different paradigms. While Critical Art Ensemble sought to expand the performative matrix from art and life to cyberspace, their conception of it remained primarily a cultural one. And although their interest in activist organization and communication technology pointed *implicitly* toward the two other performance paradigms I have just discussed, these were still cast from the perspective of artists and activists. By contrast, I have *explicitly* tried to theorize organizational and technological performance *in their own terms*, rather than immediately subjecting them to critical inquiry or creative experimentation. Second, my opening up of the performative matrix also occurs along an onto-historical or Foucauldean axis. It is here that I theorize the historical and ontological relation of the different performance paradigms. I have tried to encapsulate this dimension in the following slogan: *performance will be to the twentieth and twenty-first centuries what discipline was to the eighteenth and nineteenth: an onto-historical formation of power and knowledge*. In short, I believe performance must be understood as an emergent formation of postmodern power and post-disciplinary knowledge, which I have elsewhere called the performance stratum but am today theorizing in relation to the performative matrix.

While Foucault located the rise of discipline in Western Europe, I believe that the performative matrix emerged and took hold in the United States just after World War 2. According to Foucault, discipline produced unified subjects through a series of institutions such as school, factory and prison, each with its own discrete archive of statements and practices. By contrast, performative power blurs the borders of social institutions by connecting and sharing their digital archives. Financial information, criminal records and school transcripts once stored in separate file cabinets are now being uploaded to silicon databases and electronically networked. Bodies that once passed neatly through a linear sequence of power mechanisms are now learning to switch rapidly between conflicting evaluative grids; the resulting subjects tend to be fractured, multiple and/or hybrid. In the US workplace, for instance, we have witnessed the rise of multitasking; in schools, children are routinely diagnosed with attention-deficit disorders; and in everyday life, people have begun 'culture-surfing', moving through different styles and traditions almost as quickly and easily as changing channels on the television. From a wider historical perspective: while discipline functioned as the power matrix of the Enlightenment, the industrial revolution, liberal capitalism and European colonialism, performance operates as the matrix of the post-Enlightenment, the information revolution, neoliberal capitalism and postcolonialism.

But let me stress that performative power and knowledge is really a thing of the future; the disciplinary formation wasn't built in a day, nor has the performative matrix fully emerged. The performative matrix corresponds in many ways to the 'Empire' envisioned by Michael Hardt and Antonio Negri: a decentred network of juridical discourses and biopolitical practices, of normative performatives and performances, governed by leading industrial nations such as the G8, international organizations such as the UN, IMF and WTO and a host of multi- and transnational corporations.

Normative globalization - which I distinguish from resistant globalization or 'anti-globalization' - normative globalization operates by optimizing different performative values: social efficacy, organizational efficiency, technological effectiveness, governmental accountability, financial profitability etc. One example of such performativity is the Global Reporting Initiative or GRI. Based in the Netherlands, GRI is part of the United Nations' Environment Programme. The Global Reporting Initiative pursues sustainable development by encouraging governments, corporations and other organizations to prepare 'sustainability performance reports'. Such reports document three types of performance: economic performance (financial data), environmental performance (compliance to environmental policies) and social performance (respect of labour laws and human rights).

In a very real sense, such performance optimization across different paradigms forms the operational power behind recent forms of globalization. Now in theorizing performative power and knowledge, I draw on the work of others. For instance, Judith Butler's theory of 'punitive performatives' stresses the transgressive potential of embodied activities such as drag performance, but she also analyses the highly normative role that discursive performatives play in constituting and enforcing the heterosexist gendering of bodies. In some sense, I am trying to 'scale up' Butler's work on the relation of discursive performatives and embodied performances, using it to theorize how performativity operates in institutions and larger social formations. Though Butler's work is often read within the contexts of queer theory and the work of Austin and Derrida, I have found it useful to situate her writings in relation to two other theorists whose critical work on performance was long ignored by cultural performance scholars.

I refer here to Lyotard and Marcuse. Lyotard's performance theory lies at the core of his classic text, *The Postmodern Condition*. Famously, Lyotard argued that unlike in modernity, where knowledge and social bonds were legitimated by such grand narratives as Progress and Liberation, postmodern legitimation occurs through *performativity*, defined as system optimization, which he argues has come to dominate all language games with the demand, -be operational - or disappear'. I read the demand as a version of the performance stratum's governing order word: perform - or else. Lyotard also uses the term 'performative principle', which I hear as an echo of Herbert Marcuse's concept of 'performance principle'. Synthesizing Marx and Freud, Marcuse in 1955 defined the performance principle as the reality principle that governs advanced industrial societies. The performance principle is a repressive reality principle, and Marcuse saw the alienating performances found in factory work spreading throughout all of society, to offices, homes and into popular culture. Long before Critical Art Ensemble, long before Lyotard and Butler, Marcuse realized how pervasive and important performance was to postindustrial societies. It is not much of an exaggeration, then, to see Marcuse as a true visionary of the performative matrix.

Now Lyotard and Marcuse's theories of performativity can help us articulate two different models of normative globalization or, if you like, two different structurings of the performative matrix. Lyotard's stress on diverse language games and his suspicion of metalanguage corresponds to the globalization that reigned throughout the 1990s: a multilateral network of nations, corporations and NGOs that works cooperatively in pursuing its political, economic and cultural policies. This is also what Hardt and Negri call 'Empire'. Marcuse's theory of performance, by contrast, stresses a one-dimensional and highly conformist organizational power, a power we can see in the unilateral globalization pursued by the current Bush administration. Hardt and Negri call this, significantly, an 'imperialist backlash against Empire'. These two models are not the only ones possible, of course. Indeed, taken together, they can be combined to suggest a third, even more complex, model of globalization. I have in mind here a performative matrix that fluctuates between two modes of global performativity: the Lyotardean and the Marcusean, the multi- and the unilateral. At times, this performative matrix may operate through alliances and agreements, affirming diversity and multilateralism; at times these same alliances and agreements fall by the wayside as conformity and unilateralism reigns.

Such different modes of performativity are highly relevant to a *fourth* type of globalization, the 'anti-globalization' movement, with its many different constituencies and goals. Relevant here is what Marcuse called a 'revolution in values', in which aesthetic values come to the fore and are themselves transformed. In terms of the performance paradigms, such a revolution of values is precisely what cultural efficacy entails, at least as theorized by Schechner: rather than remaining isolated forms of entertainment, theatre and other cultural performances can potentially feedback into all of society, producing revolutionary effects there. Further, the extension and transformation of aesthetic values outside artistic and cultural institutions and into all of life and into cyberspace, as well - this is also what Critical Art Ensemble sought in first theorizing 'the performative matrix'. And to make yet another connection: it is what Hardt and Negri mean when they argue that the multitude's revolutionary force lies in its creativity.

In terms of the general theory of performance: by focusing on diverse performance paradigms and the larger performative matrix in which they operate, I try to theorize both the resistant *and* the normative aspects of global performativity. For if artists, activists and researchers are truly interested in the social efficacy of cultural performance, then understanding other types of performance and - more importantly, the matrix of power and knowledge which links them together - such understanding seems crucial for both engaging different performative values and transforming the social function of cultural production.

To return to *Alladeen*: does this cultural performance reinscribe the normative forces of globalization, or is it transgressive, transforming and unsettling them? Or might it be both? We can recast *Alladeen*'s staging of glocalization in terms of the performative matrix. Glocalization can be understood as a specific ensemble of paradigmatic performances. For starters, with Indian-based US call centres, we have the embedding of organizational and cultural performances: within the context of an outsourcing and off-shoring American business organization, we have Indian employees working, *performing*, their job, a job that requires them to role-play or culturally perform as Americans. The more efficacious, the more 'localized' and seamless their cultural performance, the more efficient and competent their organizational performance.

And to add yet another performative value: the more efficient their organizational performance, the more profitable the global economic performance of the business itself. Thus, efficacious localization of cultural performance here adds up to profitable global economic performance. What this reveals is how crucial cultural research, knowledge and education – the very stuff of the arts and humanities, of anthropology, cultural studies and performance studies – how crucial these have become to contemporary processes of globalization.

We can see how these different performances come together in Act 2 of *Alladeen*, which is set in the work space of the Bangalore call centre. On stage, the projection screen has been raised to reveal a platform holding five work stations, with characters working on flat-screen computer monitors. Downstage left and right stand what appear to be phone booths with frosted glass. The particular scene I will analyse here features a phone service called 'On the Road', which provides assistance to car rental customers. Here, Heaven Phillips stands in the booth stage left and plays an excited traveller calling from Los Angeles to get directions to Las Vegas. 'I've just won a gazillion smackeroonies in the lottery,' she exclaims, 'and I'm going to bet the whole wad.' Her jittery voice and slang expressions confuse Tanya, the worker who takes the call.

Tanya sits alone near centre stage, wearing a headphone and using a computer to access information regarding the woman's location, her specific problem and the best solution. Tanya puts the caller on hold to find out what 'smackeroonies' means, first asking her coworkers and then using her computer to find the definition. Back on the line, the caller says that she's feeling confused, even 'a little lost in space'. Hearing this American colloquialism for

• © *The Builders Association and motiroti. Photo by Simone Lynne*

being disoriented or confused, Tanya connects the caller's phrase to the old American TV show *Lost in Space*, and then she expresses a personal affection for June Cartwright, one of this show's characters. This connection to a American pop culture reference fills the lag-time of the computer system - or rather, it provides time for Tanya to call up information and provide directions to Las Vegas. Just as important, however, Tanya's reference to the TV show creates an ephemeral bond between her and the caller. The character's cultural performance consists of 'passing' as an American long enough to create personal bond and supply the appropriate information.

Obviously, also crucial here - and throughout *Alladeen* - is yet another paradigmatic performance: technological performance. In contemporary globalization, communication and information technologies are to performativity what the file cabinet and panopticon were to discipline: the dominant modes of archiving knowledge and controlling bodies. With Tanya, we see communication and information technologies embodied in the central interface of *Alladeen*'s global call centre: the interface of headphone and computer, an interface composed, precisely, with the body of the Indian worker. Tanya listens and speaks through the headphone, while her fingers enter data on a keyboard and her eyes retrieve it through the computer screen.

Now *Alladeen*'s own spectacular interface - the multimedia set that its audience must learn to navigate - displays these different performances both on stage and on the large projection screen. The workstations of the call centre are the bread and butter of the centre's economic performance, while above on the screen one can see how the other performances are embedded in this econo-organizational performance. During the first part of the scene, the screen is filled with windows of different computer programs. Stage left on the screen is a map of the geographic location of the caller standing in the booth below, with other information about the caller displayed below the map. Stage right, on the top of the screen, we see a live video image of Tanya wearing her headphone. Both below this window and to the immediate right,, we see Tanya's cultural glocalization: Tanya 'plays' Phoebe from *Friends*, and we see Phoebe's picture highlighted below. These three windows index Tanya's US cultural database, her personal reservoir of American pop-culture references that form the basis of her cultural performance, her performance as an American. In addition, two other windows in the centre of the screen reference the technological performance of the workstation, its computer system. One displays the search results for the meaning of 'smackeroonies', while the second window display shows the map that Tanya eventually uses to give the caller the directions to Vegas. These windows supplement Tanya's cultural knowledge on the fly: she can call up information as she needs it from her computerized, artificial memory.

Again, what we can see here is how the glocalization achieved by Indian call centres depends on localized entwinings of cultural, organizational and technological performances within a larger, global economic performance. Not surprisingly, such glocalized performances can confuse and disorient both customer and worker. Each becomes 'lost in space' while navigating a complex network in which the location of the other - and of the self - is uncertain and shifting. Combining this experience of being 'lost in space' with Edward Said's concept of Orientalism, one might say that the practice of glocalization produces 'disorientalism'. While Said defined Orientalism as the romanticization and misrecognition of the 'East' by Westerners, 'disorientalism' refers to a generalized sense of spatial and temporal disorientation, a confusion caused by the networking of discrete locations into multiple and at times conflicting systems, many of which are global in their reach. In some sense, disorientalism means that every place and every moment is also potentially elsewhere and elsewhen. Now and then, there and here, disorientalism.

Yet remaining mindful of the criticality of Said's concept of Orientalism, I must stress that such 'disorientalism' produces different effects on different people, differences that still divide East from West and South from North. Significantly, in this context, Ricardo Dominquez suggests a counter-movement to glocalization, one that he tags '(lo)balization', putting the local before the global without romanticizing it.

And, in closing, this brings me back to the question I posed above: *what is the relation of large-scale, multimedia theatre on the one hand, and globalization on the other?* Can theatrical events such as *Alladeen* offer modes of critical analysis and creative resistance to major processes of globalization, that is, to economic exploitation, political hegemony and cultural imperialism - and if so, how? Or, alternatively, do such large-scale, multimedia performances effectively *embody normative globalization?* I have been suggesting that while *Alladeen* explicitly focuses on outsourcing, it also reveals how largely normative tactics of glocalization can be understood in terms of specific types of performance: cultural, organizational, technological and economic. Such understanding can in turn be used to create forms of resistant glocalization, local gestures that potentially produce global effects. Such resistant glocalizations may partake of the revolution in values described by Marcuse: they are creative in a way that breaks out of the aesthetic or cultural realm and cuts transversely across technological, organizational and economic realms.

But of course, as anyone who studies cross-cultural theatre will be thinking, there's also the glocalization of the *Alladeen* performance itself. Marianne Weems told me in an interview that beyond the conceptual development of the *Alladeen* production, her collaborative work with British-Asian artists Keith Khan and Ali Zaidi gave her group access to three things: alternative funding streams, diverse technical expertise and an exchange of different performance skills.

Looked at another way, we can understand the collaborative process as mixing at least three different paradigmatic performances: the economic performance of financial funding, the technological performance of media and machines and the cultural performance of acting, dancing, singing, dramaturgy etc. And to square the circle: the collaboration of the Builders and motiroti is itself an organizational performance.

Moreover, I'd like to focus on attempts by the Builders and motiroti to glocalize the production in some of the different places it has been performed, places that include Singapore, Australia, Columbia, Canada, France, Great Britain, Germany and - as I mentioned - the United States. It has not been performed in India, although Marianne Weems told me she has tried to find a venue there but has thus far been unsuccessful. The glocalization of the performance most often occurs by connecting with local communities. In Glasgow and Bogota, for instance, The Builder's Association and motiroti conducted workshops with local artists, as well as walk-throughs of the set and demonstrations of the media technology. In New York, they joined anthropologist Arjun Appadurai to discuss the politics and aesthetics of large-scale, cross-cultural performances, in a public dialogue hosted by the Lower Manhattan Cultural Council.

In all these cases, the artists sought to contextualize their global production within local *cultural* communities. In Seattle, however, they sought to connect with a very different group: the hometown corporation of Microsoft. *Alladeen* was to have been mounted in a special performance for its employees. However, when Microsoft discovered that the performance dealt with outsourcing, it pulled out of the arrangement, for the corporation had just started outsourcing some of its positions.

In early 2004 I saw *Alladeen* at Dartmouth College. There the artists worked with both artistic and business communities. They conducted workshops and class visits with media and theatre students, and in addition creative

• © The Builders Association and motiroti. Photo by Simone Lynne

director Keith Khan participated in a panel at the Tuck School of Business. Titled 'Inside Outsourcing', this panel tried to explore the cultural, economic and policy issues surrounding outsourcing and off-shoring. Besides Keith Khan, the panel also included Jack Freker, president of Convergys Corporation, a leading US customer service company; Paul Gaffney, executive vice president of Staples Inc., a chain of large office supply stores that uses call centres; and Sonal Shah of the Center for American Progress, a non-profit research institute that promotes progressive economic policies.

The panel was, I suspect, a big success for the business people, who dominated the event with discussions of policy and economic issues. Cultural matters, however, were barely touched upon, as Khan tried to intervene critically at a few points but was, I thought, at a loss for words. Immediately afterwards, I spoke with him, and he seemed a bit overwhelmed. I do not mean to be critical of him: Keith Khan was the only artist on a panel of business people, sitting before an audience mostly of graduate business students, in a space housed in a School of Business. If you are an artist or cultural researcher, you might ask yourself how well you would have performed under similar circumstances. Indeed, it may be easier for us to fly around the world than it is to walk across a campus or a city and collaborate with researchers in other performance paradigms, where we would most likely experience another version of disorientalism.

As I do not presume to stand outside such questions, I will end by asking: does cultural performance research, research that now stretches around the world, research that has taken me, a US performance scholar, to Singapore and Tokyo, London and Berlin, Aberystwyth and Zagreb, to speak about performance, including a US/UK theatre piece dealing with the performance of Indian workers – does such a complex network of performance research embody normative or resistant globalization? Perhaps, in a range of complex ways, it does precisely both.

# *En Conjunto · from el performance to la performativa*

*El performance* rests uneasily in the Spanish language. It is a phrase that suggests intrusion, difference, masculinity and individualism. The power of *el performance* hovers claustrophobic-ally over the bodies of *la cultura performativa* that seeks to engage outside the zones of culture approved by *el mundo del performance*. Situated firmly in the academy, *el performance* reaches out with octopus arms to countries, cultures and languages in the Americas often with the well-intentioned, paternalistic goal of ethnographic retrieval, as if the 'third world' cultures of the Americas are in need of 'rescuing'. 'See this work. See this culture. See this ritual,' *el performance* says with its bright, often-privileged position of entitlement and moreover a working lexicon that excludes cultures from each other. The ship that is *el performance* carries heavy freight. Years of carefully codified, hierarchical language have determined how the study of performance is written about and discussed. *Nosotros en las Americas del sur, del centro, de las fronteras – entre tambien* the entangled Celtic, Jewish and Moor cultures of Iberia are left with the task of having to re-rescue ourselves, our very own *performativa* (imposed word from the English dominant strain of the world of *el performance*) from increasingly well-intentioned zones of silence that leave little room for the *Nosotros* within the *I/Yo*. The complicated acts of multiple retrieval (from outside and within) reinforce the double bind of seeing/not seeing culture at face value, let alone metaphorically. This struggle is made acute now by the growing rejection of the Spanish language itself by young artists (from Mexico, for example) who sing, perform, make and brand their work for their immediate audiences in English-only in order to identify themselves as part of consum-able icons of globalization.

*El performance*'s epistemology and ontology ensure and assure practitioners that to be entered into English – into the language of market and trade – is the only way to be recognized by the world. *El performance* offers visibility, but visibility, as Peggy Phelan so astutely noted, is a trap summoning 'surveillance' and holding 'the colonialist/imperial appetite for possession' (1993: 6). The opportunities, thus, to strip and mine the Spanish-speaking Americas (colonized many times over and barely still recovering from buried and unburied marks of slaughter and genocide over the centuries) displace the very acts of 'retrieval' and archaeological study necessary for the body of *la performance* to truly live. *La performance* – unlike *el performance* – exists not only within private and public poetic interventions that seek to transform and raise awareness about negative and positive acts of human history, but also within the tenuous and complex dialogues surrounding the ecological survival of the land(s). *Tierra fondo, tierra sur* ... Spanish and indigenous languages find themselves in a daily struggle to enter on equal terms – in parity – with the colonized and preferred English-dominant languages of *el performance*. Thus, the voices from within the body of the Americas – the forceful, sinuous body that represents for the inadvertent poacher's eye a chance to re-plunder its riches and re-package its legacy of violence for the empire of Authority – are almost forced into a position where they have to mobilize their creative actions through collective means. *¡La performance of el performance!* But the linguistic and semiotic challenges faced by those determined to unburden themselves from the Euro-centric structures and modalities of approved cultural thought – reinforced and reinscribed by the inculcation of the academy – face a difficult battle.

How to speak about *La performance* without the languages of *el performance*? How to be part of but respectfully separate from and, morever, recognized by the existing paradigms that limit even the ways of speaking about disidentification from a truly hemispheric stance? What structures can be re-made or newly created in the great face of changing population demographics in Iberia (the fractured European arm/link of the Americas) and *el centro, sur* and Caribbean to write and speak about the daily cultural encounters of performance itself?

We have no word for Performance Studies. *Los estudios del performance* is too disperse, too expansive, too formal, too imposed. It speaks of paradigms imposed from a language other than ours: a discourse evitably bound up with the politics of colonialism and tourism. It does not recognize its own relationship to imperialism and cultural exportation. It speaks of the Northern hemisphere, of a language spoken by 300 million as their first language, but it somehow does not recognize that it is that language spoken by a further 375 million, broken, dismembered and remembered as a second language that is the world language. One in four people on the globe have some level of competence in English but it is an English that exists with and emerges from a plethora of other languages. Spanish (as a first language) is spoken by around 350 million people across the globe, but the large proportion of these are in the Southern hemisphere, and we know that cultural exchange in an era of globalization functions from north to south, dominated by the paradigms of US- and Euro-centric imperialism. *El performance* is tainted by the agenda of our buy-and-sell culture; it is contaminated by the thrill of our search for the new; the northern hemisphere's need to search out new territories and find 'uncontaminated' performative forms. Just as tourists flock in droves to the supposedly unspoiled beaches of the far-flung corners of the globe, transforming them into the 'hip' tourist sites of tomorrow, so performance studies feeds on the need to search out ever more authentic sites and modes of performance. In the post-postmodern condition, inured to simulation and thriving on the holodeck of virtual storytelling and Second Lives, this search for the 'authentic' de-limits the complicated cultural frissons alive in countries and lands all-too-spoiled by the mighty Dig. It's about feeding our desire for the new, providing fodder for the next academic forum where we can impress, delight and challenge with our grasp of 'the other'.

*¿Pero que significa esto para el futuro de actos* decontextualized and represented for the tourist brochure of the academic circuit? Is the final destination of *las memorias y historias del sur* to be merely a Power Point slide-show re-enactment on a university dais? And how many frequent flier miles will *el performance* rack up in its quest and conquest of authenticated novelty? Moreover, how many high registration fees will lock out cultural and creative practitioners from the very sites of performativity where their work is being bartered and traded?

Performatics is plural. It recognizes that our working relationships are based on collaborations *con artistas, colegas, instituciones, producciones, artistas y espacios*. It questions the I and replaces it with the we. It is a way of doing and a mode of thinking. To make *en conjunto*. The dialogic *nosotros* v. the monologic I.

Our joint authoring of this piece comes from a decade of *colaboración*, of striving to find ways for scholars and artists to speak and respond through and across work made and experienced. Performance studies speaks so often from the view of the viewer/voyeur; it's about spectatorship, about the power of watching. Might performatics speak from the view of the makers, about making work, about conversations and encounters? Might it move beyond the culture of sampling to the possibilities offered by conversations and engagements conducted across time while finding ways of speaking about *la performance* without smothering it in the discourses of *el performance*?

Can performatics speak to our language? To our shared concerns about Spanish-language culture? To the ways English-Spanish fusion is packaged? And to why is it that we say English-Spanish rather than the other way around? These questions are prompted by a profound need to re-examine how it is we write, make and talk about the very work we do inside and outside the academy, and moreover how it is we live in the Americas and in Europe. Do we continually look only to Europe for signs of progress? Are the dramaturgical models offered from the English-speaking world more 'valid' than the ones we discover and devise based on our own collective ways of working? And when we speak about the US is it only through the lens of the transatlantic alliance? When so many languages, so many customs, and erosions of customs are being enacted throughout the Americas and Europe, *la performance* of *el performance* demands its own space. Not a contrary space. In reaction against. In rebellion. But rather simply its own within its many active pluralities.

*Dedicated to Jorge Huerta*

REFERENCES

Phelan, Peggy (1993) *Unmarked: The Politics of Performance*, London and New York: Routledge.

**MARIA M. DELGADO AND CARIDAD SVICH**

# My Performatics

TOMASZ KUBIKOWSKI

1

It is problematic to assimilate a keyword so dynamic, unstable, contextualized and culturally loaded as 'performance' when it does not have its proper equivalent within one's own language. Does one really need to do so? Can the respective fields and issues not be addressed with the local vocabulary, the native system of categories, in accordance with one's own historically rooted and naturally perceived cultural universe? It is particularly problematic when the term comes from English. Is it yet another instance of our inability to resist cultural dictates, where the inertness of our language causes us again to swallow a cliché, another bit of globalized jargon?

Is there anything natural at all in turning to 'performance studies' in Poland? Here, there could be no 'theory explosion' around the central term. It did not emerge suddenly and naturally to significance in disparate fields and raise the question, what do they have in common? When I try to explain to my students the origin of 'performance research', at first I have to explain laboriously to them various meanings of this English term and their interplay. It is complicated. After a while, I feel like someone telling a long joke, unfortunately based on some untranslatable pun, when the effort of communicating it with all its shades kills the point, leaving my willing audience bored and confused. This is when I start questioning myself: is the whole discipline based on a pun, really? Is it not too culture-specific? Can't I explain in my language in a much simpler, natural way? Do we really need this whole 'performance'?

2

My private answer is 'yes', we do need it, and that is why, for over ten years, I have tried to popularize in Poland the ways and achievements of performance studies. In other words, I have tried to create some 'performatics'. The name came naturally: it is like 'semiotics' or 'informatics', stemming from the common Greek-Latin heritage and thus acceptable, suitable for a research discipline. 'Perform' also has Latin roots. It does not necessarily, then, join the wave of globalized English terms now flooding other languages.

Some of its derivatives have already made their way into academic terminology in my country; we have 'performatives' in logic and the 'competence-performance' dyad in linguistics. The ground has been then prepared for the newcomer. Moreover, in all theoretical reflection about theatre (my own field), we have, apparently, long lacked a broader term, delimiting the field, to which theatre possibly belongs.

The native word in Polish terminology is *widowisko*: 'show' or rather 'spectacle', as it comes from *widzieć* – 'to see' (similar to some other European terminologies, for example the Italian). There exists some 'spectacle theory' (once pursued by my late professor Zbigniew Raszewski, 1991), and now there is 'anthropology of spectacle' (pursued by Leszek Kolankiewicz and his colleagues), and there are enormous problems caused by the usage of these words. How to analyse in these terms the *Actions* of Grotowski and Richards, originally not meant for display to anyone? What about Grotowski's whole post-theatrical period, after he had eliminated the 'spectator'? Wider yet, what happens to Milton Singer's 'cultural performances' when they become 'cultural spectacles', as they practically do in my country? We then miss important aspects, and we unconsciously add aspects that are neither necessary nor required. Distortion occurs. Spectacle privileges a spectator; performance privileges a performer. They may be two sides of the same event; however, they need not be.

Therefore, starting with theatre theory, in Poland, we need some broader category, not necessarily stressing the spectacular aspect of the event, and here 'performance' suggests itself. Then, there is the whole 'culture of performance', as described by Jon McKenzie (2001) and coming now from everywhere, also not necessarily identical with the Debordian *culture du spectacle*, with which we are terminologically better prepared to cope (Debord, 1994). There are even wider connotations of the term, as described in, among other places, the annals of *Performance Research*. Do they all really have a common denominator? Looking in from outside, do we, from beyond the English-speaking world, get 'performance' as a tool for analysis, or rather acquire a symptom, which is to be analysed? Something to examine with or something to be examined by? Is it a pun, after all? If so, where exactly does it begin?

3
To propose 'performatics' honestly, I had then to find my own answer to what performance really is, some convincing definition (or at least description or explanation) of the term 'performance'.

For years, my basic research interest has been in consciousness. The question, for which to find an answer, was: what mechanisms of consciousness participate in a theatrical situation (suspension of disbelief and wilful agreement for impersonation) and broader: are there any mechanisms of human consciousness that naturally cause our 'theatricality'? In other words are there any mechanisms of consciousness that make us perform? Can we find the old 'theatrical instinct' of Evreinov within our consciousness?

For some time, the best clues for developing answers to these questions could be found, again, in the English language. There used to be much interesting research in German (Ingarden 1931, Hartmann 1966, Steinbeck 1970) in the core phenomenological tradition and, thanks to Roman Ingarden and his disciples, also in the Polish language (Ingarden 1960, 1976, 1981, Makota 1964, see more in Kubikowski 1993). This ran dry, however, a generation ago. In the 1980s, new works were scarce (although in Bert O. States's *Great Reckonings in Small Rooms*, 1985, there were inspiring insights galore). The very notion of consciousness became then problematic and was deemed obsolete; the more 'objectivist' approaches prevailed (see Dennett 1981, Searle 1990, 1997, Bennett and Hacker 2003; the literature on the subject is too extensive to be fully cited here).

In the early 1990s, the anti-cognitivist counteraction opened new perspectives. John Searle in his *Rediscovery of Mind* (1992) and *The Construction of Social Reality* (1995) established firm logical ground for investigating consciousness. Gerald Edelman in his trilogy, eventually summarized in *Bright Air, Brilliant Fire* (Edelman 1987, 1988, 1989, 1992) and developed (with Guido Tononi) in *The Universe of Consciousness* (2000), provided visionary neurophilosophical concepts in accordance with Searle's logic filled out with neurological evidence. These two authors contributed the most to my present notion of performance. Not only do they use the term in unexpected, inspiring contexts (Edelman defines memory as 'ability to repeat performance' – this would only add to the collection of English examples, a database for studying a cultural phenomenon of the keyword) but they also built their whole theories on performativity. It is not surprising in Searle; in Edelman performativity gains a material shape one cannot ignore.

The famous 'explanatory inversion' in Searle's works excludes all possible teleology from our thinking and concludes with Edelman's statement that evolution works through selection, not through instruction, and therefore we never get information directly from our environment. We get answers only to the questions that we pose to the world ourselves. These questions are performatives, felicitous or not, and only from their success or failure, can we determine the world's characteristics. Through this process we submit to selection. We can die from what we did not ask.

Edelman's 'neuronal Darwinism' claims that neuronal structures in our brain compete for better categorization of the world. Those that serve the homeostasis of the organism better become augmented. Those that lose the competition, weaken. They do not vanish, however, as the living brain is never an optimized structure. On the contrary, it is 'degenerate'; it retains manifold useless structures. We survive thanks to them. When the leading structure fails, proves incompetent, not fit to newly arisen circumstances or is simply damaged, then the secondary structures take over. Anyway, it is always the fittest one that serves us in our dealings with the world. It categorizes. It creates instructions, strategies and notions, which are to help us survive selection. On the other hand, they are being selected: by their usefulness for survival or by the very survival of their bearer.

This means that our interaction with the world is always dramatic (based on actions) and performative, not narrative or cognitive. Through action, we recognize our situation. This has many consequences and interesting nuances, which there is not room here to develop at length (Kubikowski 2004). Finally, this brings me to a notion of performance as a meeting point of processes of two cardinal kinds: *performance occurs where selection and instruction meet.*

We create instructions, which are subject to selection and through which we try to master selection or withstand it; we perform. Through performatives (as Searle teaches), we create a social world and deal with it. Through performance, we deal with the world in its most general sense.

4
Although abstract, this notion of performance seems firm and useful. Firstly, I have tried to use it for insights into performing arts, into the mechanisms present both in their social practice and in their fixed instructions, culturally known as dramas. To anyone who has witnessed theatrical rehearsals or, even more, who has participated in them, it is obvious how the participants bring some instructions *a priori* but mostly form them in actual action, how a selection through this action works, how variants of the action emerge and perish and how an actor blindly recognizes a situation through 'deeds, acts and performance'. Of course, this mostly pertains to what Schechner (2006) calls a 'workshop' phase of rehearsals.

On the other hand let us take *King Lear* at its most stripped-down, as a record of a mass extinction, caused by the initial fault in the mechanism of inheritance. Both Lear and Gloucester dispose of their heritages falsely, which eventually causes the whole population to collapse. This purely Darwinian summary of the tragedy sounds ridiculous. However, it poses serious questions about the possibility of survival, and this tragedy has only one genuine survivor, Edgar (Albany is not important; Kent is old and moribund, as he admits himself). How did Edgar survive? That is the question, and the general answer is: by means of performance.

Once knocked outside the mainstream, he acquires the most 'degenerate' state, losing his old identity, categories and instructions. He lets his neuronal maps loose, to re-form them into the new patterns. He recognizes the situation dramatically, responding to stimuli both from outside and from his own deprived organism or his traumatized psyche. In the course of this, he is destructive. Finally it is Edgar who drives the old king mad. Before meeting 'poor Tom', Lear is passionate and exalted but sane. Once drawn into the 'performance of folly', he cannot stand it. Perhaps he feels that his present situation as an outcast leads to some possible solution; nevertheless, he is too old and weak to survive the whole process of a performative re-forming. For the young man it is like a deep dive from which he emerges transformed and fit; for the old man his degeneration is irreversible. Striving for his own survival, Edgar unintentionally gives a final blow to the system, which had pushed him out. The endless night in Act 3 is actually a duel, a duel in performance, or rather a competition in performance: in the basic, reduced-to-null situation of bare survival only one of the parties can remain.

Again, all this sounds unbearably naturalistic, but often Lear has been called the most naturalistic of Shakespeare's tragedies. There is still a competition between the two notions of 'nature' in the play, the one exposed by Edmund, the other by Lear. Is it 'natural' to care for our old parents or to get rid of them as soon as they become useless? There are two conflicting answers, two conflicting instructions; neither, as it proves, successful.

Then, what happens to Cordelia? As John Bayley shows in his powerful *Shakespeare and Tragedy* (1981), Cordelia is an actress who refuses performing; hence the confusion of the initial scene. She knows neither performance nor, we may add, degeneration. She keeps to the optimized strategy, one of the possible optimized strategies, and she fails along with the whole world, to which this strategy belongs. She acts according to the instructions she believes; her performance is an unhappy one.

This from the universal repertory, but some good examples for this interpretation of performance can be found in Polish drama. Especially it is in *Liberation* by Stanisław Wyspiański, a core play in the Polish tradition (see Wyspiański 1970). Wyspiański was a visionary and theatre reformer seminal to the twentieth-century achievements of Polish experimental performance (both Grotowski and Kantor staged his works and widely referred to them). The action of *Liberation* takes place at the very stage of the Cracow theatre, where the play was first staged in 1903. It is the place where figures from the national imagery meet. There is neither need nor possibility to go deeper into the action of the play. It was written by an artist who felt that his culture was on the verge of extinction (as was the Polish culture at the beginning of the twentieth century); therefore, he researched the possibility of cultural survival and development, tried to recognize the situation and to find ways out of it. The main character of *Liberation* is Konrad, the symbolic rebel-artist-hero of the Romantic heritage (coming from *The Forefathers' Eve* by Mickiewicz, 1832, see Segel 1977), and it is he who enters the stage at the beginning. On one hand, he is an eternal youth seeking his identity, life and development; on the other, just an ossified poetic cliché. For his author, he is both a *porte-parole* and a burden, a personification of traditions and instructions that for the last three generations had proved to be lethal. Konrad must select among these instructions for the felicitous performance. He tests them. He even tests in performance the traditional instruction, laying a border between the stage and the audience and creating a fictitious world on stage.

That is an exotic example (very familiar to me, however). Generally, in Polish culture, also in the performing culture, there is much about survival (which is not astonishing, given the historical circumstances). Perhaps this affects my understanding of the term 'performance'; perhaps also it makes the term relevant to better understand our condition and thus worth introducing to my country.

5

There are numerous examples of this selection/instruction performance pattern. Researching social strategies of performers and performing groups, studying theatre manifestos, provides many interesting insights. This pattern also affects the notion of performance as a tool for cultural analysis. In his *Perform or Else*, Jon McKenzie takes a feedback loop as a metamodel for performance, drawing many conclusions. In *The Universe of Consciousness*, Edelman and Tononi are careful to discern feedback (based on instruction) from re-entry (based on selection). 'Re-entry is the ongoing, recursive interchange of parallel signals between reciprocally connected areas.... This interchange, unlike feedback, involves many parallel paths and has no specific instructive error function associated with it. Instead, it alters selective events and correlations of signals among areas and is essential for the synchronization and coordination of the areas' mutual function' (Edelman, Tononi 2000, p. 48).

This longer quotation seems necessary here: what happens, if in McKenzie's cultural paradigm of performance we replace the feedback dynamics of instruction with the re-entrant dynamics of selection? Or even, when we supplement one dynamics with another and find transition between the two of them? Will the Challenger of a discourse explode again, at launch? Will it, like Columbia, explode on re-entry (McKenzie 2001)?

In Richard Bauman's (1989), widely quoted definition of performance stating the mental comparison of an actual action with some ideal or remembered pattern: which of the two serves as a criterion? Is it this 'ideal' pattern that justifies and authorizes an action, or should we rather use the explanatory inversion here and declare that the action authorizes the pattern?

In other words, Richard Schechner (2006) writes that in business or sport 'to perform' means 'to do something up to a standard, to succeed, to excel'. Is success equivalent with being up to the standard? Cordelia was up to the highest standards and failed. With the explanatory inversion, the bare existence of performer can be claimed the first sign of success. It is matching the unknown standards; it is acting, in Searlian terms, 'as if' we knew the rules, because we never really know the rules, the standards, the criteria. Once more, we do not get any information from the environment. We create information; we establish standards and rules, and all of them ultimately fail: at some point they are selected out by the turn of the unknown reality.

Half jokingly, I have called this pattern 'the principle of the Nibelung'. This refers to the Nibelung Mime, from Wagner's *Siegfried*, who was encouraged by the god to ask questions. He asked about distant things, omitting what he needed to know the most. Finally the god asked him about it, and the former oversight cost the poor dwarf his life. There was a complicated inner dialectics underlying this person. In Mime Wagner personified what he hated the most (intellectuals, Jews, hyperactive behaviour - he hated most of mankind, actually). At the same time, his unpublished notes, as examined by Adorno (2005), revealed his deep identification with his creature. In Mime he hates what he hated in himself.

From the point of view I am pursuing, we are all Mimes. We keep asking questions but are never sure if we ask the right and most needed one. We are endangered by what we did not ask about; we may always have a mental blindspot, from which our extinction comes. There is no external authority to help us localize it. Thus we have to perform.

In Shakespeare, perhaps the best summary of the performance situation is in Timon's famous words: 'Promise me friendship, but perform none. If thou wilt not promise, the gods plague thee, for thou art a man! If thou dost perform, confound thee, for thou art a man!' This is the shortest account of Cordelia's fate. She did not promise. She performed. She was doubly punished. It is the tragedy of a performative.

6

These are digressions, which I cannot resist. They still serve me as alibi for introducing 'performatics'. At this point, the then Grotowski Centre (transformed later into the Grotowski Institute) joined. In Autumn 2004, they proposed publishing Schechner's *Performance Studies: An Introduction* (2006, I have been translating the yet unpublished text of the second edition), supporting the publication of Carlson's *Performance: A Critical Introduction* (2004) and organizing a conference on Performance Studies. What were their motives? It is for them to say. Myself, I have to express my satisfaction and gratitude, and this is the most proper place for such sincere acknowledgment. We had never worked together before, and we worked harmoniously; I do not remember any disagreement about the idea, list of guests or agenda. The second issue was crucial: with limited means, we tried to invite not only a set of outstanding scholars and artists, but also to present a variety of possible approaches, to retain balance between the US and Europe, between the English and non-English speakers and finally between genders. One decision we had to make in advance: to limit our list of guests just to the US and Europe. We could not afford a worldwide conference. Our event was meant as an introduction of performance studies to Poland. We thought it reasonable, then, to have represented the country from where these studies originated (and some of the people who created them) and our own, closer European context: people who first introduced PS to this continent and people who represent other schools and therefore can discuss the need and sense of the new field here.

We were happy that we received only a few apologies and refusals (unfortunately and accidentally, they affected our gender balance). We had a last minute cancellation from Marco De Marinis, who was seriously ill, and also we could only have a recorded speech from Phillip Zarrilli, for which we were very grateful. It happens. I can only hope, the event was interesting for our foreign guests. Anyway, for some days they could feel the specific atmosphere of Wrocław and the very special atmosphere of the Centre, functioning in the spaces of Grotowski's activity, treasuring mementoes and ideas of this activity, surrounded by people whose living memory adds to an aura.

On the last day, devoted mostly to the Polish reactions to what had been said by keynote speakers, there was a heated discussion when the division between the younger and the older, the senior academic staff and the associates, became visible. Researchers in their thirties seemed to be the most enthusiastic.

Several months after the conference, we have recorded a discussion for *Dialog*, meant as a follow-up and continuation of the Wrocław debate. It took a much milder tone, however, as the opponents had softened their reservations. Generally, the tenor turned now to the apparently positive.

As for my students, many of them integrated 'performance' (polonized as *performans*) into their vocabulary. Some of them abbreviate it colloquially into *perf*. They have even concocted the unknown plural form: *perfy*. How to render the latter back into English? 'Pervs'?

REFERENCES

Adorno, Theodor (2005) *In Search of Wagner*, London: Verso.

Bayley, John (1981) *Shakespeare and Tragedy*, London: Routledge & Kegan Paul.

Bauman, Richard (1989) 'Performance' in Erik Barnouw, ed. *International Encyclopedia of Communications*, Oxford: Oxford University Press.

Bennett, M. R. and Hacker, P. M. S. (2003) *Philosophical Foundations of Neuroscience*, Malden, MA; Oxford.

Carlson, Marvin (2004) *Performance: A Critical Introduction*, Second Edition, London and New York: Routledge.

Debord, Guy (1994) *The Society of the Spectacle*, New York: Zone Books.

Dennett, Daniel C. (1991) *Consciousness Explained*, Boston: Little, Brown & Co.

Edelman, Gerard and Tononi, Guido (2000) *The Universe of Consciousness*, New York: Basic Books.

Edelman, Gerard (1987) *Neural Darwinism: The Theory*

*of Neuronal Group Selection*, New York: Basic Books.

Edelman, Gerard (1988) *Topobiology: An Introduction to Molecular Embriology*, New York: Basic Books.

Edelman, Gerard (1989) *The Remembered Present: A Biological Theory of Consciousness*, New York: Basic Books.

Edelman, Gerard (1992) *Bright Air, Brilliant Fire: On the Matter of the Mind*, New York: Basic Books.

Evreinov, Nikolai (2002) *Demon teatralnos'ti*, Moscow: Letniy Sad.

Hartmann, Nikolai (1966) *Ästhetik*, Berlin: Walter de Gruyter.

Ingarden, Roman (1931) *Das literarische Kunstwerk. Eine Untersuchung aus dem Grenzgebiet der Ontologie. Logik und Literaturwissenschaft*, Halle: Niemeyer.

Ingarden, Roman (1960) *O dziele literackim* ['On Literary Work'], Warsaw: PWN.

Ingarden, Roman (1976) *O poznawaniu dzieła literackiego* ['On Cognition of Literary Work'], Warsaw: PWN.

Ingarden, Roman (1981) *Wykłady i dyskusje z estetyki* ['Lectures and Discussions on Aesthetics'], Warsaw: PWN.

Kubikowski, Tomasz (1993) *Siedem bytów teatralnych. O fenomenologii sztuki scenicznej* ['The Seven Theatrical Beings: On Phenomenology of Stage Art'], Warsaw: Krąg.

Kubikowski, Tomasz (2004) *Reguła Nibelunga. Teatr w świetle nowych badań świadomości* ['The Principle of the Nibelung: Theatre in the Light of Recent Research into Consciousness'], Warsaw: Akademia Teatralna.

Makota, Janina (1964) *O klasyfikacji sztuk pięknych* ['On Classification of Fine Arts'], Kraków: Wydawnictwo Literackie.

McKenzie, Jon (2001) *Perform or Else*, London and New York: Routledge.

Raszewski, Zbigniew (1991) *Teatr w świecie widowisk* ['Theatre in the World of Spectacles'], Warsaw: Krąg.

Schechner, Richard (2006) *Performance Studies: An Introduction*, 2nd revised edition, London and New York: Routledge.

Searle, John R. (1992) *The Rediscovery of the Mind*, Cambridge, Mass: MIT Press.

Searle, John. R. (December 1990 )'Consciousness, Explanatory Inversion, and Cognitive Science', *The Behavioral and Brain Sciences*, vol. 13 (4), , pp. 585-95.

Searle, John R. (1995) *The Construction of Social Reality*, New York: The Free Press.

Searle, John R. (1997) *The Mystery of Consciousness: Including exchanges with Daniel C. Dennett and David J. Chalmers*, New York: The New York Review of Books.

Segel, Harold B., ed. (1977) *Polish Romantic Drama*, Ithaca: Cornell University Press.

States, Bert O. (1985) *Great Reckonings in Small Rooms. On the Phenomenology of Theatre*, Berkeley: University of California Press.

Steinbeck, Dietrich (1970) *Einleitung in die Theorie und Systematik der Theaterwissenschsaft*, Berlin: Walter de Gruyter.

Wyspiański, Stanisław ([1903] 1970) *Wyzwolenie*, ['Liberation'], Kraków: Wydawnictwo Literackie.

# A Performattic Nightmare and a Performantic Dream

My eardrums are deaf to Polish and severely challenged by English, but in my native Spanish the term *performática* strikes a nightmarish ring.

It sounds as if wanting to summon some new crossbred science spawned by computer science (*informática*) and ancient Greece (*Ática*). It seems thus to call for a renewed 'enframing' (Heidegger) of an art that has burst its banks and turned cross-cultural, boxing it again firmly inside the Western *techne*. Though it stops short of calling it 'theatre' once again, it does, to my ears, reclaim the name once more for the attic primordial *skene*. This call sounds discordant with the intercultural and non-Western turn that performance theory has brought to our discipline. A wayward turn it would seem, which, by the sounds of it, the heart of Europe may be trying to straighten back to pointing towards its centre.

To pitch, by way of illustration, my own tent far away from the European *skene*: this renaming act reminds me of 'straightening by naming' (正名, *zhèng míng*), a pivotal tool of statesmanship in the 中国: *Zhōngguó* or China's own 'central states' in the Warring States period (-475 to -221). It was a time not unlike our own. From rampant war and carnage a kind of ancient globalization emerged, led by an aggressive empire armed with a centralized language and cutting-edge technology. It succeeded there and then in subduing *otherness* for many centuries, like the modern reincarnation aspires to do here and now.

Yet at its sources in the preceding epochs, the act of naming had been the burden of multilingual performance acts inscribed in oracles, popular festivity, songs and ecstatic ritual. Such acts had been performed mostly by discriminated *others* such as women shamans and foreign-speaking migrants or captives from the peripheries still peopled by nomads, sorcerers, demi-humans, beasts and spirits.

One of the main forces driving those practices had been their prowess in foretelling, i.e., in naming the future by mantic methods such as physiognomy (including animal physiognomy), handling milfoils sticks, smelling fragrant herbs, trance and erotic frenzy, ecstatic dancing, burning of tortoise shells and oxen scapulae, divining by the weather, landscape and firmament, etcetera. Performance, captive and despised yet necessitated, had lived a potent life as a profligacy of celebratory, orgiastic and mantic arts. And my inkling is that the same obtained and still obtains in many *other* places around the earth.

So I end up dreaming: what if one day, thanks to some meandering path carved by language on the banks of our globalization, this new hybrid science became known as 'performa*n*tics' (or, in Spanish, 'perform*á*ntica') instead? A playful '*n*' culled from '*no*!', with its curly si*n*usoid turning away from the rectilinear strictures of 'I' and 'T', is all that would be required to preserve the intercultural turn. And to insi*n*uate, most forcibly in Spanish but in English (and maybe in Polish) too, a certain tension between the singularity of a techno-attic orientation to thinking about performance, and the more plural antics of a transcultural festive-mantic one.

ENZO COZZI

# The Ceramic Age
## Things Hidden Since the Foundation of Performance Studies

ALAN READ

It is with the term *theatre*, and even *the stage*, in mind that I want to ask some questions about the current reach of performance studies. This short essay is my first attempt at putting together some materials I have been working on over the last half-year since completing a manuscript with a sub-title that runs: *The Last Human Venue*. If that was, as it implies, an exploration of last things, possible endings, extinctions and problems of appearance, then this material is more to do with first things, what the Romanian writer E. M. Cioran once called *The Trouble With Being Born*. Performatics is the midwife to this generative instinct in an affirmative moment when it is less a question of seeking the troubled subjects of enquiry than of re-associating the relations of their intensity.

One thing that both projects share is the centrality of my children to my witnessing of performances and other theatre acts, the centrality of an attempt to rethink kinship, beyond family, as a way of figuring that elusive move from intimacy to engagement, from the proximity of associations, which *ethics* describes quite well, to the duty of responsibility to others further afield, beyond one's own, whose dynamics *politics* once claimed to represent.

So I will start close to home, yesterday, in the contemporary Stone Age, propose a 40,000-year jump to the first Stone Age, then come back towards today via the Ceramic Age of my title and make some simple observations about a stage that, despite all performance claims to the contrary, has somehow remained in the Stone Age. I hope that's clear as a time line. When I was interviewed for my first professorship a decade ago, I was asked by an eminent theatre historian, with a raised eyebrow, whether my approach to historical study in my monograph *Theatre and Everyday Life* was not more on the side of piracy than custom in our field deems responsible behaviour. I am afraid that, as Johnny Depp says in *Pirates of the Caribbean: Dead Man's Chest*, I see the necessary caution in plundering and pillaging time-frames less as a rule and more as a *guideline* to inform a critical practice now.

So where *was* I yesterday? Back at the Institute of Contemporary Arts for the first time since directing the talks programme there in the 1990s. Hermione, my younger daughter, now 8 years old, was booked into what was described as a 'drawing workshop'. I took this to be a salve to the local Westminster Council that the ICA did serious outreach work and took the chance to sign up, along with other middle-class parents, to some cheap crayons and paper subsidized by the central-London dispossessed. I also knew there would be a copy of Nicolas Bourriaud's celebrated work *Relational Aesthetics* in the bookshop (there were several) and, having heard it referenced over the last year at almost every performance and visual arts event I have participated in, decided it was my chance to read it and quote it to ensure the systematic topicality of this contribution to an edition on performatics.

When we arrived, and we were briefed by the ICA staff, it became apparent that this community workshop was not quite what it appeared. Hermione was with her friends Iona and Isabel, and alongside twenty other children aged between 7 and 9, they were asked by a staff member convening the workshop an apparently straightforward question: 'What is this place?' A bright spark said, 'A museum,' to which the staff member replied, 'Yes, an art gallery.' I almost interjected that this might be something of moot distinction, but saw Hermione giving me the warning eye, so I didn't. 'And do you make art?' a staff member asked. 'Yes,' said the children unanimously. 'And are you artists?' 'No,' said most of the children, forgetting the permission granted them some years before by Joseph Beuys. 'Would you like to be artists?' said the grown-up. 'Yes!' the children cried (and our inner parenting-artist-selves concurred from the sidelines).

'Right,' the grown-up said. 'Before you can get on with your drawing workshop, we would like you to split into two groups. One group will be asked to go downstairs to the gallery space, and there, without objects of any kind, you will be asked to play. Who would like to say something?' So Hermione put up her hand. 'Where's the toilet?' Hermione asked. 'No,' said the staff member, 'I mean say something in the gallery?' 'Well, if I can go to the toilet first, I am happy to say something later,' said Hermione. 'Right,' said the grown-up, 'you will step out of whatever game you are playing at the time and go up to and say the following line to anyone who comes into the gallery during today: "Hello, my name is, whatever your name is, and I would like to call the work, *This Success*.' Or you could say, if you feel otherwise: "Hello, my name is, whatever your name is, and I would like to call the work, *This Failure*." 'My name's Hermione,' said Hermione, with an economy of language that I mentally jotted down as being inherited from her mother's side.

Despite the fact that this drawing workshop had never been named, it quickly became apparent to me, from this instruction, as an insider now masquerading as an outsider to the workings of this institution, that my daughter was being briefed to become part, a speaking part no less, of a Tino Sehgal work, *Tino Sehgal 2007*, the third in his trilogy for the ICA over three years described in this way rather enigmatically in the ICA programme: 'Whether dancing museum guards, two people locked in a kiss, someone writing on the floor of an empty gallery or a conversation with a child, Tino Sehgal's situation-based pieces can be as enchanting as they are disorientating.'

As parents, who according to the staff would inhibit everything that was about to happen, we were shown the back door onto Carlton House Terrace while the shrieks and cries of our independents echoed through the building. We would be allowed back in between 6:00 and 7:00 that evening, , six hours later, to see how things ended up. This, after five weeks' continuous success and failure, was the end of the work in its ICA form, and we could participate in that ending as we wished.

I will leave it to others more expert in the reticence of Tino Sehgal's marvellous work to mine the performatics here, but I was struck by something precisely material about the success and failure of this work. And it is that materialism that I hope I hint at in my title, The Ceramic Age, though here in the ICA, the solid-state physics I am interested in are more to do with the Stone Age.

The event was being conducted in an absolutely neutral room, albeit obviously an architecturally formed exhibition space, with a white door covering the normally cherished escape route via the front desk. There was an intense display of play at work when we parents returned, with various degrees of faux theatricality and apparently innocent goodwill-brushing of girl's hair (still no objects) and clapping games. But amidst all this to-ing and fro-ing, what was inescapable was the floor, which was way too hard for its own good, or indeed for the children playing on it. At one point a boy fell and hit his head quite hard in that slightly sickening thud-like way that adults just don't do. It was pure stone, laid by the great modernist architect

48

Jane Drew in 1967, shiny and reflective of the action but unforgiving, the most utterly trapdoor-less floor that you could imagine. It was a quarried out, screen surface but one so dense as not to appear to have any light of its own nor to offer any means or hope to broach its impermeability.

And this struck me as interesting in the context of a journal issue dedicated to the promising term 'performatics', with its ring of a cross between pneumatics and pragmatics, in which the rhetorics of staging might presume that a certain *hollowness* is what supports the stage action. This is the kind of volume that the performance ensemble Baktruppen has used to great effect beneath the audience bleachers in their work across Europe in the last two decades of the twentieth century. But here, in the hollowed out, reverse figure to that ICA floor, there is an eminent tradition of exploration that links the inner-stage to the potential for revolutionary acts. The Situationists said in 1968, 'Beneath the cobblestones the beach,' and I say now, 'Beneath the stage the crocodile.' In Lindsay Anderson's 'anatomy of a public school film' from the 1960s, *If*, this hollow substage volume is the very seat of resistance for the school-boy antiheros. Beneath the school stage is a hidden world within which this kind of recovery of imagination and history, not to mention the relics of the formaldehyded anthropological machine, can be brought to light and examined. And it is from here that the revolution against the school authorities is staged in the final part of the film *Crusaders*. The liberal headmaster, whose school chaplain Malcolm McDowell has just shot on combat exercises, is meting out his own idea of discipline to McDowell and his comrades. The startling, memorable sub-stage scene that follows highlights what performative labour can give rise to by way of resistance. Off-stage is one thing, sub-stage is another, and perhaps worthy of more work where there is a volume to be explored. In the case of the ICA it was the precise quarried density that threw up the resistances on offer that day.

Well, they announced the end of the Tino Sehgal piece, and I was glad that I had taken the chance to read *Relational Aesthetics* in the café during the afternoon, above the action of my own child whom I was not able to witness in case I inhibited her prelapsarian play. For in that work by Nicolas Bourriaud I was able to establish that what Tino Sehgal is up to, alongside his contemporaries Philippe Pareno, Vanessa Beecroft, Maurizio Cattelan and Carsten Holler, is to do with what Bourriard calls 'interactive, user-friendly and relational concepts'. He asks, through exploring this work, 'is it still possible to generate relationships with the world'. His ideas of conviviality and encounter sound very much like the kind of soft performative inherent in community engagements at the fringes of theatre practice since Eisenstein occupied a factory for an event in the 1920s and Rousseau asked some years before what the public might be doing when they grouped at the village maypole.

So my first materialist model reminds me to take more notice of the ground on which action occurs, not necessarily to dig into it in a hermeneutic enterprise, the kind of archaeological model so brilliantly conducted by Mike Pearson in the works *Theatre/Archaeology* and *In Comes I*, but to account for it in my study of performances. If I am not initially interested in things hidden in the ground, I am perhaps more interested in the way in which a certain concealing is already underway in the tools that I use to encounter performance. So I will shift the focus to a method of 'grounding concepts' now on the promise that I will return to the materiality of another theatre floor by way of conclusion.

To suggest that there have been things hidden since the foundation of performance studies is to suggest that performance studies have been 'founded' in the first place, and that performance studies are somehow able to conceal things. This might be too close to an anthropomorphism of performance studies for your comfort, but all facts have a social life, and the fact of life is that disciplines have peculiarly active ones. When

Randy Newman sang in his song 'The Beehive State', 'What is Kansas Thinking? / What is Kansas for?', he was not asking whether Kansas had any *use*. I'm sure B. B. King, Dorothy from the Wizard of Oz and that wonderful song in the musical *Oklahoma* about buildings 'seven stories high' being about as far as a building ought to go, tell us what Kansas is *for*: it is a place to be striven for. Rather what might it *stand* for, what would it wish to put its name to? My question is not dissimilar: 'What is theatre thinking? What is performance for?' To what things might performance studies wish to put its name, in our name? It would be this aspirational *task* that I would consider the term performatics to describe quite well.

The history of paradigm, disciplinary or knowledge formation, is, as any *Archaeology of Knowledge* shows, one as much of concealments as of revelations. An archaeology itself is a process of disinterring those things about epistemology that have become hidden in time. But it has been the common currency of all such strategies to conceal *things*, for objects have always had a recalcitrance about them, from the chemistry laboratory to the physics chamber, that resist our humanist expectations. Things *object* to our subjecting them to experiment. The roots of the word laboratory, a word first used in English in 1608 around the time that Shakespeare was completing *The Tempest*, the 'labour of oratory', forcing things to speak, is a reminder of the violence inherent to all demonstrations of discoveries. So in its concealing of things, performance studies is in good company. It is no slight to a discipline to admit its propensity to hide things, if only in order to reveal them dramatically with the magician's exclamation 'lo and behold'. Look and behold. In this sense Richard Schechner's *Performance Studies: An Introduction* is a 'book of revelations'.

But looking is not the half of it I feel.

When *was* performance studies founded? There are no records of the earliest performances that would have been studied, they are literally pre-historic. But it is logical to assume that once the two-dimensional readings of 'media studies'

had developed, the *three dimensions* of 'live performance' would have been recognized, commented on and critically addressed for their contrasting depth and presence. To fancifully extend Philip Auslander's logic, in his book *Liveness*, that it was only at the inception of recorded television that the 'live' became identifiable as a discreet and distinct activity, it was in my view only at the inception of the first media-screen that performance could be separated out and examined for *its* difference.

The screen I am talking about here, contrary to Auslander and Bourriaud, who both presume the screen to have something to do with either televisions or computer terminals, was not the relatively recent invention of the television. But nor was it as old as the Upper-Palaeolithic cave interior at Lascaux, which Georges Bataille described as 'the cradle of humanity'. That chalked-on wall provided an early if under-illuminated prototype of the ability of human animals to picture their animal quarry and then to figure themselves as laughing at them. The shame of the hunter, the only human being pictured in Lascaux, was thus the first pictorial relationship between animal and man. But this was a bespoke artistry, unique on each extraordinary occasion from Altamira to Peche Merle. The tactility of this pigment work, the intimate relationship between hand and surface, shared more with the performance of each hunting sortie than was able to throw that performative action, restored behaviour, from one kill to the next, into any relief. We have no writing of that relationship and can only speculate with Bataille that this prehistory is our history because it announces the subject, the I, *it announces us*. Bataille figures this entrance of the human in reassuringly theatrical terms:

> What we now conceive clearly is that the coming of humanity into the world was a drama in two acts. Better still: that the second act, in which the essential matters were decided, was preceded by a much vaguer and much longer act, which is comparable in its slowness and indecisive appearance to a period of incubation. (2005: pp)

Rather the screen I am interested in here, one that was documented and can therefore be discussed sensibly and with recourse to the evidence of history, that tells us something about the foundation of performance studies, was the more modern invention of suspended narratives in mineral colour and glaze produced in the fifteen-thousand-year-old new technology of the ceramic tile. It was *this* invention, a mass-produced media technology with the limit of a prototype glass screen, that allowed commentators to distinguish between the repetitious, the mimetic and the bespoke for the first time.

The foundation of performance studies, then, if you follow my reverse logic and timeline, occurred in Egypt in the fourth millennium BC. The Near East, with its tradition of baked or sun-dried brick, was the geographical cradle of architectural ceramics. From the year 4000 BC onwards, Egyptians were producing tiles of a siliceous, sandy composition whose surface glaze was stained turquoise-blue with copper. These tiles were used to decorate the jambs of inner doorways in the Step Pyramid at Saqqara, south of Cairo. This blue, of course, was not arbitrary nor remotely abstract. For everyone who saw it, the mineral would have been instantly recognizable as concerned with contemporary conceptions of divine power and eternal life. It was readable. It signified. These tiles were written about and commented upon by contemporaries, for the first time marking them out as the first 'media' to be studied. The earlier glazed tiles used by the Assyrians and Babylonians in Mesopotamia between the thirteenth and the fifth centuries BC seem to have passed without record or notice.

Within 2000 years, by 1180 BC in the Nile Delta at the Temple of *Medinet Habu*, the tiles are picturing captured slaves of different races, fabulous beasts, real animals and symbolic signs and ornaments. The age of narrative realism begins here. The veracity of the ceramic surface and its pictorial truth-to-life from now on set off against those things that happened in front of it,

in true scale, in proximity to the spectator not abbreviated in size as demanded by the manufactured reduction of the mass-produced ceramic form.

The ceramic tile had the added dimension, critical for my argument here and any serious project that might grow from this idea today, of a porous surface to its rear-side that promised some sort of permeability with the outside world. At least it was a porosity that allowed the tile to breathe with the surface to which it was attached, which in turn would commonly be a wall with an exterior aspect and therefore prey to the vicissitudes of changing levels of damp and drought. So in the ceramic tile we have the classic bonding of a surface of impermeable aesthetics founded on a promise of interactivity with the environment within which the work takes its place.

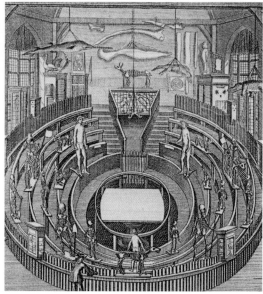

In my view we are still operating within the Ceramic Age, and not just in the operating theatres from de Waag in Amsterdam, Padua and

Uppsala for whom anatomy theatres have become tiled icons of another era of spectatorial medicine.

The Young Vic Theatre in London recently re-opened, still under the direction of the celebrated anthropologist David Lan.

It could not have escaped David's anthropological eye that the only part of his theatre's wholly rebuilt interior left untouched by the architects Haworth Tompkins were the ceramic tiles that formed the wall of a Edwardian butcher's shop integrated into the building when originally built in the 1970s.

The tiles of the butcher's shop, like those earlier in the century in more ominous surroundings across Eastern Europe, were of course well-suited to the historical delusion that the bloody transition from the life of the live to the death of the dead could be wiped clean, a

*tabula rasa* for slaughtered animals at the end of each busy day in the aptly named street in Waterloo called *The Cut*.

There is little fundamental difference between the Nintendo DS Console my daughters game with and the ceramic tile. They weigh about the same and their dimensions and opaque, milky hue are familiar. The light now emanates from *within* the screen, but the narratives are

similarly suspended close to the near-side of that screen. And of course their easy violences can be wiped clean with a single modest gesture across the surface. There is the tease of interactivity, but this like almost all gaming is fantastically limited. It's a remedial activity rather like basket-weaving would have been in a nineteenth-century home for the insane. And the porosity to the world of the tile has been traded for a specious *WiFi* link to other gaming slabs but little outside engagement.

All pictures by Alan Read

The technology at work here in the Nintendo, the *techne* or mechanics of revealing, has barely advanced on William de Morgan's Victorian tiles in my local pub. The Tabard in west London, where narratives are continued across tiles in fluid temporal dynamics. And it falls well short of the heights of soaring Moroccan mosques.

It would be the holy grail of interactivity to be in a position to announce this moment as the *end* of the Ceramic Age. Interactivity would provide us with the much-desired figure to consign the ceramic model to history. But there is little about theatre and its study, from the Greek site on, that disturbs this essentially two-dimensional model with a lustrous yet impenetrable surface and a porous back. The theatre volume could be figured as leaky to the world but only from one side at a time, and the proscenium arch reinforced the screen war in its face-off with a front-seated audience, surfaces at work rather than volumes to be entered.

A century of theatrical experiment from those Eisenstein-directed, immersive, factory pieces in the early twentieth century, through Grotowski's own para-theatricals to the current penchant for site-specific performance has done little to alter the essential face-to-face encounter of the theatrical. And all this despite the heroic efforts of Jean-Francois Lyotard in his *Libidinal Economy* to figure performance as a circulating Moebian band of energetics. 'Looking on' and wondering is the common theatrical mode of spectation irrespective of cultural origin.

It is my contention that it is this *impermeability*, like the glazed tile, that has necessitated what René Girard would have described in *Things Hidden Since the Foundation of the World* as a certain scapegoating of the theatrical by performance studies as it chases the desire of all desires, involvement in a world that it seeks to cover while hiding the resistances it encounters to occupation.

I would figure this as the *recalcitrance* of the field that the discipline wishes to enter, a recalcitrance that one rarely sees quantified in the expansionist phase of disciplines. The recalcitrance of psychology to phrenology, the resistance of astronomy to astrology and the scepticism of political materialists to phenomenology are warning signs for us here in a long-established field that would appear to have welcoming subjects when it is in fact dealing sometimes summarily with precarious objects.

Perhaps in response to this resistance to this economy of production and audience affects, performance studies always, from its earliest days in 4000 BC, figured events as privileged at the point at which they confounded this apparent distancing. More recently, in the late age of Performance Studies, the attraction of anthropology (in what has been described as the 'Schechner moment') and psychoanalytic theory (in its 'Phelan moment'), two modes of understanding that value embeddedness, participation and the allegorical interpretation of the hidden or repressed, is indicative of this urge for proximity. At least these hermeneutics announce an engagement with the 'less fake' if not the real.

Performance studies' interest in processes as contrasting as legal practices and ritual ceremonial, indeed my own interest in the anthropological machine, the architectural construction of speech sites and the performativity of the Freudian 'talking cure', share an investment in their volumetric quality, the rounded quality that can appear to be entered into, the promise of interactivity fulfilled. There is a sense in which performance studies have always wanted to *join in*, not to look on. Hence the recalcitrant, bloody-headed if not -minded obduracy of Tino Sehgal's ICA floor piece to performance thought. Performatics have used the terminology of participant observation and therapeutic dialogue to imply the interactive quality of this practice.

This emphasis is fine as long as it is not mistaken for politics. It is simply the participatory rhetorical ambience of a discipline that developed over several thousand years in tension with the dominant mode of distanced aesthetic seeing and reading that preceded it at the outset of the Ceramic Age. And while it has a welcome affirmative aspect, a collaborative social feel, it requires a synthetic conflict theory to act upon to do its work. To give its work a sense of dramatic tension beyond the obvious observation that, with a floor that dense, there is enough resistance to go around.

The melancholy ambience of a psycho-analytically informed strain of performance studies with its fascination with death, disappearance and ephemerality cannot stand in for the losses, suffering and superfluous evils that Adi Ophir has characterized as our current condition of crisis in world politics. A material inventory of loss will never be drawn up as long as the discipline of performance enquiry figures itself as infinitely mutable, unwilling to position itself at the risk of being politically identifiable and orthodox. While performance studies is unusual in its resistance to its own canonization, its willingness to sustain the fantasy of its own conflictual nature with that tired old war horse 'the stage' masks more important conflicts elsewhere.

My contention through this essay, is that Performance Studies, if it wishes to take the chance to reconfigure itself through a lens called performatics, might concern itself more actively with the longer historical material conditions for a set of 'ineffable conditions' that determine the 'distribution of the sensible', as the French philosopher Jacques Ranciére describes the policing of those who can see, speak or listen in any particular social regime. Aesthetics are politics where this distribution marks the limits of participation. In my first reading-test at school, at 11 years of age, I reached the bottom line but mispronounced the word metam*o*rphosis as metamor-*pho*sis. I was sorry that I was sent back to my desk before I had the chance to say my favourite word: idiosyncracy. My political intention is to explore the relationship between the ineffable of performance within the solid-state material of its staging as signified by the density of the floor with no trap-door, while resisting the urge to make presumptuous links between performance and politics that simply cannot hold up to any serious scrutiny.

In this project, which I conducted in some detail in *Theatre, Intimacy and Engagement: The Last Human Venue*, I take my starting point from the first line of Augusto Boal's seminal work *Theatre of the Oppressed*: 'Those who try to separate theatre from politics try to lead us into error – and this is a political attitude.' My contention is that it is only by separating theatre from politics that their potential relations can be realized. The error has precisely been to leave these two terms bonded in a fantasy of expectation and hope while patronising them both with the commiseration of failure. If performance studies sets out from anywhere, it is from the pre-condition of ecological equality, that is, from the possibility that previously discounted objects, things, materials, animals, elements, will receive attention and inclusion in an expanded collective that takes serious notice of an announcement made some years ago from within our field, regarding the 'end of humanism'.

It is in this respect that the density of the ICA floor, the image-saturated cavernous Lascaux cave and the Young Vic auditorium might be brought into a curious alignment by way of a pragmatic conclusion. Each was brought to mind the other evening watching the pre-eminent UK architectural prize being awarded at the Roundhouse in London. The spectacle of the building and good-design guru Kevin McCloud trotting out that tired old anti-theatrical prejudice in his introduction to the Young Vic Theatre segment on Channel 4's television coverage was bad enough. His fear was that this theatre would somehow confirm his suspicion about everything that is wrong with theatre and its people. But to see that prejudice compounded by the artistic director of the Young Vic, David Lan, was curious indeed. The only thing he could say to camera about this talismanic site for contemporary theatre was that he considered the rebuild a success when he witnessed two people in a 'serious smooch' on a sofa in the bar.

This Dionysian revelation was a gift for McCloud who with a smirk commented on the theatre as a great place to snog. But we had not seen the theatre at this point of the programme, and we were not meant to. We were stuck in the bar, as though the best thing to say about this project was it acted as a social lubricant – and without the pleasing irony that Tino Sehgal brings to those kissing in the gallery space referred to earlier. Well, there are many excellent bars in London, the performance cooperative Shunt runs one under London Bridge, that are much better places to snog. With a 30-second, nationally broadcast soundbite to fill, this was not the field to play on. It was as though the mocking, laughing figure of the first cave paintings had once again lessened themselves in the face of a seriously challenging rite, a rite that David Lan as an accomplished anthropologist has done so much to secure, not to sacrifice for the sake of easy social association.

For the Young Vic to arrive at the top table of international architecture in the guise of the Stirling Prize is not to succumb to this competition's own erratic terms of reference. But to be beaten out so effortlessly, as it inevitably was, by a museum of modern literature in Germany was ironic indeed for theatre enthusiasts and wholly confirming for those performance specialists who declared the institution of the stage bankrupt more than a century ago. The Marbach museum is daring in its quotation of totalitarian architectural form, but it could be anything. It does not have to be as it is, housing as it does archival objects and manuscripts that can be witnessed in a variety of ways.

But the serious absence of the auditorium from the Young Vic segment of the Stirling prize show left a void at the heart of the programme and prevented onlookers from judging in any sensible way the claims for this theatre to challenge its competition. The auditorium is not everything, but the prominence of the bar and the butcher's shop entrance in the representation of the Young Vic was telling. As telling as my own tiled diversions here in this late Ceramic Age.

There was nothing to show. That might always be the case with theatres, without the show here is no show, theatre auditoriums in this sense always disappoint the TV camera looking for its own drama. But in the case of the Young Vic, this absence hides an embarrassing reality. The venue, so critical to the recent history of British theatre, has been recovered in its recent rebuild when it should have been comprehensively re-imagined. The density of the floor, hanging as it does above a marshy, unpredictable deeper ground, retains its foundational force while sacrificing any liberty within its restraining risers.

In the case of the Royal Court in Sloane Square, the restoration project of the same partnership, Haworth Tompkins, was understandable and appropriate. A proscenium arch theatre reinforces its power in ways that meddling will not improve. This renovation reticence was the great success of the project and remains a serious pleasure for all who visit in increased numbers and comfort since its rehabilitation.

In the case of the Young Vic, the metre heightening of the auditorium is inexplicable in its modesty and conservatism. When the sunken, concrete-well auditorium of the Young Vic was originally built in The Cut, it reflected the zeitgeist of its moment. It was as solid-state as the ICA floor that preceded it by a few years. But to have mimicked that moment, as the Young Vic has been forced to do, is to have seriously lost nerve at a moment of potential radicalism and innovation, which could have stood as a serious moment of challenge to those who have all too lightly, from performance studies quarters, announced the death of the author and their texts. While Punchdrunk, Shunt and other young companies in London are seriously reinventing the scope of our theatrical and social imaginations while forgetting that all complex systems that signify have the quality of texts, the Young Vic *might*, with less fetishism of the recent past, have grasped this opportunity to look forwards not back. Down does not necessarily have to mean out.

And down (and back) it surely is: the main auditorium is apparently much loved, but it mimics that past with its stolid, serried inflexibility. The Young Vic now is the 1970s Young Vic then, with bells and whistles, which makes it close to middle age and not that young. That is a lost opportunity and one that the absence of images from the interior of the auditorium at the Stirling Prize presentation accentuated all too brutally. The theatre stands at a crossroads that the emergence of the antagonistic frames of reference exemplified by performance study mark. A crossroads that will be recognized as equivalent to the moment, more than a century ago, when the great Frank Matcham took control and revolutionized British theatre architecture from the Palace Theatre at the sea-side in Westcliff to the Lyric Theatre Hammersmith.

The architectural office of Haworth Tompkins has been rightly celebrated by journalists sympathetic to theatre's challenging cause, but with the new Liverpool Everyman to come from this practice there is still more to play for. Recognition and gratitude is timely, given the parlous state of theatre architecture in the years before this lottery-financed moment. But this respect should not turn to hagiography at the very moment when there is so much to gain.

The Young Vic, a theatre perched on the edge of a very accommodating sofa, according to its artistic director, should not have been so easily dismissed as an also-ran in this international gathering of architects. We heard nothing live to camera from Kevin McCloud about any of the candidates except for the curiously irrelevant fact that the Haworth Tompkins table at the Roundhouse ceremony had got through a few bottles of wine. Playing to the prejudices of the presenter that the theatre had turned up for a frivolously good time, while the serious heavyweight ambitions of architects such as David Chipperfield took the £20,000 goodies for the preservation of the past, was too obvious to be funny. Old Literature 1, New Theatre 0. The old story in other words. And, before it crows its oft-repeated siren warning about theatre being the extinct string quartet of another century, performance should recall that it is not even invited to the event. Its lack of architecture might be worn as a badge of peripatetic pride, but it simply marks the utter ambivalence the contemporary city has had for the pretender to tragic theatre's urban significance.

Any performance studies worth its salt would, in my view, have to account not only for its common subjects (identified historically and with an eye to victim-status by race, class and identity) but in the spirit of the democratic materialism developed in this essay begin to think through and practice the conditioning grounds of these inequalities. Subjects cannot in and of themselves tell us very much about the relations of production that gave rise to them. That the theatre has acted as the last human venue for these explorations should not privilege it in the order of performatics' other other, eclectic extra-theatrical interests. But neither should it deny the concrete stage its due weight, given that this volume is simply the denser 1970s version of what has traditionally been figured as hollow and somehow incapacitated by the demands of performance's reals. The physicality of performance here does not refer to the old binary of body and mind, practicing artist and thinking observer, but rather to the precise material conditions within which all performance does its work. The Ceramic Age within which the rhetorics of performance still operates, an apparently observable surface with the promise of an interactivity somewhere behind, is not a metaphor but a physical condition that performatics still has to get to grips with, if only to feel the slipperiness of its alluring, apparently permanent permeability.

REFERENCES

Auslander, Philip (1999) *Liveness: Performance in a Mediatized Culture*, London and New York: Routledge.

Bataille, Georges (2005) *The Cradle of Humanity*, trans. Michelle Kendall and Stuart Kendall, New York: Zone Books.

Boal, Augusto (1979) *The Theatre of the Oppressed*, trans. Charlesw A. and Maria-Odilia Leal McBride, London: Pluto Press.

Bourriaud, Nicolas (2002) *Relational Aesthetics*, trans. Simon Pleasance and Fronza Woods, Paris: Les Presses du Réel.

Cioran, E.M. (1998) *The Trouble With Being Born*, trans. Richard Howard, New York: Arcade.

Girard, René (2003) *Things Hidden Since the Foundation of the World*, trans. Stephen Bann and Michael Mercer, London: Continuum.

Lyotard, Jean-Francois (1993) *Libidinal Economy*, trans. Iain Hamilton Grant, London: Athlone Press.

Ophir, Adi (2005) *The Order of Evils: Toward an Ontology of Morals*, trans. Rela Mazali and Havi Carel, New York: Zone Books.

Rancière, Jacques (2005) *The Politics of Aesthetics*, trans. Gabriel Rockhill, London: Continuum.

Read, Alan (2007) *Theatre, Intimacy & Engagement: The Last Human Venue*, Basingstoke: Palgrave MacMillan.

Schechner, Richard (2006) *Performance Studies: An Introduction*, London and New York: Routledge.

# Performatics 1.1

Performatics studies discursive practices that are scripted and embodied.

Performatics is responding to the growing urgency to examine the constantly changing relations between discursive practices with a set script or score and the ways or the medium through which they are embodied.

The first step for clarifying the basic issues involved in this project is inspired by Roman Jakobson's seminal 1960 essay 'Poetics and Linguistics', where he distinguished between six functions, each associated with a specific dimension in the process of communication. According to Jakobson each function draws attention to, or is 'set' towards, a specific feature of this process, which when a certain function dominates the hierarchically organized system of functions defines its characteristic. When the poetic function is dominant, Jakobson argued, the communicative act draws its primary attention to the message. The 'performatic' function, adding an additional function to Jakobson's six original functions, draws attention to the fact that certain communicative acts/events are both scripted and embodied, making this combination, and the relations between 'scriptedness' and embodiment, their dominant feature.

The second step of Performatics takes up issues of representation, drawing its inspiration from Walter Benjamin's *The Origin of the German Tragic Drama*. The first sentence of this book – 'It is characteristic of philosophical writing that it must continually confront the question of representation' (2003: 27) – together with its Epistemo-Critical Prologue will serve as the theoretical basis for Performatics. Benjamin's claim that philosophical writing must confront questions of representation implies that discourses of representation, in this case embodied scripts (or scripted embodiments) must also directly confront philosophical issues. Thus the point of departure and the primary concern of Performatics is the complex, constantly re-emerging double bind between philosophy and representation.

In the first pages of his book Benjamin claims that

[i]f philosophy is to remain true to the law of its own form, as the representation of truth and not as a guide to the acquisition of knowledge, then the exercise of this form – rather than its anticipation in the system – must be accorded due importance. (2003: 28)

By emphasizing the *exercise* of this form of discourse, as an embodied practice, Benjamin the philosopher examined what it takes to perform, what its stakes are. This is his provisional answer:

Whereas the speaker uses voice and gesture to support individual sentences, even where they cannot really stand up on their own, constructing out of them – often vaguely and precariously – a sequence of ideas, as if producing a bold sketch in a single attempt, the writer must stop and restart with every new sentence. (2003: 29)

Benjamin's contested book constitutes a philosophical discourse in search of a lost script and a constantly evasive embodiment, disappearing the moment it becomes present and failing when it is most successful. The non-writing philosopher, Socrates, and in particular Plato's *Symposium*, which figure prominently in Benjamin's thesis as well as in the philosophical tradition investigating the interface between philosophy and representation, set up the third step towards the study of Performatics.

Socrates is the archetype for the performer/philosopher and the 'initiator' of/to Performatics.

REFERENCES

Benjamin, Walter (2003) *The Origin of the German Tragic Drama*, trans. J. Osborne, London and New York: Verso.

Jakobson, Roman (1990) 'Linguistics and Poetics' in K. Pomorska and S. Rudy (eds.) *Language in Literature*, Cambridge Mass.: Harvard University Press.

**FREDDIE ROKEM**

# Song from Beyond the Dark

DARIUSZ KOSIŃSKI

1

The project *Gospels of Childhood* carried out by Jarosław Fret together with Theatre ZAR is heading towards the end. Gradually the number of presentations is being limited, while the team is in an advanced stage of work on another performance and, as a matter of course, moves to quite another adventure. Despite the long, five-year period of realization and presentation in various versions, *Gospels of Childhood* has been discussed mostly in vague reviews and occasional remarks. Admittedly, in this desert, one exception did blossom in the form of Agnieszka Pietkiewicz's thesis, *Promieniowanie pamięci. Ewangelie Dzieciństwa Teatru ZAR* ['Radiation of Memory: Theatre ZAR's *Gospels of Childhood*'] written at the Adam Mickiewicz University in Poznań. But this valuable work is known to only a narrow circle of scholars and thus cannot be deemed to have influenced the performance's reception to any degree.

It may be said, therefore, that Polish theatre criticism has overlooked *Gospels* and disregarded an important phenomenon, which deserves more careful attention. It is an ambition of this text to fill the gap - at least partially. Alas this cannot substitute for the all the absent voices; to give one of the reasons, it is written from just one point of view, mine, bringing along every limitation a personal 'history' of encounters with *Gospels* imposes. In order to write about the project in full, and more in line with academic standards, one would need to go to great lengths of almost day-to-day documentation: to take part in the work, expeditions, workshops and consecutive presentations. Otherwise we are condemned to partial solutions, such as this attempt - highly subjective and uncertain even as to the factual material.

I emphasize this uncertainty in order to reduce possible expectations of the reader, as well as to find and prepare for myself a comfortable position from which to talk about *Gospels*. Thus the first - and crucial - action I should take, but am unable to, is a comprehensive description of the project. This is a severe limitation, though quite often unrecognized and underestimated. Theatre ZAR situates itself among the ensembles acting in the field whose name has been perhaps most pertinently defined by Eugenio Barba: theatre-culture. Its actions do not fall under the division of 'artistic', 'preparatory' and 'administrative', just as its work does not divide into what is connected with the performance and 'other'. *Gospels of Childhood* is not just a title of the performance, it is also the name of a whole project, which comprises work sessions with a variety of artists, workshops conducted by the team members for apprentices and guests, and expeditions - including the most important: to Georgia (Svaneti), Greece (Mount Athos) and Iran (district of the community of the Mandeans). Within this large perspective, a work of art - a performance - does not have to be a main goal for its creators. Rather, it serves as a reason for the work, as a unifying force of many different actions, essential for directing and ordering them, but not necessarily influencing the value of the experience. Even from a guest's perspective, one is able to obtain an impression that reaching Svaneti and the encounter with the tradition of funeral songs 'zar' was much more important an event that any acclaim or admiration after the performance. It is zar (and it is not an accident that the ensemble took this as its name) that is the most precious treasure and the jewel of the whole project, not only as an exceptionally powerful song but also as the fruit of a particular tradition and the intertwined cultural practices, and as a possible source for further transformations and development. Judging from Jarosław Fret's speeches, given on presenting documentation of the expeditions and work on the performance, one might gain an impression that for him the personal encounter with Svanetian culture has been an invaluable experience.

In contemporary performative arts we deal increasingly with a situation where a work of art, an artistic product, is one of many elements of a complex process or a complex project. This, naturally, has always been the case, but in the Western theatre tradition it has always been the performance that constituted a culmination point that governed material-collecting, training, rehearsals, etc. In the case of multi-stage and complex projects such as *Gospels*, creating such a hierarchy is pointless, and the performance should be treated as an integral part of a compound whole, which links artistic work with travel and anthropological and personal experience. Alas, apart from highlighting the fact that 'it should', and apart from a few simplistic remarks, I am unable to write much more about this phenomenon, since my contact with *Gospels* is, in fact, the contact of a spectator.

This first limitation does not, unfortunately, mark the end of the problems. At the first public presentation I saw (it took place as part of the celebrations of the anniversary of CTP 'Gardzienice', on 10 October 2002), a note 'work in progress' was added to the title of the performance. In fact it should be applied to *Gospels* at all times, since it is a work that - like an increasing number of contemporary theatre pieces - changes constantly, thus making it impossible for us to determine a point from which to regard it as 'ready'. Such is, of course, the nature of any performative action: while remaining always a repetition, a re-enactment, it is at the same time a unique act, happening only now, in this particular way, in these given circumstances, between itself and each spectator or witness. In this sense a theatre piece or a performance does not exist - it happens. These observations, however basic, are often forgotten or blurred in everyday theatrical and critical practice. Theatres call for, and audiences accept, the existence of a generalized theatre work that serves as a kind of a universal model for each particular spectacle. However, not only does *Gospels* not hide the differences between particular versions, it even necessitates facing them and asking the fundamental question: what was the performance you saw like, given that you say you have seen it?

Here, it is necessary to refer to the personal experience: I have seen Fret's performance eight times, of which five took place in the 'forest site' of the Grotowski Institute, in Brzezinka, some forty kilometres from Wrocław. Therefore, it is my own account, which other spectators do not have to be familiar with at all. A good many of them, after all, have only seen *Gospels* played as a guest performance in quite different spaces; moreover, among those who have seen it in Wrocław, there will be many who know only the 'studio' version, presented at the site of the Institute located in the centre of Wrocław's Old Town. This means that 'my *Gospels*' may greatly differ from 'your *Gospels*', and in writing an account or in interpreting, one must emphasize this subjectivity, rather than imply that 'my' version is 'appropriate' and, therefore, 'better'.

Another aspect of the project's variability, and what provides an additional source of complication, is related to the ensemble's composition. The original group that started to work on the project *Gospels of Childhood* was composed almost entirely of different people from today's ensemble. Changes - indeed substantial - occurred not only in the 'choir' but also among the protagonists. Among them, the most important is the change in the character of the man dressed in white garment (associated here with Lazarus), which took place in 2005. In the role formerly played by Dominik Kościelniak - somewhat angelic, boy-like, slender and fair - there appeared the stronger, more mature and resolute, dark-haired and even a little Mephistophelean Przemysław Błaszczak. The substitution seems particularly significant in respect of the monologue from *The Brothers Karamazov*, delivered by 'Lazarus' at the beginning of the performance: while Kościelniak was associated with Alosza, Błaszczak, in turn, appears more like Ivan.

When, to this maze of changes and differences, we add modifications in the composition and different ways of performing successive scenes, we receive a multifaceted, dynamic flow, which - contrary to the practice of the majority of theatre groups - presents itself as such, and even has no desire to be stopped. Thus, any interpretation, as well as any description will, patently and explicitly, form a writer's creation, his own version, added to all others, a new element of the constellation.

This does not mean, however, that *Gospels* is devoid of any consistent values that would provide a core for the variables to circle around. These constants are primarily the songs from Svaneti, the liturgical Orthodox hymns (such as *Kyrie Eleison* from the Sioni Church in Tbilisi) and the intertwined presence of the Choir that serves as a kind of support for the whole. To some extent the chronological composition of the performance's dramaturgy is also constant, as well as the arrangement and shape of particular scenes, which shall be described later. Some of the artists have not changed either: the leader of the Choir and director, Jarosław Fret, and the actresses performing the role of Mary/Martha - Ditte Berkeley (the only one who utters her lines in English thorough the performance) and Kamila Klamut. All of these constants will serve as landmarks on my way through the labyrinth called *Gospels of Childhood*.

2

Since 'my' *Gospels* is a Brzezinka performance, we need to begin with the journey and this basic fact: that in the case of watching the spectacle in Brzezinka, instead of going to a theatre located most often in the city, the audience has to decide to leave the town for more than three hours. It is, admittedly, organized and does not require any special logistical planning (as does, for instance, a trip to Gardzienice village), but nevertheless the event's character changes radically.

After an hour's drive, the coach calls into an exit off a forest road where a few people carrying flame torches are already waiting. The leader (usually Magda Mądra) informs the audience: 'We are in Brzezinka - the place where Jerzy Grotowski conducted his paratheatrical research in the '70s.' The information is important. For all of those who are familiar with the tradition of Grotowski, Brzezinka is like a legend, and *Gospels* does not move away from it. The very choice of the place, as well as emphasizing its past, implies treating the work that used to be conducted here as a tradition and as a partner in the dialogue between generations. It is a very important aspect, which needs to be highlighted before we start; often, after the performance, an opinion is expressed that *Gospels* is imitative, because it uses the achievements of Grotowski and even quotes directly from his theatre work. This criticism is based on a misunderstanding resulting from automatically falling into schemes of thinking marked out by critical clichés. There are, indeed, strong links with the artistic achievements of the Laboratory Theatre's creator. However, they are evoked in the performance clearly as part of a tradition that needs a creative, artistic response in the name of those for whom Grotowski as a theatre artist is a legend but is not part of their own experience. In some way, *Gospels* may also be read as an expression of a naïve, perhaps, but strong,

• **Ditte Berkeley in *Ewangelie dzieciństwa*.**
*Photo by Tom Dombrowski*

childlike faith in the possibility of creating a theatre in which few still believe but for which many yearn: a theatre opening a perspective of verticality and transcendence. *Gospels* (referring in the very title to the Laboratory Theatre performance that provided a departure point for *Apocalypsis cum Figuris*) provides a basis for a multi-layered dialogue with tradition, a dialogue somewhat concealed yet distinctive.

This begins during the first seconds of the performance. When, after a few moments's waiting, the audience enters into a spacious room situated in the centre of the ground floor of the old farm house, they hear a song that is ending. The Choir disperses; its members begin to put out the candles and tidy the interior after something that has just been performed. An extraordinary beginning indeed - to come in, sit down to watch, only to realize it is over. Of course nobody expects to have come to Brzezinka in vain, but still, when the actors scrape wax off the table, hang white sheets out, blow out the rest of the candles and leave, one has a strong feeling of being late for something. As seen in Brzezinka, this scene conveys the essence of the complicated situation that the generation after Grotowski faces; not being 'the sons' or the direct inheritors, devoid of the possibility of basing work on their own direct experience, they search within this tradition to find their own source. Naturally, the initial lateness refers as well to other types of legacy, including the religious. This scene finds its sources in an almost anecdotal event, which took place during one of the expeditions. In a church in Odessa the company chanced upon the very end of a ceremony and was only able to see its remains and hear its echoes. This epilogue of sorts is at the same time a prologue that provides a meaningful frame for the whole performance. Everything that happens later in the course of the performance occurs as if after, or instead. 'Those who came too late' strive to reach the experience to which they do not have access, yet of which they do have intimations, at all times struggling with despair.

Just before the initial sequence ends, the 'technical' actions, which involve ordinary cleaning of the space, take on a shape through which an icon seems to filter. A tall, slender girl folds a tablecloth covering the table. For a moment, she holds it in her extended arms, like a dead body or its shroud. A man lights the scene with a candle. After a second, with a blow, he also puts out this source of light.

It grows dark and silent, and remains thus for a moment, which seems long – as moments of silence in theatre do. At last, the first words sound, the first notes of a song reverberate through the space, and the first light appears. Standing in it, a Man (Błaszczak) speaks an abridged and musically rearranged monologue of Ivan Karamazov from Dostoyevsky's novel, which is a rebellious act of rejecting eternal glory, in respect of the intractability of human suffering. The words, uttered calmly at the beginning, become more and more enraged, culminating in a powerful point at the end, which sounds like an accusation: 'I want to be here when everyone suddenly discovers why it has all been the way it has. I want to see it for myself, and if by that time I am already dead, then let me be raised up again.'

With these words the lights go out, but after a moment's darkness, they flash once again. Subsequent sequences are constructed from short scenes that seem as if they are unfixed pictures called from the darkness by the light and the song. The protagonists of these pictures are three women. Two of them, dressed in simple red dresses, appear in the list of characters as Mary/Martha. The first, a slender fair-haired girl (Berkeley) will gradually come to resemble the gospel Martha, taking on her alleged energy and firmness. Her straight, sometimes even tense body creates an impression of something hard and expressively definite. The other character (Klamut) seems to have a limited power over herself. She is uncertain on the one hand, yet on the other rebellious. Her body fails her; one might even deem her sometimes as a little handicapped (in the initial scene of cleaning she walks with a clear limp). In order not to establish fixed evangelic identities here, I shall refer to the former as 'The Bright', the latter as 'The Dark'.

The third woman (Aleksandra Kotecka) also wears a simple, dark-blue dress. She is a strong girl who stresses her distinctiveness from the very beginning. Her relation to the other characters is never made clear. She acts in between the events and the people – therefore, the name she had in the previous versions of the character list appears to be the most accurate, 'The Third One'.

The opening, oneiric sequences seem to be not personal memories so much as common ones. One of the very first is a scene depicting an agony, resembling a pieta: a young man dies in convulsion on a woman's lap. Then, there appears a sequence of images, evoking childhood memory. They are accompanied by the Choir's song *Romelni Kerubimtasa* ('Thou, who lookest like a cherubin'), which is like a river current that carries them and – every now and then – for a moment brings them to the surface. Dynamically 'edited' images are embedded in a soft, almost contemplative song, which makes the audience feel distanced from those images, as we always are whenever we speak about our memories, even the most dramatic - being separated from them by time and our own knowledge of how it all ended. The song comes to an end, and the current of memories stops. In the reigning silence, the sisters, now as if frozen and desolate, try to warm each other. Eventually, they open the door to the large fireplace in the centre of the wall opposite the audience, letting in the warm light of the flames. The silence is broken by the sound of tubular bells, joined after a moment by the Choir's intonation of Psalm 103: *Praise the Lord, O my soul …*

As the psalm sounds, in the centre of the space there appear sequences of women in labour. In the first one, The Bright is giving birth, supported by The Dark, who holds her and cools her head. After a while, The Bright springs up to join the Choir, as if cutting through the soft song with a high-pitched voice; her intervention gives the song a new dynamic. The cohesive thanksgiving harmony is suddenly pierced by a scream from quite another space - the scream of a woman giving birth in pain. In the next moment her scream changes into words that are a fusion of the evangelic teachings of Jesus with one of the best-known verses from the gnostic *Gospel of Thomas*, 'Blessed be the womb that has not conceived, and the breast that has not given milk.'

Having uttered these words, The Bright hastens back to the 'stage', to hold up and support The Dark, who has taken over the role of the giving birth. However, after a moment The Dark is left alone. The Bright walks back to the Choir to repeat the words, this time pronouncing them more powerfully and full of determination. The Choir stirs; The Bright's intervention has disrupted the thanksgiving harmony. The psalm suspends at the vowel 'a', now prolonged, and joined by the voices - higher than all the others - of The Bright and The Third One. The sound grows increasingly louder until, reaching a climax, it changes into the word *anthropos* - 'human'. At this moment The Dark's labour is over. From the sound and the flesh, a word is born, and The Man is the one to preach it.

Half-naked, and filled with some extraordinary lightness, he delivers another famous logion from the *Gospel of Thomas*: 'Blessed is the one who stays at the beginning: that one will know the end and will not taste death.' He pronounces these words without exaggerated solemnity but more like a platitude, and even surprisingly he speaks them with a laugh - somewhat Mephisthophelean and filled with mockery. This laugh soon changes into a commanding yell, 'the Door!' The subsequent commands are broken by his laughter and knocking on the table, which gradually increases in loudness, becoming a musical, rhythmical element. It is accompanied by a high-pitched sound of tubular bells, and after a while the Georgian *Amin* sounds. Once again the loudness of the song increases, as if in order to drown out the sound of knocking. Once again, another new voice pierces the song; the sharp tone given by The Bright changes into words, which constitute a modified and musically-arranged quotation from the First Epistle to the Corinthians (15: 38-42). As a response, a monologue begins, uttered by The Man, who begins with the yell, 'The Door! The Door!', which evolves into something that resembles a sermon on resurrection. He delivers it in candlelight, which sculpts his half-naked body, making him resemble the prophet from the painting by Caravaggio. He speaks quickly, and the meaning reaches the audience's ears only with difficulty. What remains is an impression of the racing thoughts of a person struggling to grasp an incomprehensible truth.

This prophecy or sermon is accompanied by three songs: first, a calm Svan version of the Trisagion hymn *Cmidao ghmerto*, then a more dynamic *Kyrie Eleison* from Mount Athos and finally, accompanying the last words of the sermon, a Georgian song about Christ's Resurrection. Both the very selection of the songs as well as their 'editing' enhance the sermon's power and provide it with meanings deriving from the liturgy (Trisagion, in Orthodox churches, is sung before the reading of the Gospel), as well as from the prayer and from Christ's Rising. However, these three contexts do not occur as fixed or stable but rather function as additional motives to the central theme, carried out by the speaker.

As The Man delivers his lesson, The Bright repeatedly tries to separate from the Choir and walk to him but is held back by The Dark. The last sentence of the sermon, 'It is necessary to rise in this flesh, since everything exists in it', is shouted three times, and the repetitions are entwined with the hymn on the Resurrection of Christ, which then evolves into the Svan song *Dzgiragi*. It has an extraordinary structure based on an abbreviated verse that sounds like the shallow, panting breath of a dying person. The Choir moves close to The Man, lighting their candles from his, and take him in. On 'the stage', holding each other, remain The Bright and The Dark. Embracing tightly, they speak the dialogue

• *Ewangelie dzieciństwa*,
**Przemysław Błaszczak.**
Photo by Tom Dombrowski

between Mary and 'her double', equated with death – taken from the gnostic *Gospel of Mary Magdalene*. For a moment, they form a unity, and in their union they are illuminated by something that seizes and embraces them, by something to which they both belong and which both serve when they are separated – in different, though mutually complementary ways.

Through the silence that falls after both the dialogue and the song ends, there reverberates the sound of a small bell, which resembles the one that can be heard before the Elevation during a Catholic Mass. The Bright unbuttons The Dark's dress, thus beginning a sequence of preparing to leave. The sisters take their dresses off, wash their feet in a bowl of water, and put their dresses back on; they also cover their heads with black scarves. The Bright acts in a quick and determined manner, whereas The Dark is drowsy and somewhat absent.

This whole sequence, diverging from other parts of the performance in both dynamics and aesthetics, is a quotation – and one that is used very consciously. It is a re-staging of probably the only ever recorded rehearsal of the Laboratory Theatre's *Gospels*. This particular sequence comes from the film made for French television by Jean-Marie Drot, although it is more widely known from Janusz Domagalik's 1980 film documentary *Pełen guślarstwa obrzęd świętokradzki* ['Full of Sorcery Sacrilegious Rite']. It is, therefore, the only sequence related to *Gospels* – and the performance which later emerged from it, *Apocalypsis cum Figuris* – that can possibly be known to the generation which 'came too late'. It is noteworthy that in this moment, and in the following reprise of this sequence, the Marys from *Gospels of Childhood* will never reach the Sepulchre and lift the shrouds left inside, as occured in the filmed rehearsal and (in a slightly changed form) in *Apocalypsis*. After a long while of preparation, the two sisters stand next to each other, ready to go. They start walking, but soon The Dark runs back to collect the flask she has forgotten. One clumsy movement and the oil flask falls to the ground and smashes. The Dark, somewhat piqued at this, exclaims, 'I'm not going!'

At these words, the Choir walks to the door. A Polish dawn song is sung – a little noisily, to a coarse accompaniment of a trumpet and an accordion. The Choir stops by the open door, through which the forest, enveloped in the night's darkness, can be seen. Meanwhile, The Bright stands by the other door, gazing at the centre of the space, where The Dark nestles in the arms of The Man, whose white shirt is now roughly unbuttoned.

This whole scene is pervaded by the atmosphere of Polish folk piety, which blends together the high with the low, the solemn with the crude. As Fret mentioned, it is connected with his personal memories from folk weddings, which usually ended with the band and the drunken wedding guests walking out of the house to sing the dawn song. However, here, this band, into which the Choir has transformed, resembles an amateur parish orchestra, which often accompanies the traditional Resurrection processions on the Easter Sunday. In a sense, this dawn song talks about waking up from a dream, which is a shadow of death. It is, therefore, not accidental that in the performance it breaks off on the verse, 'We still wake up ...'.

This ending is closely related to the action taking place on the stage. The initially gentle caresses and hugs of The Dark and The Man grow evermore violent. The Man's mounting aggression leads him to attempt a rape. She tries to break free; he is stronger, however, and finally tears off her dress. She falls to the floor. At this moment the song breaks off, and the members of the Choir turn back to look. The Bright runs to her sister and tries to help her up. She lifts her on her back, but The Dark falls down inertly like a sack. After another attempt, The Bright throws accusations at her sister, which are a slightly changed version of the complaint in the Gospel Martha (Luke 10: 40), 'You don't care about anything, you have left me here to serve on my own.' Being unable to lift her sister, she seats her by the wall. The Choir, playing at a quick tempo a fragment of the dawn song, moves a step towards the centre of the space. The door is closed. After a short while the song *Szen giga lobt* begins - a Georgian call for the prayer.

The Dark stands up and, leaning against the wall, faces the Choir. With a voice filled with anger and pride, she speaks a monologue which, in a way, reveals her true identity as the powerful, eternal female force. The last words ('I am the one you have been looking for') are shouted out twice. The song then breaks off, to be substituted by the sound of the accordion, and subsequently, by an almost lyrical song of the Choir and the high, prominent voice of The Bright, growing ever louder. The Man drags The Third One to the centre and sets her into a spinning movement, whose rhythm is governed by the sound of the stones falling on the wooden floor of the stage. Each thump is a blow landing on The Dark, who stands against the wall. Her body is stoned with the sound, wounded with it, until it is dead. The Dark, while remaining Mary the sister of Martha, and Mary Magdalene, becomes also the harlot - stoned to death, because no Innocent stood by her.

As The Dark falls under the blows, The Third One falls down as well, and her body is covered with a shroud. After a moment's silence, The Bright quickly closes the iron door of the fireplace and opens the door in the wall to the audience's right. Rays of candlelight burst through, as well as the thumping of a hammer, like the sound of a nail being driven into a coffin or a cross, the sound of death. As if in response to it, the Leader of the Choir starts a song from the Catholic funeral liturgy, a prayer that is sung at the cemetery moments before lowering the coffin to the tomb. The solo intonation, set against the indifferent background, is immensely powerful, as it refers to the most traumatic personal experience. The clash of the solemn prayer with the technical, professionally cold service is like putting a finger back into the wound we have long thought to be healed.

When the song ceases and the doors close, The Bright lights a candle and puts it next to the place where her sister lies. Meanwhile, The Third One stands up, walks to the table and - with one slow movement - throws all the objects lying on it to the floor. The Bright pours water into a bowl and washes her hands. After a while, The Dark rises, walks to her, and washes her face, hands and shoulders. The Third One covers a part of the table with a clean tablecloth. The sisters prepare, once again, to go. The Dark puts on the dress The Man tore off; The Bright, acting briskly and decidedly as ever, helps her. The Third One puts bread on the white tablecloth and pours wine into a glass. All three put on their black headscarves. They are ready.

But the expected supper does not take place. The Third One tears the loaf in two and puts the halves back on the table, then spills the wine on it. The Bright runs to the table in anxiety, but The Third One stops her and lays her head on the table by force, in a puddle of wine. The Choir, standing now almost in the centre of the stage, gives a single, wordless tone that lasts for a long time and underscores The Bright's words - taken from Simone Weil. This famous fragment, used also in *Apocalypsis cum Figuris*, focuses on a teacher who did not teach anything to the one who awaited him, and who had come to her by mistake. However, its ending differs here from the original version. As The Bright reaches the words, 'Sometimes I cannot refrain from recalling to myself, with fear and guilt, fragments of what he had told me', she is disturbed by The Dark, who says, 'Don't touch me. He said, don't touch me'. This intervention (the only time anything is uttered by The Dark in English) obviously refers to the evangelical 'Noli me tangere' (John 20: 17), thus confirming the equation of Mary, the sister of Martha, with Mary Magdalene.

The Choir's song evolves into *Kyrie Eleison* from the Sioni church, which is one of the two musical pillars of the performance. The three women sit at the table, on which the torn bread lies. The Bright takes *The Bible* from The Dark's hands, opens it, and with a breaking voice reads in English the fragment of the 'Gospel of St John' about the illness and death of Lazarus. When she reaches the words 'Mary and her sister Martha', The Dark interrupts, shouting 'Mary!', 'Martha!' The Bright insists, but The Dark does not give up: 'Mary!', she shouts again and takes over the reading in Polish: 'It was Mary who anointed the Lord with ointment', she says, transforming in a way Martha and Mary into two Marys, one of whom is Mary Magdalene, the harlot. After this, The Bright intercepts the reading once again and continues until the sorrowful Martha's statement, 'Lord, if thou hadst been here, my brother would not have died.' At this moment a significant divergence from the Gospel account occurs. The words that should follow, an expression of Martha's confidence in Jesus' power, are not uttered, and the summoning of her sister only enables Mary to shout her grudge out as well. Thus, she repeats ever louder, 'If thou hadst been here.' The words evolve into a lamentation, and from it, into an incomprehensible plaintive wail that is bound with the song, creating a great polyphonic expression of resentment. It builds to reach a very high chord and then breaks off.

Silence and darkness fall. And through this darkness, *zar* - a Svan funeral song - reverberates. As Jarosław Fret says, it is a song like a column of spirits, like a stairway the soul ascends. In the performance it sounds like a response to the lamentation *Kyrie*; the two songs appear in this moment like two persons made of flesh. They are neither signs nor symbols. What is crucial is their tangible presence, beyond the reach of words, beyond images, beyond meanings. For *zar*, together with the accompanying female lamentations and cries, are heard in the *Gospels* in complete darkness. There is no image here to be seen - we are surrounded by the song, which is an absolute fact, which we are to live here and now. *Zar*, in my deepest and repeatedly confirmed experience, is an act of encountering death and overcoming it within the song, which, ultimately, not only fills the darkness but also illuminates it, although the vision is obscured.

While *zar* evolves, in the darkness, a clatter and the sound of a spade digging repeatedly in the ground can be heard. In the end, a low tone of a tubular bell sounds. The Leader of the Choir intones the initial verses of *Megistis Pascha* - a paschal song from Mount Athos. From the Choir, and still in total darkness, The Man's voice emerges, speaking the initial part of the gnostic *Hymn of the Pearl*. This time, he speaks calmly, as if revealing a truth that constitutes the very core of his knowledge. But he speaks only about the quest, about the letter his parents gave him in order to remind him of his mission. There are no words that speak about the fall and the return – there is only the imperative to strive.

Slowly, the light is brought back. The Choir leads an Easter liturgy of Resurrection, which is accompanied by the sounds of tubular bells. The Bright and The Dark lower steel cart-wheels from below the ceiling and, one after another, light thin Orthodox candles. The sound and the light announce: *Christos anesti* (Christ is Risen). This is certified by the images: an excavated tomb and shrouds lain on the floor by the women. In the finale, the sound mounts once again until it reaches a climax; the last sound is a single chime of the biggest bell. Before it dies away, all the actors leave. Left alone in the illuminated and suddenly quiet space, is the audience; usually staying long in the silence, sometimes somewhat anxious for a continuation of some kind, very rarely breaking impatiently into conventional clapping, but against convention, nobody comes back to thank the audience for it and bow.

3
On completing this unavoidably linear report, I am overwhelmed by a feeling of having oversimplified the experience of *Gospels of Childhood*. What does vindicate me to some extent, however, is that this loss was inevitable, because of the differences between the multi-channelled and multi-directional, spatial, sensuous and spiritual experience and the verbal and intellectual task, which writing about any performance has to be. It is precisely this difference of dimensions that creates a fundamental problem. In writing about a traditional dramatic theatre, a writer may count on an important support, namely, the linearity that results from theatre's strong connections with literature. A theatre that respects writing, also lends itself to writing. The problem arose when theatres started to appear that did not base their work on script and the stress was shifted from permanent and timeless (a record) to specific and contemporary (a performance). Artists began to seek new dramatic means, instead of using a text to be pronounced, they intended to create a kind of environment of experience built not of signs but of those means that impact on the extra-intellectual, sensory organs of perception. The most important of those means is music – traditionally contrasted with the word as one that permits a direct perception of the inexpressible.

A detailed elaboration of the differences between a theatre that is born from the word and the theatre 'from the spirit of music' needs to be put off for another occasion. I mention it here, from necessity cursorily and superficially, because ZAR is a theatre 'from the spirit of music', being one of the most prominent ensembles in Poland that develop in their own way the idea of the theatre of musicality, which finds its source in the experiences of 'Gardzienice'. *Gospels of Childhood* is a work in which the music, or more generally the sound and its dramaturgy, plays a crucial role. It is composed on music principles and could certainly be analysed with the use of music terminology.

Still, this does not mean that it is an exclusively musical opus. In addition to the songs, there are also words and actions referring to the Gospel scenes – therefore carrying a lot of cultural symbolism – as well as sequences functioning as personal metaphors, which are ambiguous, triggering equally personal associations. Yet all of them are intertwined in a composition that works more like a musical piece than a literary one, for it produces a specific overall reaction, which lies very far from 'comprehending' and, thus, is extremely difficult to verbalize. This difficulty is also connected with the discontinuity that characterizes this work and provides its uniqueness. Variability of rhythms, sudden shifts from calm and soft scenes to dynamic ones, lengthy spaces granted for silence and darkness, a relatively extensive geography of acting areas, a variety and variability of means of expression – all of this creates an impression of dispersal and discontinuity, which fades only towards the end of the performance, together with the appearance of the sequence of scenes that refers to the most renowned motif, derived from the canonical Gospels.

This discontinuity was intentional, as the creators gave the performance the subtitle 'Fragments on Intimations of Immortality from Recollections of Early Childhood'. While being a paraphrase of the title of the ode by William Wordsworth, the subtitle refers also to a famous Polish example, Adam Mickiewicz's *Forefathers' Eve*, whose title was originally intended to be *Fragments from the Poem Forefathers' Eve*.

This subtitle of *Gospels of Childhood* must be read as a suggestion for the audience not to search for ways to integrate or unify but rather to be open to encountering 'fragments' and 'intimations'. Both of these terms allude to a surface absence of what is most important. I referred to the fragmentary nature of *Forefathers' Eve* purposefully, because this masterpiece is probably the greatest example in Polish literature of an open and unfinished opus, which at the same time is a challenge and an indication of a powerful yet undisclosed force, of a core that exists, even though it seems to be empty – in other words, of a mystery. As Krzysztof Rutkowski used to say, one cannot speak the mystery out; one can only aspire to corner it. This aspiration – of not expressing directly – cannot have the structure of a linear and complete dissertation, for as such, it could only succeed in talking the mystery away. It has to be discontinuous, fragmentary, based on intimations. It aims not at signifying and communicating but at building a space for possible experience, creating opportunities, leading to ambiguities.

Such is the nature of the Theatre ZAR performance, which is not only site-specific, but also time- and sound-specific. Referring to it with the word 'performance' is only partly justified, for *Gospels* is more a sound-spatial environment, in which the events that take place are complemented by the spectator's experience. This complementary addition is, in a way, the mystery's polar opposite of discontinuity and fragmentariness. The inexpressible silence, which is the project's core, correlates with the silence scattered on the peripheries. Between them, the effect of the sounds, bodies and words is located, which, therefore, cannot be anything other than fragmentary, incomplete and discontinuous.

To respond to the character of the piece as described, and intending also – at least partially – to delimit the advantage of linearity, I would like to lend voice to the experience itself, in all its extensiveness, and to recall, to evoke my experience of *Gospels* as a certain remembered whole. What dominates is the music – above all, *zar* and the final Orthodox Greek hymns. That they 'dominate' means here simply that when I think of Fret's performance, the first thing to appear is the darkness and *zar* reverberating through it, and then the light of the paschal hymn and the lit candles swinging on the metal wheels. That they 'dominate' means also that for me *Gospels*, like the ethno-oratories of 'Gardzienice', is primarily an experience of musicality – an experience available more to a listener than to a spectator.

If I were to synthesize the effect this performance produces, the action it performed within my own experience, I would use the expression 'looming out'. I see *Gospels* as a bright seed, looming out from tangled, hazy and unclear fragments. Their dramaturgy is not a dramaturgy of journeying to reach something but one of looming out, lightening, uncovering, and – eventually – being born. From the scattered initial scenes, from the variety of their themes, a main line gradually appears, which is detectable in the darkness, and in the light of the concluding scenes. This line leads to the core of the spectacle, namely, to the death and

• *Ewangelie dzieciństwa*, Przemysław Błaszczak and Kamila Klamut.
*Photo by Tom Dombrowski*

resurrection of Lazarus, which is the situation I shall remember most distinctly. *Gospels* for me is an endeavour to cross the borderline of death, to open the door that slams shut after those who pass away. Maybe this is the reason why, out of many details I am able to recall, the one that is engraved in my memory particularly firmly is the cry, 'The Door!', woven surprisingly into the logia of the *Gospel of Thomas* - the cry that does not seem to belong to any character's line and at the same time sounds like a battle cry.

I also remember images, of course, and I was able to describe some of them. However, from the iconography of *Gospels*, what lodged itself most strongly in my memory is not so much any concrete image but the very repetitive situation: faces and bodies looming up from candlelight in the darkness, with the dynamic structure of light-shade oppositions that is present as well in the paintings by de la Tour and Caravaggio. This is connected in an astonishingly obvious manner with what I have said above about the dramaturgy of *Gospels*, namely, with the performance's basic figure of looming out.

The song and this looming out. The song that occurs in the darkness and in the light, and this that passes between the two, surfacing for a moment like a dolphin's head.

4

From among a wide range of different subjects raised by *Gospels*, I would like to point to the issues related to the dramaturgy of the performance and, consequently, to the dramaturgy of the experience of encountering it. I believe that this dramaturgy may be analysed by referring to the characters involved, together with the actions they perform and the 'model' structure that lies at their base.

The very type of existence of the *dramatis personæ* in *Gospels* is a peculiar one; it is contrary to the expectations of an audience raised on traditional dramatic theatre, accustomed to the uniformity and consequences of characters and believing in the axiom that the unity of the person with a body is tantamount to the unity of identity. Conversely, in the performance of Fret - who refers creatively also in this respect to the achievements of Grotowski and Staniewski - the identity, the body and the voice of a performer are not equated with the identity, the body and the voice of the character, which he or she allows to emerge. The audience spontaneously seeks in the performance homogenous characters 'implanted' in the bodies of the actors, while, in my opinion, it would be far more appropriate to focus on each of the performing persons and observe their journey through various situations, actions and relations with one another.

Besides being more appropriate, it would also be easier, because if one searches for 'characters', *Gospels* lays false trails. To show this strategy, let us first look at the most active participants of the events, to whom I have earlier referred as The Bright and The Dark. It is worth remembering here that they, as the only 'characters' in the performance, have kept the name that was originally proposed by the creators. Their character is, therefore, still named Mary/Martha, and written in this way. That the character's name is recorded in this way, coupled with duality presented by the performers, creates an expectation that the identity of the character will be fluid but also points to its dual unity. However, during the performance we often encounter scenes that suggest that The Bright is Martha, whereas The Dark, Mary. Sequences in which they seem to change their roles do appear, naturally; however, these occur rarely and by no means do they belong to the main course of actions. Most of the time, the two persons act - and are perceived - as Mary and Martha, even evoking directly the roles of the sisters of Lazarus in the final scene. At the same time, however, to see them as representing these specific characters throughout the whole performance would oversimplify, if not distort, the sense of their stage presence, since what is by far more important than the obvious differences between them, is what they have in common. The key scene here is, of course, the 'dialogue' from

*The Gospel of Mary Magdalene.* In the performance's synopsis it is called *Hesychia*, which on the one hand may refer to the ascetic and meditative practice of the Christian Anchorites; on the other hand, however, it is the name of the Greek goddess of quiet and stillness, the daughter of Dice. The unity that the two women characters achieve in this scene comprises both of these aspects: their communion is like a spiritual elation, like attaining mystical knowledge; but at the same time it appears as an embodiment of the goddess - of a unity built from two. Adopting the traditional Christian interpretation of Mary/Martha as a representation of two paths leading to God - of action and of contemplation - we will see that their coalescence in the act (and the figure) of Hesychia will become an image of Completeness, arising from having rejected neither possibility. Rejecting neither possibility also means resigning from choosing, as opposed to actively choosing. Here lies the great difficulty of attaining fulfillment, which appears only momentarily in the performance.

The duality and opposition of The Bright and The Dark have yet quite another aspect, which also refers to evangelical examples. It is beyond doubt that by her actions The Dark gradually comes close to those traditional interpretations that equate Mary of Bethany with Mary Magdalene. This process is clearly in evidence and made manifest through many signs. However, a question arises here, whether - in respect of such an evaluation of The Dark - we are able to track a similar change in the Bright; whether - to express this more precisely - in view of the transition of The Dark towards Mary Magdalene, some other pattern emerges connected with The Bright. I believe that the gradual emergence of Mary Magdalene out of Mary of Bethany helps us discern that in Martha another Mary is present, namely, the mother of Jesus. This process is of course not in the least as spectacular as The Dark's transition, yet placing the two characters within such a perspective allows us to understand better some aspects of The Bright's actions - the initial 'Pieta' with the tablecloth/shroud, or the fact that it is she who is later to 'teach' of, among other things, the Immaculate Conception. It is also worth remembering here that in the Christian tradition both Marys function as oppositions that gradually - and owing to the repentance of Mary Magdalene - approach one another, eventually attaining unity in their love for Jesus.

This does not mean, of course, that The Bright 'plays' Mary, the Mother of Jesus. The point is that in the case of these characters, there is no permanent 'entering into roles'. Neither The Bright nor The Dark loses her identity, described probably most accurately by Richard Schechner's formula 'not-not-me'. They are not actresses acting in their own name, but neither do they become any of the evoked characters. Through a crack in identities, which traditional theatre struggles to avoid, these characters emerge into the space, in which they can exist simultaneously in various aspects and dimensions, and point to the indissoluble unity they form. Perhaps the *modus operandi* of this process is most visible in the scene of reading the Gospel. Doubtlessly, the women who read are not the ones they read about, but at the same time - and this simultaneity needs to be emphasized - they are. Their lamentation is the lament of Mary and Martha at the grave of Lazarus and - simultaneously - the lament of Mary and Mary Magdalene over the dying Jesus ('if thou hadst been here' sounds like Jesus' own cry at that later event, 'My God, why hast thou forsaken me?'), as well as the lamentation of all mourners reverberating through the centuries. It is being sung from the crack between the characters.

Quite similar in nature are the two remaining characters I have singled out, who share the feature of losing their proper names in the course of the performance. Thus the female character that appears in the performance beside The Bright and The Dark used to bear the name The Third One, which I have taken the liberty of retaining. The Third One serves as a counterpoint to Mary/Martha. Even when she takes part in their actions, she is perceived as different. During many stage actions she alone situates herself at the opposite pole to the sisters, opposing, but at the same time, complementing them. Moreover, although all three move dynamically between different roles and registers, The Third One has much greater latitude, functioning like a trickster who can easily change shape and identity, yet who often also thwarts and counteracts the actions of The Bright and The Dark that aim at attaining something clear and permanent. The Third One, juxtaposed with The Two, is a mysterious element, a shadow and a distortion of their unity, something driven out, yet essential. Her silent presence (silent in the sense that she does not utter a single word) introduces a peculiar dynamic to the relations between characters, distorting the rising connection and equilibrium between The Bright and The Dark and at the same time in a sense opening the way for another person – The Man.

I regard The Man as an axis, around which the other characters' actions happen. Moreover, he functions as a figure that, in a sense, induces these actions. Adopting the original name of this character and assuming that The Man is Lazarus, it seems beyond doubt that the actions of Mary/Martha should be concentrated around him, while the central events – the death, the funeral and the complaint directed at the Absent – refer to him. Yet such clear-cut assigning of the character is in direct opposition to the words uttered by The Man – in relation not only to their meaning but also to their nature and place in the dramaturgy of the performance. The first monologue is, after all, a fierce accusation of God and a rejection of his order. The second monologue, the 'sermon on resurrection', is in turn a speech of a teacher and a prophet. And the third and final monologue has an air of revelation and, also, of some resignation. In addition, between those monologues delivered by The Man, his various actions take place, including the rape of The Dark and his participation in stoning her to death. All these actions and speeches seem inconsistent, although functionally they do concur in each individual situation. Perhaps The Man, therefore, is not an axis but rather a beam of various voices that speak depending on a given situation, something more of the trickster nature of The Third One; perhaps 'The Fourth One'?

That is a tempting speculation, yet it does not accord with the character's function in the realm of the performance. The Man, after all, occupies a very important place, to which the roles taken on by the other characters allude through their words and actions. It is the place of Jesus, although occupied by somebody who does not assume the role of the Absent, yet whose presence emphasizes the Absence still more strongly. The Man, even when acting as a prophet, is a person who does not act instead of, but rather during Jesus' non-presence. His four actions correspond with the four models of reaction to the Absence: rebellion, theological speculation, cruelty and striving. Among them, the least Christ-like is the action related to the stoning, where The Man brings death into the situation into which Jesus brought rescue. For this is probably the ultimate sense of the presence of The Man in the place where Christ should be – crucial for this presence is the resurrection, or, more specifically, its lack. The Man is Lazarus in the sense that he dies and cannot rise from the dead; therefore, unlike Christ, he cannot survive death. He may rebel against it, or try to rationalize it, or bring it or strive to accept it – but he cannot overcome it. His presence is at the same time the absence of God, and the journey he is on appears as a kind of recapitulation of human choices. The Man is therefore an Everyman located in the place of Jesus, yet, unable to overcome death, he is unable to replace him.

Such a reading of these four characters alludes to what I regard as the fundamental theme of *Gospels*, which is – as it has to be – resurrection. Everything that has been said here so far may suggest that it is a performance about an impossible resurrection, about a lost battle with death; that it is a lamentation over the irreclaimable 'intimations from recollections of early childhood'. But this is not true. Although *Gospels* is filled with cries of despair, its finale is comprised of resurrection, which at the same time forms an act of revealing the presence of Jesus as the one who is not subject to death. For it is not true that Christ the Saviour is absent in *Gospels* - he is present at all times in what determines and imbues all of the elements of the performance, namely, the music.

I remind once again: in the performance of Theatre ZAR, the music, the song and the sound do not constitute an illustration, or even an equivalent means of expression. It is these elements that govern the whole opus and are (literally) the dominant voice. They also delineate a dramaturgical model that is superordinate to the characters' actions, which I regard as a liturgical model. To avoid possible misunderstanding, I want to emphasize that I am not suggesting that in particular moments of the performance the Choir sings hymns and epiphonema that could suggest a reading that certain sequences are counterparts to elements of either the Catholic Mass or the Divine Liturgy. Such an operation would be unoriginal, even banal. In fact, there is only one moment in the performance in which one could try to make an assumption that the song builds an analogy between the performance and the liturgy. This moment is Trisagion, which, during the Divine Liturgy, is sung before the reading from the Gospel, and which is heard in the performance before and during the 'sermon' of The Man, preceding the scene of Hesychia. Another example, also sonic, though not a song, is the sound produced by a little bell, which can be heard before the scene of the preparation to go.

In order to comprehend the superordinate dramaturgy of the sound in *Gospels*, one would need not to watch it but rather listen to it, treating it as an opus constructed entirely from sounds. It would turn out, then, that deprived of direct analogies with the liturgy, *Gospels* is, and likewise the Mass, an action that leads to a central experience, in which the revelation of the constant Presence is symbolized here not by the Host but by the sound and the light. The journey that the people who perform in *Gospels* set out on and take throughout the performance ends on the threshold of darkness, on the threshold of the visible. Beyond, there is only the song - *zar*. If it alone is able to transcend the border between life and death and to remain in the space occupied by death, then it is beyond any doubt that the Resurrecting, to whose (un)presence all the elements of the performance allude, is present only in the song. It should not be surprising therefore that, in the synopsis of the performance, the sequence of *zar* is entitled *Lamentation of Jesus*. In this context, it seems entirely logical that the scene of the Resurrection is accomplished entirely by the song, this time directly alluding to the liturgy. One can of course see this sequence as a staging of Resurrection, but one cannot hear this scene as such. The image here emerges directly from the sound, and among the performers the characters that have earlier been singled out no longer exist. Candles are lit by 'three Marys', but also by a girl from the Choir. The performers, immersed in the song, come back to the position of operators who carry out the actions that emerge from the song and complement it. The song announces: 'Christ is Risen', and this message is confirmed by the light, which is raised to a high level to illuminate the darkness. The ultimate sense of this figure, which I have always intuitively considered as essential for *Gospels*, is therefore that from the darkness the light and the song emerge as signs of the presence of the Resurrected.

What is very important is the fact that these actions do not have the character of a ritual and do not belong to any rite. Moreover, they do not even require faith. They are provided for a direct experience which, together with the preceding journey through the darkness, forms a sensuous analogy with a liturgy construed in a direct way that leads, through symbols completed by faith, to the recognition of the Presence.

Translated by Tomasz Wierzbowski and Andrei Biziorek

# Die neuen Wissenschaftsdisziplinen der Performatik ['New Scientific Discipline: Performatik']

*The systems are dying.* Slaven Bilic

Die Virtualität nähert sich mit Hilfe immer schnellerer Prozessoren der Wirklichkeit an.

So verwischen sukzessiv die Grenzen zwischen Spielvirtualität und Realität, und genau wie im richtigen Sport und anderen kulturellen Praktiken interagieren über das Computer-Medium die Spieler mit ausgeklügelten Taktiken und Systemtricks mit- bzw. gegeneinander. Im Zentrum der heutigen posttheatralen Handlungsforschung stehen Interaktion und Code, womit gleichzeitig das globale Genre des Computerspiels als Metatechnik ältere Dramaturgien des bürgerlichen Illusionstheaters wie auch des postdramatischen Theaters abgelöst hat.

Als exemplarisch stellt sich dabei die Lage bei den weniger kampfbetonten und eher philosophischen Gesellschafts- und Weltherstellungsspielen dar, z.B. *Second Life*, denn deren System beinhaltet die Herausforderung, eine soziales, ökonomisches und kulturelles Gebilde und Zusammenhänge zu formatieren und spielerisch zu er-leben. Dabei kommt es in *Second Life*, der virtuellen Spielwelt im globalen Internetzeitalter, zu wenig überraschenden wirtschaftlichen System-Verhaltensweisen (man muss „Resident" werden, Mieten bezahlen, und die Bewohner beginnen damit, Besitzobjekte und Liegenschaften je nach „Marktwert" in der virtuellen Landschaft anzubieten und zu vermieten). Das digitale Spiel-System hat sich demnach den spätkapitalistischen Bedingungen des Ersten Lebens und seiner künstlerischen Virtualitäten angepasst. Das *Second Life* ist eine Börsenwelt des Kunst- und Avatarbetriebs und der menschlichen Projektionen oder Vorstellungshorizonte, die als dynamische Regelkreise beschrieben werden können.

Performatik ist die Wissenschaft von Handlungs-Wahrscheinlichkeiten, -Möglichkeiten und -Beschränkungen (durch Regelsysteme). Der mediale Kampf um Aufmerksamkeit und Präsenz erfordert vom einzelnen Akteur, sich in den Netzwerken von Raum-Zeit-Dynamiken zu positionieren. Und das immer wieder neu: Anhalten, Raum dimensionieren, selbstbestimmte Bewegung im Raum erzeugen. Die augenblickliche Verlinkung ist das Zeichen der Selbsterhaltung in erhöhter Abhängigkeit von Umweltinformationen, internen Arrangements der Informationsverarbeitung, Informationsauswahl, der Entscheidungen und der Zeitregie. Die Gestaltung von Umgebungen, die immer wieder neue Bezüge zwischen Anwesenden und den sie umgebenden Koordinaten Zeit und Raum generieren, fordern Ansätze zu einer performatischen Phänomenologie der Begegnung in virtuellen Umgebungen heraus.

Vergleicht man die Performatik mit der Informatik, ist auch letztere nicht vorwiegend mit Computern beschäftigt, sondern benutzt diese als Medium dazu, um theoretische Konzepte praktisch umzusetzen. Die Informatik war sozusagen ein Schnittpunkt der Mathematik, Elektro- und Nachrichtentechnik und konzentrierte sich auf die maschinelle Realisierbarkeit von theoretischen (mathematischen) Konzepten. Eines der interessantesten Teilgebiete der Informatik war die Künstliche Intelligenz (KI). Die KI, die mit Hilfe der Logik, Linguistik, Neurophysiologie und Kognitionspsychologie, auf maschineller Ebene versuchte einen (möglichst großen) Ausschnitt menschlichen Bewusstseins zu simulieren, unterscheidet sich hauptsächlich in der Methodik von der klassischen Informatik: Während in der klassischen Informatik eine vollständige Lösungsbeschreibung vorgegeben wird, wurde es zum Anliegen der KI, dass der Computer selbst nach einer Lösung sucht. Was ist nun Taktik (Spielsystem) des Computers, um ihm gestellte Aufgaben zu lösen? Ein grundlegender Ansatz ist die Anwendung von Expertensystemen, die im Wesentlichen die Erfassung, Verwaltung und Anwendung einer Vielzahl von Regeln zu einem bestimmten Gegenstand leisten.

Die Performatik ist die im 21. Jahrhundert entstandene Verbindung von anthropologischer Kybernetik und Informatik, die Begriffe wie "Regelung' oder

"Selbststeuerung' als Metatechniken auf das kreative und künstlerische Spielverhalten des Menschen überträgt und eine neue Wissensform ermöglicht. Weil das Leben und die Regelung als gleichursprüngliche Grössen in Erscheinung treten, sind performatische Prozesse, Handlung und Wahrnehmung nicht mehr eindeutig einer Kultur- bzw. Naturwissenschaft zuzuordnen. Vielmehr erhält die Performatik ihre zentrale Stellung in der nachmodernen Ordnung des Wissens dadurch, dass sie eine Vielzahl unterschiedlicher Erklärungsmodi bündelt und die technische Existenz des Menschen klarstellt, d.h. sie als Struktur für jene Virtualitäten erkennbar macht, mit denen Menschen konstitutiv und ständig Umgang haben. Im heutigen digitalen Verständnis der Performatik ist Virtualität jene Matrix, in der alles eingetragen wird, was Menschen und Maschinen mit einem Aussen, also mit einer Welt, bzw. einer Umwelt im Sinne sämtlicher Systemtheorien in Beziehung setzt.

Die Formen, mit denen Menschen performatisch mit sich und der Welt umgehen, die Formung, mit der sie sich Dinge vorstellen oder veranschaulichen (vorführen), bis hin zu den Moden, mit denen sie ihr Leben gestalten, wie sie dieses Leben in seiner Ganzheit ebenso wie in seinen Teilabschnitten entwerfen und planen, wie sie ihre Interaktionen und Kommunikationen auf ein Kalkül der Chance oder des Erfolges abstellen, wie sie Risiken minimieren und Erfolgschancen erhöhen, wie sie Individuen oder Gruppen lenken, wie sie Anschlüsse herstellen, all dies wird mit Kriterien der Performatik vor dem Hintergrund der Bewegung, der Dynamik, des Entwurfes und des Sich-vorweg-Seins, d.h. der Virtualität beschreibbar gemacht (vgl. Vilém Flusser's *Universum der technischen Bilder*, Peter Weibels *Imachinationen*, u. Stefan Riegers *Kybernetische Anthropologie*).

Da die Performatik, ähnlich der Systemtheorie, keine eigene Disziplin, sondern ein interdisziplinäres Erkenntnismodell ist, erstrecken sich deren Ansätze auf vielerei Disziplinen, wie Biologie, Soziologie, Informatik, Physik, Elektrotechnik, Psychologie etc. Da es keine abgeschlossenen Kunstwerke mehr gibt sondern nur noch die ständige Dynamik vernetzter digitaler Performanz, versucht die Performatik, komplexe Phänomene zu beschreiben und zu erklären. Darüber hinaus können durch die Analyse der Struktur und Funktion eines dynamischen oder emergenten Systems Vorsagen für das Systemverhalten getroffen werden können, wie etwa bei der Wettervorhersage oder bei Übertragungen von Sport- oder Kunstevents oder bei Grossausstellungen der

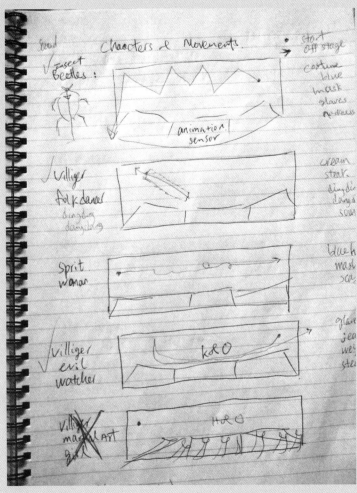

*Suna no Onna, Dans Sans Joux*, diagram for sensors and machine vision, 2007
© J. Birringer

Zombiekultur (Museum). Bei der früheren Körperkunst ist es ähnlich, denn differenzierte Analysen dynamischer raum-zeitlicher Aufführungen von Körpern können nur durch mediale Transfers und Aufzeichnungssysteme geleistet werden, die habitualisierte Muster wie auch das Agens der Wirklichkeitsproduktion erkennbar machen. Bei nichttrivialen Anschlüssen zwischen Mensch und Maschine wird es dann interessant, wenn relative Nichtvorhersagbarkeit die Phantasie der Performatik erhöht. Ziel der bis dato entwickelten Performatik ist die Erarbeitung einer formalen Theorie, die möglichst umfassend das Maximum an möglichen Variablen berücksichtigt und gleich einer Simulation sich der Realität so weit wie möglich annähert.

Um mit dem Beispiel der tschechischen Medienkunstperformance V.I.R.US (Regie: Pavel Smetana, ENTERmultimediale 2, Prag, 2005) zu schliessen: Die posthumanistische Eigenschaft magnetischer Bewegungserfassungssysteme (*motion capture*), die in einer Performance-umwelt eingesetzt werden, liegt darin, neue Erfahrungen für unseren gesamten Körper zu schaffen und unsere Körperlichkeit, wie auch die Materialiät virtueller Bilder, neu zu definieren. Die Performatik arbeitet im Sinne posthumanistischer Philiosphie daran, die Entstehung von neuen Organismen (ähnlich wie in der transgenetischen Kunst) zu beschreiben; sie kann bei V.I.R.US die Modellierung von hybriden Seinsformen, von einer verteilten Identiät, feststellen, die in der Mensch-Maschine-Interaktion eine zeitgenösssische Vorstellung der Evolution als Prozess einer Symbiogenese verdeutlicht, die nicht nur organische, sondern auch anorganische Daseinsformen benutzt. Diese neue Form der Verkörperung in Echtzeit (*real-time*) Aktion lässt auf Hybridisierung zurückschliessen, nicht nur in dieser spezifischen Performance, sondern weitgreifend in der Verschmelzung von Tanz, Technologie und Wissenschaft im Fall des Experimentierens mit Bewegungserfassung, die auch auf politische Dimensionen der "Erfassung' im Zeitalter verteilter Identitäten reflektiert. Die Performatik leistet damit auch einen Beitrag zur politischen Gesellschaftsanalyse spätkapitalistischer Macht- und Kontrollsysteme sowie der Mechanismen der Selbstregulation.

**JOHANNES BIRRINGER**

• *Suna no Onna, Dans Sans Joux*, close up of digital scenography, 2007 © J.Birringer

# Yahoo! Babel Fish, 31st July 2008 http://babelfish.yahoo.com/translate_txt

*The Virtualität approaches with the help of ever faster processors of the reality on. Thus gradually the borders between Spielvirtualität and reality smear, and exactly as in the correct sport and other cultural practices the players interact with thought out tactics and system-cheat along and/or against each other over the computer medium. In the center of the today's posttheatralen action research interaction and code are located, with which at the same time the global category of the computer game replaced older Dramaturgien of the civil illusion theatre as Metatechnik as also the post office-dramatic theatre. As exemplary thereby the situation presents itself Second Life with fewer combatstressed and rather philosophical society and world manufacture plays, e.g., because their system contains the challenge, social, to experience economic and cultural thing and connections to format animals and playful. It comes into Second Life, the virtual play world in the global Internet age, too little surprising economic system performance ways (one must become „resident ", pay rents, and the inhabitants begin to offer possession objects and real estate properties depending upon „market value "in the virtual landscape and for letting). The digital play system therefore adapted to the latecapitalistic conditions of the first life and its artistic Virtualitäten. The Second Life is a stock exchange world of the art and Avatarbetriebs and the human projections or conception horizons, which can be described as dynamic automatic control loops. Performatik is the science of probabilities of action, – possibilities and – restrictions (by monitoring systems). The medial fight for attention and presence requires from the individual participant to position itself in the networks from area time Dynamiken to. And that again and again: Continue, area dimension, certain movement in the area produce. The present/immediate linking is the indication of the self-preservation in increased dependence on environmental information, internal arrangements of the data processing, information selection, the decisions and the time direction. Beginnings provoke the organization of environments, which again and again generate new purchases between present ones and them surrounding coordinates time and space, to a performatischen Phänomenologie of the meeting in virtual environments. If one compares the Performatik with computer science, the also latter is not predominantly busy with computers, but uses these as medium to convert around theoretical concepts practically. Computer science was as it were an intersection of mathematics, electrical and communications technology and concentrated on the machine feasibility of theoretical (mathematical) concepts. One of the most interesting subsections of computer science was artificial intelligence (AI). The AI, those with the help of the logic, linguistics, neuro physiology and cognitive psychology, on machine level tried to simulate (as large ones as possible) a cutout of human consciousness, differs mainly in methodology from classical computer science: While in classical computer science a complete description of solution is given, it became the request of the AI that the computer looks for a solution. What now is tactics (play system) of the computer, in order to solve it tasks posed? A fundamental beginning is the use of expert systems, which essentially carry the collection, administration and application out of a multiplicity from rules to a certain article. The Performatik is in 21. Century developed connection of anthropologischer cybernetics and computer science, which transfer terms like "regulation' or "self-regulation' as Metatechniken to the creative and artistic play behavior of humans and a new knowledge form made possible. Because the life and the regulation go as equivalent sizes into action, performatische processes are not to assign action and perception any longer clearly a cultural and/or a natural science. Rather the Performatik receives ...*

'The invitation to contribute definitions encouraged authors to write in their 'mother-tongue' and explore the term from the perspective of their own language. This definition was written in the language system (German) where the new transdiscipline – PERFORMATIK – has emerged. Johannes Birringer did not want a full translation to appear in English and, to his knowledge, the new transdiscipline does not exist in the UK. The editors offer the first page of a Babel Fish translation which approximates the original definition but for which no guarantees can be made.'

# Surrogate Stages: Theatre, Performance and the Challenge of New Media

CHRISTOPHER BALME

It is well known that Marcel Proust spent the last decade of his life in almost complete seclusion, living in a cork-lined room, attended by a few loyal servants. Almost completely unknown is the fact that, although he seldom left his apartment, Proust participated actively in the theatrical life of Paris. He was able to comment authoritatively on concerts, opera and operettas. How was this possible? How could one attend the live art of theatre and yet be cloistered in the confines of an almost hermetically sealed room? The answer was a medium. Not the radio, which had not yet been developed for private use, but the theatrophone. Proust subscribed to a service of the same name, by means of which he listened to live theatrical performances from home. A recent biographer describes the theatrophone as 'a large black ear-trumpet connected through telephone lines to eight Paris theaters and concert halls' (Carter 2000: 497) (see fig. 1). Of course, the theatrophone is not the real thing; it is a kind of surrogate theatre for those who cannot attend the live performance. Yet for Proust, it was enough, I suspect, to hear theatre with the help of a medium. It was short-lived broadcast technology soon to be surpassed by radio and television; yet its very invention should give us pause for thought. The success of the theatrophone in the late nineteenth and early twentieth centuries suggests that the medium of theatre - even if reduced to its acoustic track - is such that it can be transformed into other media. It was also a live experience, albeit at several kilometers removed from the listener. As this rather extreme example suggests: theatre can be and has been mediated; even in such surrogated forms it can find an audience. As I hope to demonstrate, the image of Proust listening to theatre in his cork-lined room may have relevance to contemporary questions concerning the relationship between performance and new media.

Anyone visiting the theatre in the last ten years on a regular basis has become aware of the increasing use of technologies - both visual and acoustic - that in different ways 'mediate' the theatrical experience. The technologies of mediation begin with the use of surtitles, both in opera and in productions employing different languages; they continue with actors and singers equipped with headmikes, and culminate in video projections where actors may not even be physically present; spectators watch instead a digital double. Brecht's observation in 1931, 'the technification of literary production is irreversible' (1967: 156), has with slight modification - the replacement of literary with theatrical - finally come to fulfilment.[1] There are of course sites of resistance - Gallic villages of tradition valiantly defying the march of technological progress that conceive of and practice theatre as an art form in a technologically unadulterated pristine state. Unlike Asterix's lone village, however, the islands of resistance comprise remarkably large sections of mainstream theatre and - I would argue - theatre studies as well. Much experimental theatre and performance, however, does embrace

[1] In 1931 Brecht published a report on the trial surrounding the film adaptation of *The Threepenny Opera, Über den Dreigroschenprozeß*. The citation reads: 'The film viewer reads stories differently. But he who writes stories is also a film viewer. The technification of literary production is irreversable.'

and explore new technologies, and for this reason alone the questions such experiments pose are acute and should be discussed seriously within the discipline. As a discipline we cannot afford to rest on essentialist assumptions, which on closer inspection may turn out to be not ontological truths but merely attempts to reify a particular historical status quo.

In this paper I wish to discuss a number of issues surrounding the relationship between theatre, performance and technological media. Any discussion of theatre's relationship to and integration of new media technologies must engage with concepts such as 'liveness', immediacy, interaction, because they have for decades provided the defining and distinguishing concepts for our discipline. The first part of the paper will therefore review recent discussions of these concepts. Immediacy and interactivity are central to new media theory and shall be discussed with reference to Bolter and Grusin's study *Remediation* (1999). The quality of 'liveness' has been the focus of a very intense debate in theatre and performance studies on the part of both artists and academics alike. It received new nourishment with the publication of Phil Auslander's book, *Liveness* (1999), in which the author takes issue with conventional distinctions – 'mediatized' television versus 'live' theatre – and the highly value-ridden judgements associated with them. He wishes to challenge those who 'reassert the integrity of the live compared to the 'corrupt, co-opted nature of the mediatized' (1999: 39). As well as discussing Auslander's important intervention, I will also include discussions of more recent contributions such as Fischer-Lichte's *Ästhetik des Performativen* (2004).

In the second section of the paper, I wish to concentrate on two examples. The first is a recent and much acclaimed adaptation of Proust's *A la recherche du temps perdu* directed by Guy Cassiers at the ro theater, Rotterdam, entitled *Op zoek naar de verloren tijd*. It employed extremely sophisticated digital projections that went beyond a scenographic function to become genuine surrogates of the actors. It could be argued that the digitally enhanced stage is the only medium (apart from the book) that can begin to approximate the complexity of Proust's novels. The second example, *Call Cutta*, was a performance coordinated by the German-Swiss performance group Rimini Protokoll, which involved a city tour of Berlin while being directed from a call centre in India.

Using these two performances as examples, I shall in the third part of the paper discuss the disciplinary implications they – potentially – involve. The two examples – the first using a conventional stage-audience setting, the second involving site-specific interaction between an individualized listener, a medium, and a cityscape – have been chosen to illustrate that in German theatre studies, there is no dichotomy between theatre on the one hand and performance on the other. Both types of performance can be studied within the parameters of theatre studies.

• *Fig 1, The Theatrophone.*
*An Illustration from* Le Magasin Pittoresque *(1892)*

## FROM MEDIA ESSENTIALISM TO INTERMEDIALITY

Although we tend to think that the relationship between media and art is a relatively recent phenomenon, dating mainly from Marshall McLuhan's interventions in the 1960s, the question is in fact much older and lies at the heart of aesthetic theory as defined in the eighteenth century. Most of us were raised and trained in the paradigm of media specificity. The term refers, in the words of the film theorist Noël Carroll, to a form of medium-essentialism: 'It is the doctrine that that each artform has its own distinctive medium, a medium that distinguishes it from other art forms … the medium qua essence dictates what is suitable to do with the medium' (1996: 49). Attempts to define art forms in terms of specific, incontestable medial characteristics is symptomatic of high modernist aesthetics and is rooted in its fundamental move towards form at the expense of content, or towards the medium, not the message. The concept of media specificity is, however, by no means an invention of modernism. It in fact goes back to a much older 'common place' of aesthetic theory that finds its first comprehensive formulation in Lessing's Laokoon essay of 1766, where he makes a fundamental and famous distinction between temporal and spatial arts. By critiquing the old formula of ut pictura poesis, which enabled one artform to be the model for another, Lessing introduced a new precept in aesthetic theory that privileged arguments of difference and delimitation over concepts of analogy and exchange. German idealist aesthetics refined Lessing's very general distinction by establishing a clear hierarchy of artistic expression whereby the medium of the work of art is its most unimportant aspect. Friedrich Schiller, for example, argued that the work of art (his example is acting) can be divided into three levels. In his letter to Körner of 28 February 1793 he states:

> The great artist, one could say, shows us the object (his representation is purely objective), the mediocre one shows himself (his representation is subjective), the bad artist shows his material (the representation is determined by the *nature of the medium* and the limitations of the artist).
> (Schiller 1984: 137, emphasis added, C. B.)

Schiller argues that the artist must erase the nature of the medium in order to attain the highest form of artistic expression. Let us compare Schiller's hierarchy with Clement Greenberg's famous definition of modernist painting: 'A modernist work of art must try, in principle, to avoid dependence upon any order of experience not given in the most essentially construed nature of its medium' (Greenberg 1961: 139). Needless to say, the modernist artist is one who emphasizes colour, texture, the materiality of the canvas or whatever materials are being used. Modernism adopts the concept of media specificity but reverses the hierarchical implications characteristic of German idealism.

In the 1960s we find also in theatre a similar search for and attempt to define 'the most essentially construed nature of its medium'. There are also precursors such as Copeau or Meyerhold who posit space (the *Tréteau nu*) and the body (bio-mechanics) as the essential media of the stage. In our time, i.e., the 1960s and later, we find media essentialism in Peter Brook's search for an immediate theatre in an empty space, or Grotowski's poor theatre for a few chosen spectators: both can be seen as attempts to formulate both in theory and practice the theatrical equivalent of medium-specificity. Peter Brook's search for an immediate theatre opens with the famous words: 'I can take any empty space and call it a bare stage. A man walks across this empty space whilst someone else is watching him, and this is all that is needed for an act of theatre to be engaged' (1968: 11). Jerzy Grotowski's poor theatre for a few chosen spectators is a theatre bared to the basic essentials:

> By gradually eliminating what we found to be superfluous we discovered that theatre can exist without make-up, without costumes and stage

settings, without a separate performance area (stage), without lighting and sound effects etc. It cannot exist without the actor-spectator relationship, a perceptual, direct living community.
(Grotowski 1986: 15)

Both can be seen as attempts to formulate both in theory and practice the theatrical equivalent of media specificity. Both directors, in this period of their work at least, were working with a concept of theatre reduced to its basic essentials. Both positioned their concepts explicitly and implicitly in opposition to the ubiquity of cinematic and televisual media.

At almost exactly the same time, theatre studies (and I am speaking particularly of German *Theaterwissenschaft* here) was redefining itself within the same paradigm. One can observe significant tendencies to define the scope or even essence of the subject as the problem of intratheatrical communication, i.e., what happens between stage and spectators. Theatre was defined as a special form of face-to-face communication and therefore clearly distinct from other art forms or media. The theoretical basis of this discussion is sociological theory, in particular the Chicago school of symbolic interactionism. One of the major proponents of this movement in Germany, Arno Paul, wrote in 1970: 'It is necessary to ask precisely and systematically what the constitutive moment of theatre is and from there to determine the central object of the discipline' (1981: 222). The central object is the performance and more exactly the face-to-face communication between performers and spectators. This almost fundamentalist obsession with the live performance was motivated by three strategies of demarcation: Firstly, to free the subject from its entirely positivist-historicist orientation; secondly, to draw a clear line between itself and literary criticism and, thirdly, and this is the point which is of concern here, the essentialization of face-to-face communication meant drawing a clear line of demarcation between theatre and the new, technical, audio-visual media. That this debate is by no means dead, or just a teutonic spleen, can be seen from the on-going discussion within performance theory over the status of liveness. The basic positions – for the sake of brevity we shall call them Auslander versus Phelan – restate the same debate twenty-five years after Paul, albeit with different examples and a wider frame of reference.

While the shift from symbolic interactionism to interactivity may only seem to involve a change of suffix, the gap is in fact much greater. The former refers to human beings in situations of face-to-face communication, usually without technical mediation, whereas the latter is inextricably linked to the rise of digital technology and the promises, among other things, of digitally enhanced or, depending on your ideological position, degraded versions of reality. Whatever else the digital revolution promised, it certainly delivered on its pledge to reconfigure all information according to the same code, thereby making texts and images easily storable and accessible. Little, except perhaps the actual material world of animals, vegetables and minerals seemed to be invulnerable to the all-encompassing processes of digitalization.

In the face of this genuine media revolution it is perhaps little wonder that two books appeared at the end of the decade, in 1999, that discussed the interrelationships between rather than cementing yet again the specificity of the individual media. Bolter's and Grusin's study *Remediation: Understanding New Media* and Phil Auslander's *Liveness: Performance in a Mediatized Culture* both posited intermedial rather than essentialist theories of mediatization, and both focus on notions of supposedly non-mediated experience, immediacy and liveness.

Bolter and Grusin proceed from the assumption that modern culture is defined by 'our apparently insatiable desire for immediacy' which manifests itself in increasing numbers of live broadcasts, reality television and such like. Like most US media theorists, including

Auslander, they posit television as the medial norm from which all other media deviate. To achieve immediacy, media must efface themselves by making the action of mediation invisible. Remediation is their term to describe this somewhat paradoxical process whereby 'our culture wants to erase its media in the very act of multiplying them' (Bolter and Grusin 1999: 5). This process is not, however, an invention of the digital age but can be observed in 'old' media as well. Their prime example is the technique of linear perspective in painting, which renders invisible the means whereby three-dimensional space is emulated. They also have a McLuhan-like evolutionary view of media history whereby each new medium attempts to emulate, absorb and surpass the remediation techniques of the previous one.

The spectator's desire for immediacy and technology's ability to fulfil this desire forms the subject of Auslander's study. He takes issue with conventional distinctions – mediatized television versus live theatre – and the highly value-ridden judgements associated with them. He wishes to challenge those who 'reassert the integrity of the live' compared to the 'corrupt, co-opted nature of the mediatized' (Auslander 1999: 39). Firstly, Auslander argues, the relationship between theatre and the mass media is determined by rivalry and competition. On the first page we read: 'at the level of cultural economy, theatre (and live performance generally) and the mass media are rivals, not partners' (1999: 1). Secondly, 'liveness' is not an immutable given but rather a historically contingent category that does not emerge as a distinct concept until the 1930s. One could argue in fact, according to Auslander, that today the situation is reversed. Television dominates the market for 'liveness' with its news and sports broadcasts. He shows that television, historically, drew heavily on theatrical forms for its entertainment formats, and of course originally all television was live. Performance on the other hand, and his main example is the rock concert, is increasingly reliant on technological extensions such as video screens and head mikes. Clearly, the two concepts are much more intertwined and mutually dependent than they may appear at first glance.

Auslander's book has engendered much controversial comment. Auslander develops his argument that there is no fundamental difference between live and mediatized performance by critiquing Peggy Phelan's influential book, *Unmarked: The Politics of Performance*, where he finds a convenient formulation of what he terms the ontological approach to liveness and performance: 'Performance cannot be saved, recorded, documented, or otherwise participate in the circulation of representations of representations: once it does so, it becomes something other than performance. To the degree that performance attempts to enter the economy of reproduction, it betrays and lessens the promise of its own ontology' (Phelan 1993: 146).

The controversy engendered by Auslander's intervention suggests that he touched a neuralgic point in our own disciplines. A recent sustained critique of Auslander's position can be found in Erika Fischer-Lichte's book, *Ästhetik des Performativen*, published in 2004, which has been translated as *The Transformative Power of Performance: A New Aesthetics* (2008). Fischer-Lichte defines the performative in terms of the physical co-presence of performers and spectators as a basic pre-requisite for performance. She further differentiates this given by introducing concepts from system theory and cognition studies. In place of a work accessible to hermeneutic interpretation, Fischer-Lichte describes the performative as a kind of self-regulating system. Performers and spectators feed off each other in a perpetual and self-referential feedback loop. From this position she engages with two central arguments made by Auslander:

> 1) Live events are being increasingly shaped by the demands of mediatization so that they emulate mediatized representations and thereby become second-hand representations of themselves.
> 2) Live events incorporate technologies of

reproduction such as amplification so that the live itself becomes dominated by the mediatized.

Fischer-Lichte argues that theatre and television may both be interactive media but that theatre with its potential for genuine intervention offers the more effective use of interaction. She buttresses her argument with reference to a performance by the German performance artist Christoph Schlingensief who staged a live version of the reality television show *Big Brother* by placing a container with real asylum seekers facing deportation in the middle of Vienna. Entitled *Please Love Austria: Foreigners Out*, one was supposed to 'vote out' individuals who would then be deported. The live performance clearly 'fed off' a television format, but its liveness provoked genuine interventions – at one point a group of demonstrators tried to liberate the asylum seekers. Therefore, Fischer-Lichte argues, far from being second-hand emulations, the live quality and actions produced by the performance surpassed the television original.

With regard to the second argument – the domination of the live by media technologies – Fischer-Lichte analyzes a production by the German director Frank Castorf – an adaptation of Dostoyevsky's *The Idiot* – which made such extensive use of live video that for a prolonged period actors were not physically present on stage but only visible on monitors. This was a clear interruption of the feedback loop. However, the reappearance of the actors on stage for the curtain call demonstrated that the live does not disappear in the mediated as Auslander argues. On the contrary, such interruptions produce an even stronger desire for the unmediated performer body. The reappearance of the actors in the stage lights of the curtain- call created, according to Fischer-Lichte, a kind of apotheosis, a transfiguration of the actors which in fact reinforced the aura of the live.

It is clearly necessary for Fischer-Lichte to defend liveness against both Auslander and the experiments of Castorf. Her personal response is clear: the live actor is infinitely preferable to the video version. Performance lives from the immediacy of the feedback loop of performer and spectator who literally feed off each other. My question would be: why defend the one against the other? Why is it necessary to formulate the relationship between live performance and media technology in such confrontational terms as though media and performance were engaged in a kind of agon in which the winner takes all. As I shall argue in the final section of the paper: our current discourses are determined by disciplinary exigencies and less by contemporary performance practice. As I shall demonstrate from two recent performances, the relationship between the live and the mediated is far less confrontational in artistic practice than it is in academic discourse.

## PROUST ON STAGE

In September 2005 the Dutch theatre director Ger Thijs attended *De kant van Marcel*, the fourth and final production of the ro theater's cycle *Op zoek naar de verloren tijd* based on Proust's *A la recherche du temps perdu*. He was intrigued by the many positive reactions. But during the performance he became so annoyed by what he saw and heard that he decided to instigate the annual Emperor's New Clothes Trophy for the most terrible performances that are highly praised by critics. The first award went to Guy Cassiers and the ro theater for their production *Proust 4: De kant van Marcel* [Marcel's Way]. In an article for the Dutch theatre magazine *TM*, Thijs expounded why he disliked this production so much. He criticized the lack of a dramatic story and the excessive emphasis on aesthetics and the musicality of the performance. It is devoid, he notes, of tension, confrontation and dynamics. Instead it dwells on anecdotal particularities about Marcel Proust and his housekeeper Céleste Albaret. According to Thijs, the work of Proust was neither performed nor critically approached. Instead Proust was celebrated. He writes that it all looked beautiful but continues that looking beautiful cannot be the only criterion for a work of art. He ends by saying that the performance 'is about nothing. It is always the same atmosphere, a fragment of meaning is all that remains. Elegy, melancholy. Yes the time is lost, but how pretty ... In other words: just kitsch' (Thijs 2005: 51).

Thijs also problematizes the use of projections. Drama is dialogue, he argues, interaction between actors, not between a reciter and a camera. He argues that in *Proust 4* the movements of the actors are dictated by the cameras and so no longer relate to the position of the spectators. As a consequence he calls the highly technological setting a gruesome technical corset. Nor do the projections add to our understanding of the performance; they have an entirely aesthetic function.

The controversy and debate between two theatre makers – Ger Thijs and Guy Cassiers – reveals fundamentally different ideas about what theatre should be and in particular what function technology in theatre should occupy. The hierarchy is clearly defined. The video images, if they are allocated a place at all, must be subservient to the text and the actions of the actors. As a consequence Thijs reduces the function of video in *Proust 4* to illustrating the texts of the reciters/actors (e.g., projecting images of waves when the characters talk about the sea) (Goeyens 2005).

*Op zoek naar de verloren tijd* was created by Guy Cassiers, the Flemish artistic director of ro theater, Rotterdam, over a two-year period from 2003 to 2005. The production combines actors, live music performed by a string quartet, and highly sophisticated video projections. Cassiers set himself the task of specifically adapting Proust's notoriously intractable work for the stage. But perhaps more importantly he wanted to explore how the process of *remembering* can be represented through the interplay of actors, music and both live and pre-recorded video, which together begin to approximate the dynamics of memory in at least some of its complexity.

The four parts could be termed variations on Proust and his novels rather than an adaptation in the strict sense of the word. The four parts are entitled: *Proust 1: Swann's Way*; *Proust 2: Albertine's way; Charlus' Way* and *Proust 4: Marcel's Way*. The focus, as the titles suggest, is on central characters in the novels but not on the individual novels themselves. Each part is self-contained and can be viewed independent of the others, although viewing them together, as I did at the 2005 Holland festival, reveals numerous intertextual connections between the four parts.

I wish to focus on the fourth and final part. Not only because we can take the critique of Ger Thijs as a point of departure but because this part demonstrates the possibilities that digital technology can offer as a means to represent the multi-layered dynamics of memory and remembering. The focus in this part shifts from the level of events and characters in the novels to the process of writing and remembering itself.

Levels of time and memory include:
- Proust's housekeeper Céleste Albaret's memories of her life with Proust, looking back from the 1970s
- The older writer Proust recounting his memories to Céleste,
- The young Proust himself remembering his childhood.[2]

Scenographically the stage represents on the left side Céleste's small room in Proust's apartment from 1912 until Proust's death in 1922. It is also her apartment in the 1970s, the time of narration. The middle of the stage comprises a large screen, which is further subdivided into smaller projection areas. On the far right there is a chair in which the older Proust sits and narrates into the camera. Above the screen a timeline is visible counting back each year from 2005, marking important events in each year. The timeline (and the performance) stop in 1871, the year of Proust's birth.

The progression of time is thus represented visually on two counteractive levels: the time of memory and remembering is representing as retroactive: moving backwards, whereas the

[2] See Albaret (1973). The book formed the basis of a German film by Percy Adlon, *Céleste* (1981), starring Eva Matthes.

• Fig 2, Proust 4. De Kant van Marcel. Directed by Guy Cassiers, Ro Theater.
*Photo credit: Pan Sok*

empirical progression of time on stage roughly parallels the ten years Céleste spent with Proust. Characteristic for the complexity of time and memory is an early scene where Céleste tells how she first met Proust when applying for the position of housekeeper. (Fig. 1) Lower stage left the real actress sits in the *chambre de concierge* and speaks into a camera while drinking a cup of coffee. Above we see a video image of her in close-up. Onstage the actress playing the young Céleste is being interviewed by the older Proust represented by a video projection. He specifies in precise detail how he likes his coffee and croissants. The coffee cup the older Céleste is drinking from is represented as a close-up on the large middle screen.

The coffee cup serves here as an illustration of the Proustian observation that small, quotidian objects, such as famous Madeleine cakes, can serve to set in motion the dynamics of memory, and consequently, how much there is in everyday existence to notice, relish and learn from. The plethora of projections, real bodies and faces overlapping with virtual simulacra, conveys an experience similar to reading the novels, which convey the otherworldly feeling that its events are floating in time, in and yet somehow outside of it. In point of fact the production is highly structured in terms of its temporal coordinates. *Proust 4* ends with Proust's death and his birth (on the timeline) and in the year 1972, when Céleste wrote her recollections. The timeline notes also, for the year 1984, her death.

If we turn now to the main aesthetic device in the production, the doubling of the live actors by means of video projections, we must ask what is gained by it. Thijs criticized the lack of interaction between actor and actor, as it was replaced, he argued, by interaction between a reciter and a camera. This criticism echoes Fischer-Lichte's observation that Frank Castorf's production of *The Idiot* created a yearning for the real performer body, not its digitized double. Both criticisms are predicated on, as we have noted, an antagonistic relationship between the live and the mediated, whether this is intended by the production or not. There are of course productions that focus on such questions. *Proust 4* does not, however, I would argue, thematize an adversarial relationship between the real and the projected body, although the two levels are present throughout. Instead, it makes a genuine attempt to find a theatrical equivalent for the complexities of Proust's novel and beyond. It introduces an explicitly auto/biographical approach where the novels themselves are of course fictional, albeit autobiographically inflected.

A 'theatrical equivalent' means that in this production the director takes full advantage of theatre's hypermedial potential. A hypermedium means that theatre can contain and represent most other media. The experience of reading Proust remains by definition intensely personal and private. As phenomenology taught us at the end of the nineteenth century, reading is an apperceptive activity, appealing to the ability of the individual to complete the act of perception in ways which transcend and even distort any objective or empirical qualities pertaining to things perceived. I would argue that the production makes use of video projections plus other devices to represent the multitudinous apperceptions generated by remembering. The juxtaposition of real bodies and their projected doubles demonstrates not a deficit relationship of pure original over diluted projection but rather the complex simultaneity of memory in action: Céleste's memory, Proust's memory and the spectator's memory of the three earlier sections of the four-part production.

If we are to regard the production in terms of an agon, then perhaps it should be between theatre and cinema. The production demonstrates that theatre can contain and manage levels of media interaction that cinema seldom, if ever, attempts. Flashbacks and framed narratives are only fairly simple devices in comparison to the levels employed and arranged in *Proust 4.* At certain points, up to half a dozen different kinetic images are visible simultaneously, interacting with one another. In cinematic terms this would be the equivalent to six split screens, something seldom attempted in even Peter Greenaway's wildest dreams. In comparison with Greenaway's kaleidoscopic visions, the images in *Proust 4* linger, provide the audience with time to contemplate and immerse themselves in the levels of voice, music and image.

3 For an analysis of this performance and of the genre of audio theatre, see Balme (2006).

## CALL CUTTA

My second example with which to interrogate the relationship between theatre and media is *Call Cutta*, an audio performance coordinated by the German-Swiss performance group Rimini Protokoll in 2005 that involved city tours of Calcutta and Berlin respectively, in the course of which the participants were being directed from a call centre in Calcutta. Rimini Protokoll is a performance collective made up of Helgard Haug, Stefan Kaegi and Daniel Wetzel. The performance is a further variation on an early audio performance developed by Kaegi and Bernd Ernst entitled *Kanal Kirchner*. They term their concept an 'audio theatre play', in which the viewer/listener, equipped with a tape player and headphones, takes an urban journey. Following the instructions on the tape, the viewer/listener wandered through the real world of the different cities and through the fragments of a detective story provided by the authors. The audio experience and real visual impressions combine to form a private experience on the streets of the respective cities. The narrative the audience followed on the tapes was centred around the fictitious librarian, Mr Kirchner, who had allegedly disappeared three years ago. Using text, sound effects and a music soundtrack, the tape superimposed a second, virtual reality on the well-known (or not so well-known) sites the audience walked through.[3]

*Call Cutta* followed roughly the same idea but expanded the concept from an exploration of perception to include political and economic dimensions. In February 2005 the three artists staged part 1 of their idea at the Goethe Institut in Calcutta in conjunction with local artists and call-centre workers. I quote from the Indian website:

> The world's first mobile phone theatre takes place in Kolkata from February onwards. Theatre that transforms the city into a stage. A mobile stage. Or into a game. Or into a film. You start off as the audience, but you might become the player, the user, the hero, of your personal scenography: Kolkata. Calcutta … [T]he city you thought you knew

becomes a movie which you shoot with your own eyes. The soundtrack is the conversation you are having with a person you have never met, who nevertheless is remote-controlling you within a certain matrix. Or it could turn Kolkata into something like a computer game but this time for real. No screen, no keyboards, just you and the city.[4]

In April 2005 the experiment was continued in Berlin where spectators also went to the theatre, this time the historic Hebbel Theater, and were also guided on a walk from Kreuzberg to Potsdamer Platz by call-centre employees located in Calcutta. The guides had never been in Berlin, but they provided the participants with detailed instructions, initially in German and then in English. Special city maps were developed for the project. All necessary information was prepared for the performers in the call centre in the form of a Power Point program on a monitor in front of them.

If the weakness of *Kanal Kirchner* lay in its trivial narrative line (the detective story without resolution), then *Call Cutta* more than compensates with its concern for global and historical interconnections as well as explorations of the theatrical relationship between client and agent in the special dynamics of call-centre business. Participants are guided from a garbage bin to a section of an old pre-war wall on which photos are visible. They show the Indian national hero 'Netaji' ('leader') Bose: first beside Gandhi, then next to Hitler. The Indian Berlin expert on the telephone explains Bose's significance for the struggle against British colonial rule, in which a pact with Hitler was just as expedient as the ideology of non-violent resistance.

Another important level is the relationship between participant and call-centre employee. In the *Kanal Kirchner*, the audiotrack was pre-recorded and hence locked the participant into a fixed itinerary. In *Call Cutta*, the point of departure is the supposed theatrical relationship on which this form of economic activity depends. In reality call-centre employees are trained to simulate propinquity, even though the caller and agent may be thousands of miles apart. It begins with carefully trained accents and proceeds to the point of genuine role-playing. The agents do not just speak perfect English but they even engage in small talk about the local weather or the football results in the customer's country. They sometimes even assume in real life their fake Western names in order to strengthen the illusion that they are direct neighbours of the American or English customer on the phone. Immediacy, authenticity, even in simulated form, are in the call-centre economy good for business. Perfect role-playing and identification with character, long since derelict in the theatre itself, are being resuscitated and revalued it seems in the global economy.

The relationship between client and agent or between participant and performer was integrated into the performance. The intimate relationship between two subjects, although separated by several time zones and difficult cultures, could become particularly intense, as one German review indicates:

> Yet, what part is instruction, what part invention?. Step by step Sarah [the assumed name of the Indian call-centre employee] leads me through the council housing estate in western Kreuzberg, which has – she explains - close links with India's struggle for independence. The tone alternates between service-line, autonavigation, blind date and confession. I am walking through a small park, when Sarah tells me her real name. 'My name is Shuktara.' She says I have a nice voice – hers has changed a lot since working in the call centre. Is that in the script? Shuktara asks: 'Have you ever fallen in love on the phone? Have you ever lied on the phone?' She shows me on the phone the trees with the sad eyes, guides me past a fence, makes the sounds of train station, sings, takes me down a slope and warns me about the road with a perfect imitation of traffic congestion. Was this all learned, all just read off a script? (Krampitz 2005: n.p.)

Like all of Rimini Protokoll's work, *Call Cutta* is predicated on the fundamental idea of situating performance in the real world and thereby problematizing the borders between reality and fiction. While such performances invariably begin in or around the theatre, they

[4] www.rimini-protokoll.de Last visited 26 February 2007.

either move out into the real world or they bring the real world into the theatre. In *Sabenation*, another performance by Rimini Protokoll, employees of the bankrupt Belgian airline Sabena came on stage and told their stories. A crucial factor in such experimentation with reality and fiction (which can be observed in much experimental theatre and performance) is the place that modern media play. If the function of media technology in the theatre has been, following Bolter and Grusin, to intensify the experience of immediacy, then a performance such as *Call Cutta* is continuing this tradition with the important difference that it is not content just to create immediacy and then make the medial means invisible. The medium – in this case the mobile telephone – becomes foregrounded rather than effaced because our experience of the world in the sixty-odd minutes of the performance's duration is determined by the medium. One cannot discuss a performance such as *Call Cutta* in terms of competition between the live and the mediatized: the relationship between the two is entirely symbiotic; they are imbricated into one another like Siamese twins and cannot be prised apart without severe damage ensuing.5

5 An interesting postscript: *Call Cutta* was presented at the 2006 CEBIT in Hannover (no performance) in association with DESCON Ltd.: Hall 6, Stall K53.5, 8-15 March 2006. DESCON is the software and telecommunications firm that provided the call-centre technology and personnel.

DISCIPLINARY IMPLICATIONS

In conclusion I would like to discuss some possible perspectives and areas of research for theatre studies proceeding from an intermedial paradigm. These two productions demonstrate, I would argue, the necessity to look at theatre and performance in the context of intermedial relationships where not rivalry but mutual enrichment are at stake.

1) The theatre spectator is a spectator with competence and knowledge in a variety of media. Taking cognizance of this circumstance does not mean becoming the pied piper of theatre studies, playing seductive tunes taken from MTV video clips. Nor does it mean that the theatre must subscribe to the same aesthetic of quick cuts. On the contrary: the seven to eight hours of the *Proust* production requires an exceptionally patient spectator, willing to adapt to quite heterogeneous ways of seeing and hearing. From the point of view of research, it is necessary to examine more closely different media aesthetics as a question of conventionality, i.e., as historically emergent practices of seeing, hearing and behaving rather than as essentialized properties determined by material factors.

2) If intermediality is to be taken as a historical paradigm, then theatre must be understood in the first instance as a hypermedium that was always capable of incorporating, representing and on occasion even thematizing other media. This ability is not a just a recent discovery of Erwin Piscator, the Wooster Group or Robert Lepage. An intermedial perspective could be productive for theatre historical research if, for example, the question of technical apparatus were examined more closely, not as a separate question but in relationship to other aspects of the theatre. Well before the so-called new media were invented, theatre was a technological medium in dialogue with other media. The exchange is clearly evident in the question of writing, and more importantly of the invention of printing. McLuhan's Gutenberg Galaxy fundamentally altered the medium of theatre in the early modern period with wide-ranging implications for interrelationship between language, performance and reception. The interaction between media is, however, more obvious in the area of illusionistic technologies such as the laterna magica, panoramas, dioramas and of course photography. Although the development of these media has been intensively researched in isolation, our knowledge of their interrelation with the theatre remains fragmentary.

(3) On a theoretical level a shift towards intermediality would require that theatre studies engage with the complex and often contradictory discussion of media theory. If there are two points of gravitation in the labyrinthine field of

media discourse - text-oriented and technology-oriented media theories - then it is difficult to fit the theatre into either. Therefore, one must ask if there is not a third path to explore, which would necessitate examining particular features of theatrical mediality. If we define theatre as a hypermedium, then one of these features is the potential of theatre to realize and represent all other media. A live television broadcast incorporated into a performance is live television but, thanks to the theatre's ability to recode anything it enframes, also theatre - as semioticians and phenomenologists never tire of telling us.

CONCLUSION

If theatre today is exploring the interstices of intermedial relations, then theatre and performance studies cannot afford not to follow in the wake. This means that the subject cannot define itself in counter-distinction to other media by assuming a defensive posture. On the contrary, the discipline must define theatre as a medium whose basic disposition is intermedial, that is, open to exchange. All theatre spectators today, or almost all, have at their command plural media competence. Theatre and performance, such as explored by Guy Cassiers or Rimini Protokoll, open a new perspective on the relationship between performance and the technical media, which have since the beginning of the last century posed its greatest challenge. If theatre is to gain access to a new generation of spectators and not become the string quartet of the twenty-first century, then it must define its relationship to the other media in terms of openness and productive exchange. As critics and scholars of theatre, we must do the same.

Note: An earlier version of this paper was published in Japanese in: Engekiron no henbo (Changing Aspects of Theatre Studies)' ed. Mitsuya Mori, Toyko: Ronso-sha, 2007

REFERENCES

Albaret, Céleste (1973) *Monsieur Proust*, Paris: Robert Laffont.

Auslander, Philip (1999) *Liveness: Performance in a Mediatized Culture*, London: Routledge.

Balme, Christopher (2006) 'Audio Theatre: The Mediatization of Theatrical Space', in Freda Chapple and Chiel Kattenbelt (eds) *Intermediality in Theatre and Performance*, Amsterdam: Rodopi, pp.117-124.

Brecht, Bertolt (1967) *Gesammelte Werke*, vol. 18, Frankfurt am Main: Suhrkamp.

Brook, Peter (1968) *The Empty Space*, Harmondsworth: Penguin Books.

Bolter, Jay David and Grusin, Richard (1999) *Remediation: Understanding New Media*, Cambridge, Massachusetts: MIT Press.

Carroll, Noël (1996) *Theorizing the Moving Image*, Cambridge and New York: Cambridge University Press.

Carter, William C. (2000) *Marcel Proust: A Life*, New Haven: Yale University Press.

Fischer-Lichte, Erika (2004) *Ästhetik des Performativen*, Frankfurt am Main: Suhrkamp.

Fischer-Lichte, Erika (2008) *The Transformative Power of Performance: A New Aesthetics*, New York and London: Routledge.

Goeyens, Hein (2005) 'Staging Video: On Intermediality in Theatre and the Use of Video in the Proust Performances', M.A. thesis, Department of Theater Studies, University of Amsterdam.

Greenberg, Clement (1961) *Art and Culture*, Boston: Beacon Press.

Grotowski, Jerzy (1986) *Towards a Poor Theatre*, London: Methuen.

Krampnitz, Dirk (2005) 'Callcenter-Mitarbeiter in Kalkutta führen Theatergänger per Handy durch die deutsche Hauptstadt', *Welt am Sonntag* (3 April).

Paul, Arno (1981 [1970]) 'Theaterwissenschaft als Lehre vom theatralischen Handeln', in Helmar Klier (ed.) *Theaterwissenschaft im deutschsprachigen Raum*, Darmstadt: Wissenschaftliche Buchgesellschaft.

Phelan, Peggy (1993) *Unmarked: The Politics of Performance*, London: Routledge.

Schiller, Friedrich (1984) *Über Kunst und Wirklichkeit: Schriften und Briefe zur Ästhetik*, ed. Claus Träger, Leipzig: Reclam.

Thijs, G. (2005) 'Speel, verdomme, speel!', *TM* 6 (September): 50-51.

# Towards Nu-Academia

The problems of the modern world become more and more complex. The possibility of not being able to solve them bears growing danger and dramatic consequences. There are too many limitations one faces when sticking to the practices and strategies as we know them. 'Interdisciplinary' was (and still is) the all-around strategy of the past years. The horizon of specific (academic) disciplines is supposed to be too narrow. Cooperation with other disciplines and practices is needed to cope with the ever-growing complexity of problems human societies are facing in the modern world. 'Performativity' is the magic word that promises unexpected solutions. Practice seems to have a strange magic that promises surprising results and new ways. Trust in the known practices and processes is shattered. Everything becomes performance and performative. This tells about a strong need for new strategies. High-ranking among the offered concepts are performative strategies, strategies which produce results that can be measured according to categories of their performance.

The interactive processes and active practices that are meant by the abundant use of the words 'performative' and 'performance' signal towards a dramatic shift of paradigms.

And here comes performatics, the new superscience of interactive practices and processes between everything. Embracing all fields of human existence probably, as well incorporating interactive practices between man and machine, processes between data and machine, thus going beyond borders of organic/non-organic. A holistic approach that promises an understanding of a world that slips out of the hands of mankind's abilities to describe it and finds solutions for the problems that are presented to us by that same world. It reminds of the times when cybernetics was the magic word that made scientists of all academic disciplines dream the dream of a superscience. The question remains what and above all how the new superscience will observe and describe? Is it the aim of performatics to observe dynamics, annotate rules and find repetitive structures? And isn't it that it will miss the very point of the observed practices and processes as, by definition, an academic discipline as we know it always has to keep the distance of the observer? Performatics might be the superscience that allows us to think together the best parts of other academic disciplines and combine the strategies and fields of research of various if not all academic fields. But in the end of the day it sticks to the old paradigm.

The kernel has to be practice. If not, performatics will not differ on structural levels from the approaches of the known academic disciplines and other strategies. The possibility of performatics might be to introduce practice as a strategy of (academic) research and beyond. But then it has to face that thus it shoots itself out of the realm of academic disciplines as we know them. At the same time, only then will performatics meet the mentioned change of paradigms on eye level and be more than just another derivative of all the 'performances' and 'performative' situations that surround us nowadays.

**FLORIAN FEIGL**

# A Debate between Włodzimierz Staniewski and Leszek Kolankiewicz, led by Grzegorz Ziółkowski

**Ziółkowski:** Over ten years ago, on 19 June 1994, a conversation with Włodzimierz Staniewski was held on the stage of the Stary Theatre in Cracow - among the props of *Wesele* ['The Wedding' by Stanisław Wyspiański]. A few years later, on 30 May 2000, there was an encounter with Staniewski in an Old Court Chamber of the Wrocław Town Hall, led by Ludwik Flaszen. The characters of *procurator Dei* and *advocatus diaboli* had been cast, so in this case the space played its role as well. Today, looking at the platform where you are sitting, one has an impression that we are in a boxing ring.

But let me recall yet another meeting with the same guests as today. On 6 October 2003, there was a public discussion at the Polish Institute in Rome during which Marina Fabbri, who led the talk, used a very fertile comparison. She named Leszek Kolankiewicz and Włodzimierz Staniewski Castor and Pollux.

I paraphrase: The twins Castor and Pollux were brought up rigorously. They were trained in running, archery, fighting with javelin and spear in the inaccessible, forested Tayetos mountains, which gave them supernatural health and strength. Pollux was fearsome in fist fighting; Castor unrivalled in riding the wildest horses. Inseparable, exemplars of brotherly love, they performed great deeds and became widely known by a single name, the *Dioskouroi*, the sons of Zeus.

When Castor was killed in a battle, Pollux implored Zeus not to be left alone in the world, and both were put among the stars as the Gemini constellation. Another myth says Zeus resurrected Castor, but from then on the brothers had to spend in turn one day with the gods, one day in the Underworld.

This comparison to the *Dioskouroi* seems to me right, as the paths of Włodzimierz Staniewski and Leszek Kolankiewicz cross very often. The artist ventures into *hidden territories*, and his expeditions led to the creation of theatre essays, as he calls his works. Leszek Kolankiewicz sets off on expeditions in the world of the academy, mainly on the pages of books. So - hands in gloves - an artist and a researcher. But while the passion to initiate events in the world of the academy is characteristic for the artist, the researcher responds in a creative way to the undertakings of this and other artists.

This was the case of a densely woven performance of *Carmina Burana*, directed by Włodzimierz Staniewski, and the equally dense, two-part text of Leszek Kolankiewicz, *Ave, mundi rosa!*, originally printed in *Dialog*, and later as a chapter of his book *Wielki mały wóz*. With this essay Kolankiewicz takes up the gauntlet, faces the challenge that Staniewski's performance set for researchers and critics.

Hence a question arises about crossing borders in the areas discussed. What dangers do you notice when you push them and make the domains of art and research enter into a dialogue with each other, and overlap?

**Staniewski:** The word 'expedition' was spoken. We were talking today about Juliusz Osterwa. I have the pleasure of knowing the second daughter of Osterwa, Mrs Maria Osterwa-Czekaj. Maria's idea was that Gardzienice should wander to the Eastern Borderlands [of Poland] following routes of Reduta. In fact, the expeditions of Gardzienice do not resemble the movement of a people that Maria Osterwa evoked. Our ramblings were closer rather to the plainness of the procession with Thespis's cart from his Icarian village to the city of Athens. However, she must have noticed some likeness; maybe in the desire to search for, as I called it once, 'a new, natural environment for theatre'; maybe in the fascination of the Borderlands, with the almost mystical sensation, which appears from time to time, that our roots are there? It must have been similar with Zorian Dołęga Chodakowski who travelled to the villages of the Borderlands at the turn of the eighteenth and nineteenth centuries and collected relics of pagan customs. Stanisław Pigoń sees Dołęga Chodakowski as the herald of romanticism and one of those who might have inspired Adam Mickiewicz to create a Slavic master-drama of sorcerery *Dziady* [Forefathers' Eve]. Today we have a book launch of Osterwa's *Przez teatr – poza teatr,* edited by Ireneusz Guszpit, with his excellent introduction, and by Dariusz Kosiński. There is also an outstanding book by Leszek Kolankiewicz, entitled *Dziady*.

To me all these circumstances interweave and complete each other in some way. Not necessarily because we are present here today, but because all those people searched for *valuables* of culture in the Borderlands. Borderlands understood geographically but also as belonging to the spiritual sphere and non-material culture. As if we were searching for shadows of forgotten ancestors. And suddenly it turns out that while penetrating 'ethnic' culture we all land in the culture of ancient Greece.

I have such an image that in the times of Julian the Apostate, that is during the declining years of the ancient civilization, these non-material *valuables* of Mediterranean culture were deposited with various peoples so that the songs of the ancient times could escape untouched.

1 This book is the first printed chronicle of the Poles.

I imagine that it was immersed in an aura of tragic mystery, similar to the one that accompanied the events when holy relics of the imprisoned Knights Templar, who had been sentenced to death, were secretly taken out of Paris. This contraband can be symbolized by the famous hay cart known from Breughel's painting. Let's say that in the fourth and fifth centuries the remnants of still-living ancient culture were taken out somewhere to the Balkan mountains, to the Carpathians, to Illyria, to the steppes of the Borderlands. And this is where we search today for the relics of sounds of ancient music or the remnants of the forgotten art of *cheironomy*, whose practitioners are 'those wise with hands' (*cheirosophoi*). This is a system of hand and arm movements (a dance of hands and arms) in which a word and a gesture are interconnected by invisible strings. In his book, Leszek Kolankiewicz, not for nothing associates the ancient Castor and Pollux with Lelum and Polelum.

**Kolankiewicz:** It was Miechowita's *interpretatio* from his *Kronika Polaków*[1] from the beginning of the sixteenth century. Mickiewicz adopted it in *Pan Tadeusz*. Indeed, these divinities could have a very old structure, even Indo-European: like the Indian Ashvins, like the Greek; Leli and Poleli, Castor and Pollux, like the Roman Romulus and Remus, like the Nordic Frey and Freya etc. The name of Leli has a respectable etymology: the Old Polish *lelejać się*, 'to wobble, to stagger, to rock', from the old Indian *lēlāyati*, 'to wobble' and *lālāyati*, 'to hold, to take care of'. If Leli and Poleli were really divinities of such archaic structure, they would appear in the third function in the classification of Georges Dumézil: fertility, favourable living. An oak figure from the eleventh or the twelfth century was discovered on the Fischerinsel [island] on Tollensee [lake] near Neubrandenburg, where the ancient Slavic Radogoszcz could have been located. It represented a double male bust with moustache, joined at the head and torso – interpreted as the Slavic image of the divine twins, maybe Leli and

Poleli. It was accompanied by yet another figure representing - typically for the Indo-Europeans - a female figure with breasts.

However, in my *Dziady: Teatr święta zmarłych* [Forefathers' Eve: Theatre of the Day of the Dead], I added the fourth function to the famous Dumézil scheme of three functions, as this resulted for me from the sources - and not otherwise! - that is, the function of the spirit world represented by Nija (or rather Nyja), about whom Długosz wrote in *Roczniki*[2] that his most important temple was in the city of Gniezno, the destination of pilgrimages. He must have been also an archaic divinity. The Old Polish *nyć* means 'fade, decay, die', including also the pre-Indo-European root *\*nu-*. Nyja - I agree with the interpretation of Mikołaj Rudnicki - was a god who caused living creatures to die (*nyją*) and who ruled *w nawi* - from the same word-group - that is, 'in the land of the dead'. The specific character of the pantheon of the ancient Polish divinities, in my opinion, consists in a close connection between eschatology and the third function, which should be assigned to Łada, as the patron-goddess of prosperity, with her twins Leli and Poleli (but also possibly to a duplicated goddess of growth or to a divine guardian of the human race represented by progenitors, forefathers - these deities seeming to be so archaic that they are reminiscent of the Great Mother). Like her, they are connected with the underworld and with the dead ancestors.

This relation of the third function [fertility, favourable living] and the postulated fourth [the spirit world] comes to light in the cycle of holidays from the winter to the summer solstices, from wandering groups of carolers to the Sobótka dances, with the culmination on Whit Sunday (the ancient Polish Whit Sunday), which was the celebration of life, and at the same time the proper celebration of Dziady. This relation underlies a mythological potential that was used with such a creative power by Mickiewicz.

This research in the sources was for me like an expedition that after years took place once again in a different way. The expeditions of Gardzienice in the late 1970 were a great, essential *novum* in Polish theatre, culture and - I presume - social life. From the very beginning Staniewski was inspired by academic studies. And this continues today.

First of all in the beginning there was a book by Michail Bakhtin, *Rabelais and His World*, the Polish edition of which - a great editing work of Stanisław Balbus - was published right at that time, in the mid-1970s. It was a very important work not only for historians of culture and literature of Middle Ages and Renaissance. The innovative character of Bakhtin's interpretation consisted first of all in cutting Rabelais's novel from the development of the epic form - somewhere between Boccaccio and Cervantes - and placing him in a completely different context of market-familiar speech and - more widely - of ritualistic-performative forms, specifically a celebration of carnival nature, or in a general context of the folk culture of laughter. In this way Bakhtin cast new light on the text of Rabelais that turned out to be a late artistic synthesis of this vast phenomenon of folk culture, still functioning in sixteenth-century Europe. On the other hand, he painted an extremely suggestive, fresh and alive picture of this culture. It is amazingly inspiring, especially the concept of the carnival celebrations, symbols and functions of holidays. For instance, from Bakhtin's book, Jan Kott learned a new way of reading Shakespeare. Bakhtin was the key to his second interpretation of *Midsummer Night's Dream*, from the beginning of the 1980s, *Blind Cupid* and *The Golden Ass*. This inspiration - visible also in the interpretation of *Doctor Faustus* - was shown even in the subtitle of Kott's book, *The Bottom Translation: Marlowe, Shakespeare and the Carnival Tradition*.

But surely nobody expected Bakhtin's book on Rabelais and folk culture to meet with such creative reading as it received in the artistic interpretation of Staniewski. We did not suspect that this work on the history of literature and culture could fall into the hands of someone who would translate it into practice. From his reading

[2] In his *Annals* Jan Długosz describes the history of Poland from the legendary times to 1480.

• **The Village – Gardzienice (Spring 89).** *Photo by Hugo Glendinning*

of it Staniewski drew far-reaching conclusions. He applied Bakhtin's theses on the functions of folk celebrations to contemporary theatre practice. It was a revolution in theatre life and in our ideas of what theatre could be and how it could function. In the late 1970s, in the moment of creation of Gardzienice, we – I mean theatre researchers and critics – had to move from the city and look for this group in the field. Because Gardzienice made expeditions. So in order to see their performance one had either to set off on an expedition with them, or to be in the right place at the right time – in a village that the group was to visit. The outdoor *Evening Performance*, the first work of Gardzienice – based of course on *Gargantua and Pantagruel* but already using the text of the Sorcerer from *Dziady*: *Purgatory souls!* – could have been watched only in this manner, that is, while participating in at least a fragment of their expedition.

The late 1970s to early 1980s was the time of expeditions. It was also the decline of Gierek's epoch, constant so-called 'temporary difficulties' in big cities, but in villages there was poverty, real penury – and it was exactly this environment that Gardzienice chose for themselves. Courage was needed, not only artistic but also human. And true romanticism. It charged the unprecedented village programme of Gardzienice with extreme intensity. None of us had thought before that a gathering in a village is a ready theatre environment, that it is almost a proto-theatrical phenomenon. It changed the minds of scholars significantly.

It is worth remembering two important researchers who in that pioneering period faithfully accompanied Gardzienice's search, participating in the expeditions: Zbigniew Osiński and Włodzimierz Pawluczuk. Their works inspired the ensemble (for instance *Wierszalin: Reportaż o końcu świata* by Pawluczuk) but *vice versa* as well. They both wrote texts on Gardzienice that are important in the bibliography of the group as well as in the bibliographies of the authors: *Wyprawa jako sposób życia*, *Pójście za Graalem* by Pawluczuk,

96

*Gardzienice: więcej niż teatr, Gardzienice: praktykowanie humanistyki* by Osiński.[3] These are examples with meaningful titles. And the involvement in Gardzienice's activities, especially in the expeditions, had - I guess - a deeper meaning for their own works. For example, for Professor Osiński's studies on the theatrical doctrine of Mieczysław Limanowski and Juliusz Osterwa.

Therefore, from the very beginning for Staniewski and Gardzienice, academic studies - even as sophisticated as monographs on ancient Greek music by Martin West or John Landels at the course of work on ancient material - constituted very important artistic impulses. (These studies appeared in Polish as a consequence of - it is known fact - a fashion initiated by Gardzienice). Moreover, Gardzienice organized important international conferences, all with the presence of researchers and invited artists. They created yet another field of exchange, because interactions have always been mutual.

If I can refer here to my own example, there would not have been *Dziady: Teatr święta zmarłych* were it not for my earlier experience with Gardzienice.

**Staniewski:** There would not have been my expeditions to the Tarahumaras were it not for the very beautiful, extremely inspiring and imagination-opening book by Leszek Kolankiewicz on Artaud, entitled *Święty Artaud*. The chapter on Artaud's expedition to the Tarahumaras was a challenge for me. I managed to realize my dream because I could use the map of Artaud's itinerary sketched by Kolankiewicz. I was able to take the same route: from Mexico City to Chihuahua, from Chihuahua to Creel, from Creel to Norogachic, to the settlement where - as rumours say - Artaud, who understood nothing of the language of the Tarahumaras, as they did not understand his language - spoke idiolect, *languages*, and they carried him on their shoulders like a divinity.

There are some sentences in that book, so close to me, that speak about the metaphysics of the Sierra Tarahumara landscape. And this is the honest truth. Yes, rocks, sun, the dust of the road, precipices, flora, silence - all this breathes metaphysics there. Yes, the culture there is an integral part of nature.

This journey and all that I witnessed were an intense experience for me. Actually, it reaffirmed my conviction that an expedition is one of those experiences that naturalizes theatre and sublimates an artist's ideas; it tames the imagination and brings thinking about a work to a pattern of simplicity, to a *dithyramb*. What is a *dithyramb*? A *dithyramb*, in ancient Greece, is singing and dancing of essential matters by a chorus and an actor as an exponent of the chorus's messages.

This is how I envision Artaud there - I see him shouting and gesticulating his poems against a background of the choir of the Tarahumara Indians. This picture consists both of my personal experience and of a message about Artaud inscribed by Leszek Kolankiewicz in his book.

When an academic, a scholar, writes a book about a place where he has never been, he does it through travels in a library. Still, it is also an artistic work, similar to what Bakhtin said about a philosophical and artistic experience. If a researcher does not find documentation, he should start thinking artistically and add what cannot be found in archives. Kolankiewicz's *Dziady* is such work, which not by chance was called 'satanic verses of theatre studies'. It is a treasury of knowledge and a captivating artistic work. Extremely inspiring.

**Kolankiewicz:** Once Staniewski reads about a place, about an area where there is - or might be - something precious, something that works or worked strongly for someone else, as in the case of Artaud, he just goes there straight away, or organizes an expedition. And this is how it was with his expedition into these impressive mountains of the Tarahumara Indians.

This is an attitude of a true researcher, but not

[3] Respectively the references for each work mentioned are: for *Wierszalin: Reportaż o końcu świata* ['Wierszalin: Reportage About the End of the World'] first published by Wydawnictwo Literackie in Cracow in 1974. For 'Wyprawa jako sposób życia' ['Expedition as a Way of Life'], published in *Kontrasty* 10, 1979. For 'Pójście za Graalem' ['Following the Grail'], published in *Kontrasty* 2, 3, 1983. For 'Gardzienice: więcej niż teatr' ['Gardzienice - more than theatre'], published in *Radar* 12, 1979. For 'Gardzienice: praktykowanie humanistyki' ['Gardzienice: practicing the humanities'], published in *Parateatr* II, Wrocław 1982.

all researchers have the guts to do something like this. Staniewski's curiosity, his stubbornness, his perseverance in trying everything that might lead to a fullness of experience - all this impresses me greatly.

Among his many expeditions there was one in which regretably I did not take part. Staniewski read an autobiography of Carl Gustav Jung, *Memories, Dreams, Reflections*, that Robert Reszke and I made available to the Polish readers. (By the way, I considered this one of my most important duties). Staniewski found in it this wonderful, exceptional chapter about a tower. At one point writing books was not enough for Jung; he felt that he should commemorate something in stone, something that was coming to the fore. The question was: what was it? And so, without any premeditated plan, he built a tower. When something important in his life happened, he would rebuild or extend it. When his wife died, he built another floor between two little towers. Only with time did he discover that the building had evolved over almost twenty-two years - from the death of his mother till the death of his wife - along his own path of evolution. He says that he was building the tower as if in a dream, in order to eventually discover a form full of significance - a symbol of fullness. He calls the tower his *credo* carved in stone. In the autobiography he speaks about how it turned out that the tower was connected not only to the important women in his life but also to the dead. So, this tower, lost somewhere on the shore of an upper Zürich lake in the town of Bollingen, does not appear on the maps. It is difficult to find.

Staniewski read about Jung's tower and organized an expedition to Bollingen. They found and reached this place. It is a private property that belongs to Jung's family, but of course Staniewski got there.

**Staniewski:** Over the fence. I guess I had read Jung's autobiography before the Polish edition.

**Kolankiewicz:** So typical of him - over the fence. I know Jung's tower quite precisely, including its interior, but unfortunately only from description, in a library. I regret this a bit. One should visit personally the place supposedly connected with the dead to feel it for oneself. Well - Staniewski was there. I must say, though, that participation in Gardzienice's expeditions was extremely instructive for me - even if, different from my outstanding colleagues Pawluczuk and Osiński, I participated only in the Polish expeditions. I know how to take action in the field mainly from this. I have learned a lot from you, Włodek. I have learned discipline, stubbornness in search, ways of overcoming difficulties. Wherever I was afterwards, for example in Brazil, I coped using these experiences.

The phase of the field expeditions of Gardzienice has been completed; today it is a historical matter. But please look: in the course of work on *Carmina Burana*, Gardzienice expeditions transformed into expeditions in time. These also require courage, resourcefulness, perseverance. These expeditions go further and further into the depths of time. Exploration of medieval myths was a consequence of reading Bakhtin and of the romantic attitude adopted by Gardzienice. With *Carmina Burana* Staniewski once again opened our eyes to the reality of medieval culture. It was a superb synthesis of legends and traditions of the Middle Ages, bursting with life, moving. I had a chance to find out what hermeneutic work stood there in the wings when I described and analysed it. Staniewski not only recalled the legend of Tristan and Isolde with all its archetypal depths - down to its tribal Celtic roots - but he also plunged it in the element of medieval *ludorum* (plays) of goliards, seeing that as the proper performative environment. He recalled, or actually rediscovered, *Codicem Buranum*. Afterwards, in my description of the performance, I had to translate the songs from medieval Latin that had not been known in Polish before! Włodek, you mentioned the Knights Templar. I think that a hidden treasure of *Carmina Burana* was the legend of the Holy Grail, which was not evoked directly.

The expedition into the depth of time did not stop and it brought the next two performances which were called - what a meaningful name! - *theatre essays*. They resulted from a vast exploration and a dazzling interpretation of ancient Greek culture. And Gardzienice entered this distant historical reality as they entered the geographical reality. A reality that is distant, yet that we come closer to and finally enter as if we were eyewitnesses. It is still an expedition! That is why this vision is still so suggestive, so refreshing - at least for me.

**Ziółkowski:** Shall we start the second round?

**Kolankiewicz:** Wait! Is anybody here named Andrew Gołota?[4] Is the fight fixed?

**Ziółkowski:** Kolankiewicz wants to hear that, indeed, the fight has been fixed. All right then. Yesterday, I was 'examined' regarding today's meeting. The examiners were my two teachers. You might call it a 'High Committee'. Leszek Kolankiewicz supervised my thesis *Argonauci współczesnego teatru*, a chapter of which was devoted to Gardzienice. And one of my most important theatre initiations took place on the meadows and in the ravines of Gardzienice village, where people run together at night. This was inspired by the practice which you, Włodek, met in Mexico.

**Staniewski:** A group run resulted from an intuition that not only can it serve the proper regulation of emotional athletics (to use Artaud's term) but rehearsals can be done this way, raising an actor's state of readiness to the level of elation, without any psychological manipulation.

It happens also that if you do not practice the run, something that can be called ardour, or passion, slowly dies down. This intuition was confirmed when I ran with the Tarahumaras, or rather I took part in a performance-ritual (I do not hesitate to call it this) that was happening while running. It was called *raramuri*.

**Ziółkowski:** The High Committee wanted to know what questions I was going to ask today. So the fight has been fixed and now it is time for the second round.

We had a chance to see fragments of Gardzienice's *Metamorphoses* yesterday from the CD-Rom attached to the book *Hidden Territories*. Most of us saw this raw material for the first time. Among fragments shown there was a scene of a clash between Dionysus and Christ. It is one of the key sequences of *Metamorphoses*, besides of course the final one, the dance of the Bacchae. The scene with the dancing Dionysus and the distressed Christ seems to me emblematic for this performance.

In Leszek Kolankiewicz's book, *Dziady*, there are two chapters in which the author also recalls the character of Dionysus; these are: *Szałem pijany ty mnie unosisz, Bachusie* [You are raising me drunk in rage, Bacchus] and *Co to ma wspólnego z Dionizosem?* [What does it have to do with Dionysus?]. At the same time, the archetype of Christ is constantly evoked in his book. Therefore, let me pose a question: about the hero. Who is a hero in the latest performances of Włodzimierz Staniewski and in Leszek Kolankiewicz's *Dziady*.

**Staniewski:** I have the feeling that we live in a time when there is a deficit of heroes, that we live in times when heroism, on one hand as an ethical attitude and on the other as an artistic figure, is completely anachronistic, outdated. Today we deal with the debasement of the character of a hero. Heroes are either tired or relegated to the shadow of the stage. On one hand it seems that there is some desperate need for creating an ethical canon, as for example Osterwa wrote, in which an individual, a human being, a character, *dramatis persona*, would be an example, a challenge; it would set a certain level that we can refer to and be equal to. On the other hand we avoid this, admitting that it is a challenge beyond our powers. The fruit of these dodges are the melodramas of life. The point lies not in that we deal with the debasement of heroic attitudes but

[4] Andrew Gołota born in 1968 is a famous Polish Heavyweight contender who has been in a number of controversial fights notably with Riddick Bowe, Mike Tyson and Chris Byrd.

• **Gardzienice -
Metamorphosis.** *Photo by
Zbigniew Bielawka*

in the ambiguity of situations and choices that a hero of our times faces.

It seems that this is how Euripides perceived his characters. His Orestes is supposed to be a heroic character; he is supposed to fulfill an act of justice. Yet, we see him torn by doubts. He is to fulfill a duty designated by a god, by Apollo. However, he hesitates in doing this, being in a dilemma, timid to the point of cowardice. He doubts the imperative of the gods. A hero can doubt neither the imperative of the gods nor the imperative of history.

The question is: does it happen because the hero's mettle is weak, or is it reality that is so tangled? I guess it's the latter. No less ambiguous is Electra. Despite the demonic consequences in pursuing her goal and some transfixing inner strength, her melodrama is even more paralysing because when it seems that it is she who is the pure tool of justice, suddenly we notice that she is driven by clear self-interest. As if she were driven by a passion of suspicious nature, which trivializes her seemingly heroic attitude. What is the origin of such passions? Where does the imperative come from that makes her bring things to their fatal end? Maybe to escape from unbearable conclusions, I reached a conclusion that Electra had been raped by her step-father, Aegisthus, in her early childhood.

This convergence of conditions that make a melodramatic character of an erstwhile hero would perhaps be worth no more than a shrug of the shoulders, were it not for one condition: that a homicide in the heroic story is an act of ritualistic purification, an act of worship, while in a melodramatic story it is an atrocious murder.

**Kolankiewicz:** I will not enter into answering this question: is there any hero of our times? Or a question: what kind of a hero is needed in our times? I shall focus exactly on who is a hero of the last performances of Gardzienice and who actually is a hero of my *Dziady*.

Grzegorz, you spoke about Dionysus and Christ in *Metamorphoses*. We should not forget though about Lucius (that is, Apuleius himself, that is, the Ass) and – maybe above all – about the

Bacchae. In *Electra* we have of course a title character that Włodek has just spoken about, but also we have a character that we should not forget - Euripides himself. I just recall it as a formality, because now I would like to focus on the fact that in both performances we deal with an extremely far-reaching (and very timely) analysis of the female element, of various personifications of femininity. That is why it is necessary to speak here about this element. This analysis perfectly chimes with our times. After all, we are witnesses of a great wave of research in humanities called gender studies, which introduces the great theme of gender. Actually, it cannot be omitted now. These performances of Gardzienice get down to the same subject, showing that it is possible - and how it is possible - with this ancient material.

I recall an unforgettable scene from *Metamorphoses or the Golden Ass*, the scene of the dance of the Bacchae. This genius image of the *secret dances in honour of the god* that Euripides speaks about in the Bacchae. What dances were they? What did these dances cause?

Originally Dionysism was a female religion. It had been so before theatre became a form of the Dionysian cult. The cult was already urbanized and performed by men who actually treated it as an entertainment. According to Edward Zwolski, whose book *Choreia* was so important for Staniewski, a tragedy is 'playing fear and agony'. The enthusiasm of the Bacchae turned into the passion of a hero. But in the original cult, which appeared still in some rituals of the holiday of Anthesteria, Dionysus was inseparable from his female worshippers; they supplemented him and were his helpers. Plutarch evokes their song: 'Arrive, Dionysus the hero.' As a hero Dionysus was arriving from the land of the dead. However, in order to resurrect he had to be woken up. And it was precisely the Bacchae who would wake him up. This awakening resembled the awakening of Osiris and the archaic rituals of the Egyptian Old State. A scholium to *Acharnians* by Aristophanes reveals the story of the resurrection: 'according to the mystery, the phallus has been raised for Dionysus'. This is what his female worshippers were doing, holding their highjinks in the Korkyrian cave that Pausanias mentions. They would wake up the god who threw them into a frenzy. This frenzy had an erotic tinge. Let us not forget that it was a religious experience, a seasonal and collective one. It had to be an experience as deep and strong as an earthquake that wakes up the earth from winter sleep in the early spring. A bunch of women seized by seasonal ecstasy crying *'Euoí!'* were evoking the dead hero from the underworld.

And exactly in *Metamorphoses* of Gardzienice we have a scene that begins with a song *Euoí, Bacchae!*, at first inconspicuously. Afterwards though, this scene develops extraordinarily. It has to be experienced! You have to be a witness of it directly in the theatre; no recording can convey this. In such moments theatre has the advantage over other media. By duration and persistence of the dance of the Bacchae, in the unchanged rhythm, gradually greater and greater intensity accumulates - a perceptible and hypnotizing intensity, so that this wind, this stream of power reaches a spectator, exactly like *manía*, a ritualistic Bacchic frenzy. There is no other more suggestive artistic reconstruction of this phenomenon. I always remain dumbfounded in the face of this scene.

And we also have this femininity in *Electra*, in which the characters of Electra and Clytemnestra become prominent. Femininity is shown here in all its diversity, I would say: from one pole of possible expression to the other. I recall the daring duo of Electra and Clytemnestra: they are sitting on upright chairs next to each other, in turns bending towards spectators and throwing or spitting out their lines in which reason and emotions create a dangerous mix. I recall a great, moving scene in which Electra persuades Orestes to kill their mother, who is breast-feeding him at the same time. Most impressive, though, is probably Electra's lamentation, an incredible rising line, where desperation becomes frenzy, divine rapture. Staniewski always places psychology in an archetypal frame, and at the same time he can restore the power of expression to ritualistic forms.

Now, I can continue about my *Dziady*. Its hero is obviously Dionysus, among others, as a patron and a divinity of theatre. But in the whole richness and diversity of his manifestations. Theatre in its proper notion originated, according to Aristotle's *Poetics*, from a *dithyramb*, mentioned here by Staniewski, and from a satyr drama. The *dithyramb* as a song in praise of Dionysus had as its base the Dionysian ritualistic madness, which was preserved by Archilochus, who said that he intoned a *dithyramb* when wine - meaning Dionysus - struck him like lightning. On the other hand, satyr drama was supposed to have originated from a masquerade. Its costumed participants pretended that they were in a Dionysian frenzy. Regardless of whether this genealogy of tragedy can be confirmed - and it is questioned for example by Richard Schechner - these two sources, *manía* and masquerade, seem to be quite beyond doubt. And behind them there are two symbols of Dionysus: a phallus and a mask. What was Anthesteria, the most ancient Athenian holiday in honour of Dionysus? It was Dziady - Forefathers' Eve - after all. The transformations of Dionysus and this passage from rituals to theatre, which in Athens took place every year from one Dionysian holiday to another - from Anthesteria to Great Dionysia - fascinated me; for me it was the central theme, and a topical one, when I was writing *Dziady*.

The hero of the book is of course a sorcerer. A sorcerer - one who evokes ghosts, who makes apparitions appear - it is a proto-theatrical function. The prototype of theatre is the evocation and appearance of apparitions. And this is a distinctive feature of the Polish theatre tradition - from Mickiewicz to Kantor.

But in *Dziady: Teatr święta zmarłych*, I must admit, there is one more important person hidden. Who, for the Greeks, ruled the land of the dead? Hades and Persephone. Actually, nowhere in the text do I emphasize the fact that the hero of my *Dziady* is Persephone - a divinity that has attracted me, that, in my opinion, holds some great power, and is mysterious. Persephone is a perfect female character, not only as Kore but also as an essence and source of what the Greeks called the Two Divinities, 'a girl and a woman', Persephone and Demeter at the same time. And not only these but also Hekate (or Artemis), associated with sorcery, an incredibly ancient, even a prototypical female divinity. Already in the fifteenth century B.C., there must have been a Mother Goddess, a goddess of grain, connected with the land of the dead and evoking visions. This 'inexpressible lady,' *árretos koúra*, Persephone, is for me a mysterious figure. She is this beautiful girl, kidnapped to be married. (The kidnapper was Hades, but Hades is the underground Zeus, or Dionysus, which is signalled in the myth by the fact that Demeter does not want to drink the wine she was given in Eleusis to regain strength - as if she knew who was the perpetrator of the kidnapping.) This maiden, though, is also 'terrible Persephone'. Homer and Hesiod call her this and so does Apuleius. She is the one whose very name - Brimo - could terrify; the one who sends ghosts and who herself has the horrible head of the Gorgon. It is this real mother, terrible, who - as Karl Kerényi says - sends every living creature to the world once only.

Actually, I do not know how to speak about her.

So I will speak about my field research in Rome. Dealing with the Eleusinian mysteries, I read about the Lovatelli Urn, which is an important source to understand the *mýesis* rituals - initiation to the small mysteries, which took place in spring in the suburbs of Athens and preceded the autumn Grand Mysteries in Eleusis. The relief on this small marble urn (described as 30 cm high) shows three rituals of initiation, probably of Hercules, who had to be initiated into the Eleusinian mysteries in order to come back alive from his labour of bringing Cerberus up from Hades. By the way, in one of the three rituals the hero is sitting on a stool with his head covered - exactly like Demeter, who sat in this way longing for her kidnapped daughter.

Everyone initiated in the Eleusinian mysteries had to imitate a woman. At the end of the initiation, even someone as virile as Hercules had to enter the fate of the Mother in order to visit the Daughter. I knew these scenes from the photos, even from Kerényi's monograph; they are also printed in the book by Walter Burkert. I wanted to see the urn personally, because its details are interpreted in different ways. I knew that the Lovatelli Urn was kept in the Museo Nazionale Romano. I went to the Museo alle Terme, viewed all their collections carefully, I saw two urns, unfortunately smooth. But no one there had heard of the Lovatelli Urn. Undeterred I searched the Museo *delle* Terme. From top to bottom, nothing. I searched all the departments of the Museo Nazionale Romano, including the wonderful new department at the Palazzo Altemps (which I had the honour of describing to Tadeusz Różewicz). No Lovatelli Urn. Then I called the headquarters of the Museo Nazionale Romano at Piazza delle Finanze. And I heard,'Yes, indeed, we used to have something like this, but we do not know where it is. We will look for it, please call in a few days.' I called numerous times and finally an aware employee said that the Lovatelli Urn had been found. It had been closed in some room and a special permit was needed. I thought, I need to take action. I'll approach through two independent channels: through the ministry and through archeologists. The first channel turned out to be blocked. Meanwhile, we managed to deduce that the situation was worse than I had thought. Many years earlier, the Lovatelli Urn had been sealed in a box: 'Open for conservation only'. Practically, there was no chance to see it. Still, I pressed a certain professor who finally found the person who could open this little box. Naturally, this would be a woman. But I discovered this just before my departure. I have not reached this dottoressa. I have not seen the Lovatelli Urn.

With Persephone, the mystery of the Eleusinian mysteries, it is the same as with my search for the Lovatelli Urn.

• Gardzienice - *Metamorphosis.* Photo by Zbigniew Bielawka

**Staniewski:** It is fantastic - ecstasis and torment

– as in the famous journeys of Lévi-Strauss to the Bororo and Nambikwara tribes, hidden in the wilderness of the Brazilian savannah and in thickets of the Amazon jungle. An anthropologist creates a goal, and the attempt to achieve it verges on the miraculous. His journey is like a search for the Grail. The journey is more exciting than the goal itself. However, it is also full of quandaries, the feeling of loss of sense, of depression, physical suffering and intellectual torment (what is all this for!?); so the initiation has its full dimension. With Lévi-Strauss, it is a journey deep into the jungle, where – as he learned from scattered chronicles – a descendant of a once-great people lived, who could be a key to knowledge of civilization in its virgin state. When finally, as described in one of the chapters of *Tristes: Tropiques*, as far as I remember, one day he stands face to face with the natives. We have every right to expect the lost paradise. But the picture that emerges is in fact purgatorial. The natives look like souls in purgatory: paralytic, swollen or emaciated, evoking the feeling of terror, mercy and disappointment.

The story of the Lovatelli Urn is beautiful, but maybe it is better that the urn stays hidden in the labyrinths of museums. You never know what kind of purgatorial evil spirit could emerge from it to meet you.

**Kolankiewicz**: I do not remember exactly who it concerned, but certainly it does not refer to his journey to the Nambikwaras. Lévi-Strauss visited the Nambikwaras in the second half of the 1930s, before the World War II. There is a wonderful picture album with black and white photographs by Lévi-Strauss (partly known already from *Tristes: Tropiques*), published only about ten years ago and entitled *Saudades do Brasil* [Missing Brazil], like the piano piece of Marius Milhaud. The pictures of the Nambikwaras are very beautiful, above all pictures of Nambikwara girls walking naked in a jungle. But all of these photos were taken, you can say, with love. There are a lot of portraits, also of men in their prime, with characteristic feathers stuck in the nasal septum. These portraits present a real abundance of human experiences, feelings, thoughts, shown on people's faces. The Nambikwaras were Lévi-Strauss's beloved people, an incarnation of 'good savages'. When after half a century – I guess in the mid-1980s – he returned to Brazil, he got a proposal to visit them again, but he did not want to go back. He did not want to see the decay of the Indians under the influence of the white man. He wanted to keep the image of them when they were still happy.

**Ziółkowski**: I will ask now about the horizon that always remains unreachable. Włodek, your last statement – I mean the talk led by Tadeusz Kornaś for *Didaskalia* – was entitled *Port: Grecja*. That is exactly how you called it: Greece is the point of arrival, foothold and reference. And as with every port, it is a place where handling takes place – transferring goods from the seaway to overland routes and *vice versa*. Does it mean that this area sets the boundaries within which you will be moving now? Or maybe there are other territories which you would like to penetrate because you suspect that they can be inspiring and challenging? Are there any other Nambikwaras, whom you have not reached yet?

I am directing this question also to Leszek Kolankiewicz, who for some time has been moving in the sphere of antiquity. For instance in a publication dedicated to professor Janusz Degler on the occasion of his sixty-fifth birthday, *Między teatrem a literaturą*, we can find your very thorough text *Eleusis. Oczy szeroko zamknięte*, dedicated to the Eleusinian mysteries. Having been asked about it, you said that ancient Greece is an abyss. If so, what is the next 'urn' impossible to reach but still mysterious enough to tempt you?

**Staniewski**: Leszek spoke here about our journey, a journey in time, about stepping back. There is nothing strange in this, when we turn to the culture of fathers, then consequently to the culture of forefathers, great-forefathers, grandfathers and great-grandfathers. Our common source is the Mediterranean culture. It is worth remembering how, having regained liberty, the whole of Poland shouted with a thunderous voice that we were a part of the Mediterranean culture. It elevated us somehow.

Leszek, you say in your book that the Athenian democracy in some moment was recognized as a theatre democracy, that theatre dictated not only a sense of culture but also a sense of civilization, that right after the election of a strategist, *choregoi*[5] were chosen – those who presided over the most important theatre holidays.

**Kolankiewicz:** Let me interrupt. A theatre festival was the biggest civic gathering in Athens – 15,000, maybe even 17,000 people! After the political reform of Cleisthenes at the end of the sixth century B.C., each of ten *phyles* staged two fifty-person dithyrambic choirs: one of men and one of boys. These were voluntary choirs. Even if a *phyle* entered only one choir, as some scholars suggest, still, each year in the dithyrambic contest – counting conservatively – 500 people took part. So every citizen had finally to dance and sing a dithyramb during the Great Dionysia.

**Staniewski:** That is the point – to dance and to sing. Not to recite. The Greek theatre is – contrary to common opinion – not only literature, not only words to be interpreted, but also, or even above all, musical and dance themes. The power of the Greek theatre was *action*, the renaissance of which we experienced in the avant-garde theatre of the twentieth century.

Let us admit that there is some resistance in comprehending and assimilating only the word in Greek drama. Seeing and hearing what is *happening, what is being done*, not only brings us closer to the ancient art but also allows us to imagine its amazing, striking power in the time of its full bloom. The power consists in the music, the relics of which have barely survived, and in movement and gesture. It is impossible not to believe some testimonies that suggest that the songs from the dramas of Euripides were seen as musical hits by his contemporaries.

We have tried to *resuscitate* music of the ancient Greece in *Metamorphoses*. Now we deal with *cheironomy*, the ancient art of message through gesture, gesticulation. This is the basic means of expression in *Electra*. I suspect that what was used in the ancient performances was some kind of alphabet of gestures analogous to the alphabets of today's theatres of the East, for example *kathakali*.

In 2000, I brought a group of the aged Samaveda singers from Kerala in India for the Festival *Mysteries, Initiations* in Cracow, which I programmed. The technique of musical realization of the holy theatre strongly influenced *kutiyattam*, the ancient theatre of Kerala. They performed their mysteries in the Tempel synagogue. It was a simple and touching ritual. Four old men singing the Vedas in sounds over two thousand years old and gesticulating sequences of notes, as if the wind were playing with the leaves of a tree and dancing them. Nobody understood anything, but the shock was tremendous, with purifying power. It cannot be ruled out that similar means of expression were used in ancient Greek performances. In the *Electra* of Euripides, we come across an indication like this: *illustrates words with gestures*. Maybe accompanied by singing and music? One of Aeschylus' actors became legendary because he could perfectly show words with gestures.

There are some interesting things still to be discovered in the techniques of ancient theatre. Professor Lengauer pointed in *Didaskalia* to a seemingly trivial, yet essential thing. He recalled that an ancient actor could perform equally majestically and impetuously, rapidly, shouting and straining his voice when singing to the limits of his possibilities. He could move dynamically and gesticulate fully. Our vision of a performance in ancient theatre has probably been overshadowed by great amphitheatre buildings. In their context, the means of expression seem to be hieratic, slow, and actors reciting text resemble marionettes.

What would happen if we looked at the ancient

[5] Choir leaders.

theatre from the point of view of rehearsal, if we pondered over what rehearsals might have been like. Without buskings, without thousands of people in the audience, without mask. Only a director and an actor, or a few actors. And not in the amphitheatre but in a peristyle of a private house or in one of the gymnasium's rooms where fist fighting was practised, as well as acrobatic movements, grace, tempo, speed and agility of the body. Where it was taught how to paint characters whose movements are caught in various positions, and then to imitate and compose them in so-called live pictures. Euripides took up such an education.

Let's imagine the rehearsals then. A director, author of the text, creator of the music and choreographer - all in one person. Euripides, for example, struggles with the material of a performance. There is an anecdote about Euripides, who reprimands a naughty actor during a rehearsal: 'If you weren't an insensitive ignoramus, you wouldn't laugh when I sing in the Mixolydian mode.' It is worth mentioning that in today's categories we would consider Euripides a courageous and provocatively experimental theatre-maker. In the music that he composed for his performances, he was no less *moderne* than his friend Timotheos who aroused controversies among his contemporaries.

Ancient theatre seen through rehearsals is a completely different research adventure.

**Kolankiewicz:** You can hear how Staniewski is entering the topic - exactly like a scholar. It is because Staniewski is a kind of scholar of antiquity - the artistic scholar, hence this peculiar form created by him: a theatrical essay. *Metamorphoses* and *Electra* are really essays. Nothing can be added to this lecture, Włodek, because indeed it is a fascinating lecture.

I would just disagree with this point of departure. Because Mediterranean culture is an ideological construct. We have various visions of ancient Greece. Ancient Greece of secondary and high schools, a shining city. This is, for instance, the Greece of Jan Parandowski. In our times Zygmunt Kubiak created his own version, an existential one: Greece appears in it as tenebrous; a human being is abandoned by the gods there. But these are ideological constructions. Włodzimierz Lengauer thinks that in fact Greece is alien to us, as alien as some distant tribes, and this is why it is just an illusion that there is a cultural continuity between Greece and us. This is what many researchers of antiquity state nowadays. We find it for instance in the studies of Jean-Pierre Vernant and Pierre Vidal-Naquet, where the Greeks are shown as if in an ethnological perspective - almost as if they were some African tribes.

And on the other hand, please see Lengauer's *text on Gardzienice gesty* in the October issue of *Didaskalia*. *Electra* in the perspective of Gardzienice proves - we read in Lengauer's conclusion - that 'characters of the Greek myth can find their place in our world'. And earlier, that 'a spectator totally involved in Gardzienice's performance experiences *katharsis*. I couldn't believe my eyes, so at the first opportunity I accosted the author: Staniewski could not have received a better affirmation than your statement. And professor Lengauer answered, 'Indeed, I consider attributing the cathartic effect to a theatre piece the highest praise - and that is what I meant.' However, this means that there is a possibility of breaking through to this reality, of reviving ancient Greece by a creative reconstruction.

It is fascinating isn't it, how Staniewski revives antiquity, directs it and also tells us about his vision.

I would say that *Electra* is a semiological treatise, something like Roland Barthes's essays or Umberto Eco's dissertations. Włodek has been talking a lot here about *cheironomy*, about the Greek system of gesturing by hands and - more widely, in the original meaning of the word - of signs given by a movement of a body. But this is his artistic discovery, because we did not know this code. It is not a pantomime; it is something completely new. Taking the patterns from the vase paintings and Greek sculptures, the artists of Gardzienice have created a true code of gestures. The signs may seem purely arbitrary, but they are presented to the spectator as a precise code. And afterwards, the actor's energy is freed through these signs, and we see how this energy changes and concentrates into the signs, articulated, as if a life process were coagulating into a sign, but only for a moment because this indomitable energy overwhelms it immediately. The process keeps going, incessantly, until the next momentary concentration into a sign. Thus the essence of art as an articulation of the life process is being revealed.

This game takes place in *Electra* on many levels. Conventions are recalled and then immediately blasted out. There is irony in this, as well as self-irony. Like in the scene of the first meeting of Electra and Orestes, where the character of Electra, pretending to be a virgin, is played by a transvestite. It is generally an imitation game on many levels, which reveals the semiotic, multi-storey construction of theatre art. After all, we all seem to know that in the Greek theatre only men performed and, if there was a need, they dressed up as women. But in Gardzienice's *Electra* this dressing-up gains new meanings. We receive a clear lesson of what performativity of gender is, but we also realize something of an unresolved mystery of the female element.

We used to consider Gardzienice an exuberant theatre whose performances are sequences of explosions, with actors giving their best. And *Electra* is also full of explosions, and the actors also do their utmost in it; it is a performance full of concentrated, extreme emotions, incorporated above all in the actions of the women: Electra, Clytemnestra. Here, emotions come to expression with full power, as if unbridled. Except that we have here a constant tension between these emotions and arbitrary gestures, between individual energy and a social code of signs. From this kind of tension - between an immovable structure and the energy that enlivens this structure - great works are born.

Staniewski reaches here from the other side to what constitutes, for example, the *Noh* theatre. (This comparison is surely not surprising: Greek tragedy was already compared to Japanese *Noh* in the nineteenth century. I wrote about this in *Dziady: Teatr święta zmarłych*.)

In Tokyo, I had a chance to witness an absolutely exceptional *Noh* performance. Iga Rodowicz - an outstanding specialist of *Noh*, author of *Aktor doskonały: Traktaty Zeamiego o sztuce nō* and a former actress of Gardzienice - was wondering what performance I should visit. Finally she chose *Yōkihi*, edited in the end of the fifteenth century by Zenchiku Ujinobu Komparu, Zeami's son-in-law. Why did she pick this one? Because its plot resembles the myth of Orpheus and Eurydice. The title character is a mistress of

• Gardzienice – *Carmina Burana*, Dorota Porowska, Marcin Mrowca, Ela Rojek, Mariana Sadowska, Mariusz Gołaj. *Photo by Zbigniew Bielawka*

the Chinese emperor Gensō (Xuanzong) who - under pressure from forces around him - sentences her to death. But inconsolable with grief, he sends a taoist sorcerer to search for her spirit. The sorcerer - played by a secondary actor (the *waki*) - finds Yōkihi's spirit on the Island of Immortality. Here the plot begins. The performance was proceeding normally until a certain moment. The emperor's emissary reaches the Island of Immortality, learns where to look for the Jade Princess and finds her singing a lamentation. Having sung it, Yōkihi's spirit appears - the main actor (the *shite*) in a mask emerges from a curtained litter, placed on the stage at the beginning of the performance. At this point something seemed wrong to me, because the actor appeared to be having some difficulties, and also his swinging step was not as fluid as usual. And in the scene where the ghost gives to the sorcerer an ornamental pin for the emperor, the actor fell. I noticed him fall, but a friend who was with me, and did not known the convention of *Noh*, did not see anything wrong in it. He just thought that the *Noh* actors have this kind of expression. The actor sank to the floor as if he had fainted, but he did not tumble, he just sat down heavily. A serious problem arouse on the stage then. From the moment when the *shite* puts on a mask in so-called mirror room (that is a changing room), he is considered a character - in this case a spirit of the dead - whom you mustn't address personally. The privilege of touching him belongs to *shitezure*, his helper and understudy who tidies up his robes or passes a fan to him during a performance. It turned out though that the helper was not able to lift the actor on his own, even if he tried holding his elbow. He needed the help of the choir conductor who was sitting on the right side. The conductor ceremoniously left the second row and took hold of *shite* by the other elbow (afterwards I learned that he was the only person entitled to help the *shitezure*). Together they took the actor out, not without effort and completely atypically through the choir exit. By that time I was sure that something amazing was taking place. And it

continued until the very end. For the performance had to be completed. After all it is a ritualistic theatre, and a ritual must be performed till the very end. The *shite* was substituted by the *shitezure* - an understudy who always sits at the back, as if invisible, ready for substitution at any moment, even though there is hardly ever an occasion for it. And maybe this was the only time ever. The understudy of course did not wear any mask. He was to perform the most important sequence of the dances of the dead Yōkihi. So, we saw a ghost dancing without a mask. And then it was possible to see his full expression and witness the energy that fills all actions of the *Noh* actor but is never perceived so directly. This event also revealed the place of an accident in the art of *Noh* that seems to be so utterly codified. Except that probably in all Japanese arts - in calligraphy, arranging flowers or archery - a convention joins what is aleatory.

So, in *Electra* of Gardzienice we deal with something exactly like this, that is with deconstruction, analysis of these blends, this mixture of codified and energetic elements. That is why I call this performance a semiological treatise.

**Staniewski:** Thank you, Leszek, but allow me to disagree a little with the thesis that the Mediterranean culture is an ideological construct, strange and distant like a culture from another planet. It may be so if we think about a comprehensive civil-socio-cultural model with which we would like to identify somehow. This probably would not work.

We need to remember that there can be (and probably there are) numerous ideological constructs that make Greece more distant or bring it closer to us. Each epoch and each culture does it in different way. In Poland we have also the Greece of Tadeusz Zieliński - resembling a heroic fairy-tale. (It is worth remembering now that professor Zieliński was Meyerhold's guide during his travel to the monuments of the ancient Greece.) The nineteenth-century Germans are accused of making Greece pompous, elevated and static, while the twentieth-century English try almost to touch it. Peter Green tells a fragment of the Greek history (well, the whole of Greece!) in his book *Alexander the Great* in such a way that we can almost touch these people. Even though this is also an ideological construct created by setting in motion a fashionable mechanism that links politics with sensation, intrigue, corruption, ambitions, sex scandals and the pursuit of utopia. Devouring this Greece, I finally felt what it was like to be a Greek. The point is to get closer, to be able to touch the people of the epoch.

The genius of Greek drama consists in going beyond the ideological context. Because we have people involved in very precise actions, and not in some Greek ones. Oliver Taplin was writing about it in his *Greek Tragedy in Action*, which is almost a classic today. They really are archetypal, mythic, and at the same time madly of flesh and body. They cry, moan, yelp, shout, beg, mock, laugh (in tragedy rarely), tear their hair, run in, run out, sing, enter, exit, hum, thunder, gesticulate, scream at one another, fall in despair, in enthusiastic joy, in disease, in nervous chaos, grab each other by the throat, hate and love so much that they are ready to make any offering on the altar of love, commit adultery, undress, touch, address each other, god, people, us.

They address you, Leszek, and me. And they touch us. And also you.

Polish text edited by Ireneusz Guszpit
Translated by Justyna Rodzińska and Andrei Biziorek

*The debate took place on 27 November 2004, as part of the conference* Teatr - przestrzeń - ciało - dialog. Poszukiwania we współczesnym teatrze *[Theatre - Space - Body - Dialogue: Research in Contemporary Theatre], organized by Wrocław University and the Grotowski Centre (26-28 November 2004, Wrocław).*

*This is an edited version of the debate first published in Polish in:* Teatr - przestrzeń - ciało - dialog. Poszukiwania we współczesnym teatrze *[Theatre - Space - Body - Dialogue: Research in Contemporary Theatre], edited by Magdalena Gołaczyńska and Ireneusz Guszpit, Wrocław: Wydawnictwo Uniwersytetu Wrocławskiego 2006, 11-33.*

REFERENCES

Kolankiewicz, Leszek (1999) *Dziady. Teatr święta zmarłych* ['Forefathers' Eve: Theatre of the Day of the Dead'], Gdańsk: Słowo/obraz terytoria.

Kolankiewicz, Leszek (1988) *Święty Artaud* ['Saint Artaud'] Warsaw: Państwowy Instytut Wydawniczy.

Kolankiewicz, Leszek (2001) *Wielki mały wóz* ['Big Small Vehicle'], Gdańsk: Słowo/obraz terytoria.

Kolankiewicz, Leszek (2004) 'Eleusis. Oczy szeroko zamknięte' ['Eleusis: Eyes Wide Shut'], in Adolf Juzwenko and Jan Miodek (eds) *Między teatrem a literaturą* ['Between Theatre and Literature'], Wrocław: Ossolineum pp. 31-91.

Kornaś, Tadeusz and Staniewski, Włodzimierz (June - August 2004) 'Port: Grecja' ['Harbour Greece'], *Didaskalia* n.61/62, pp. 61–2.

Lengauer, Włodzimierz (October 2004) 'Gardzienickie gesty' ['Gardzienice Gestures'], *Didaskalia* 63, pp. 54-55.

Osterwa, Juliusz (2004) *Przez teatr - poza teatr* ['Through Theatre - Beyond Theatre'], Kraków: Towarzystwo Naukowe Societas Vistulana.

Rodowicz, Jadwiga (2000) *Aktor doskonały: Traktaty Zeamiego o sztuce nō* ['A Perfect Actor: Zeami's Treatises on the Art of Noh'], Gdańsk: Słowo/obraz terytoria.

Ziółkowski, Grzegorz (1995) *Argonauci współczesnego teatru* ['Argonauts of Contemporary Theatre'], Łódź: Towarzystwo Kultury Teatralnej and Łódzkie Spotkania Teatralne.

Zwolski, Edward (1978) *Choreia: Muza i bóstwo w religii greckiej* ['Chorea: Muse and Divinity in the Greek Religion'], Warsaw: Instytut Wydawniczy PAX.

# Letter to Adorno: on the question of *performatics*

Aberystwyth, 16 October 2007

Lieber Herr Professor Adorno,

Many thanks for your letter. I agree with you that the question of *performatics* reverberates beyond the discursive field of contemporary performance theory and aesthetics and must be examined for its cultural value and ideological implications. Emerging as a new concept from within the field of performance studies, the term *performatics* suggests a terminology which is at once precise yet also abstract in a curious way. The connotation (or deliberate illusion?) of precision is mainly provided by the term's scientific overtones deriving from its resemblance to fields such as informatics, mathematics, semiotics, etc. The German rendering of *performatics* as *Performatik* indeed seems to give the concept the kind of heightened legitimacy usually pertaining to analytic, scientific fields of study. Indeed, in German-speaking countries the humanities have frequently sought legitimization through direct reference to scientific models and terminologies, as can most clearly be demonstrated by the literal translation of *Theaterwissenschaft* as theatre 'science'. To what extent this might be a linguistic reflection of the deep-rooted values of the Enlightenment in German culture is a related and indeed interesting question.

With regards to your disapproving description of the term *performatics* as a *Jargon* that conveys a sense of 'empty' authority or pseudo-scientific absoluteness, I would say that rather than criticizing the term for what it conceals (owing to its 'aura', as you would say), it might be more productive to examine the concept as an expression of an identity 'crisis' that produces its own creative mechanisms for re-definition. I think in this context pertinent references could be made to your own great analyses of the ways in which modernist art embraces the idea of crisis (failure, impossibility, collapse of meaning) into its own structural laws of expression. I think that the possibility of *performatics* as a new designation for performance studies lies in its finely tuned demonstration of self-reflexivity – in an awareness of the very disjunction or resistance between the quasi-scientific appearance of the term and the actual experiences or performances that the field examines. It seems that the term's abstract scientificity is very cunningly pitched against the everyday-ness of performance, thus producing a kind of negative dialectic, if you like. As you imply in 'Versuch, das Endspiel zu verstehen', the performance of Beckett's *Endgame* continually exhausts its own totalization of meaning – hence the introduction of *performatics* would perhaps merely highlight the irony of a term that suggests the rationalizing language of the Enlightenment project but whose practice continually undermines both that practice and language. Another case would be one of the clowns you liked in your youth: Charlie Chaplin, for example, whose film *The Great Dictator* continually shows the means by which the language of power overshoots and undershoots its mark, thus destabilizing dictatorial claims to absolute power. In order for *performatics* to establish itself as a new term of critical reflection, it would perhaps be necessary to insist on the failure of the term to cohere and be a logos.

Perhaps the inevitable gap in my translation of the German that we speak, back into the English that we also speak, is like the incongruity between the concepts *performance*, *performatics* and *Performatik*, as opposed to the everyday performances we must all live within and through.

Mit freundlichen Grüßen,
Ihre Karoline

**KAROLINE GRITZNER**

# The Key to All Locks
## Conversation between Wojciech Dudzik, Dariusz Kosiński, Tomasz Kubikowski, Małgorzata Leyko and Dobrochna Ratajczakowa

**Kosiński:** We are meeting several months after the Wrocław conference 'Performance Studies: and Beyond' and the publication of the Polish translation of Richard Schechner's book, *Performance Studies: An Introduction*, to continue the discussion that we started in Mickiewiczian fashion - that is, as something which burst, flickered and was extinguished. During all these months there were no spectacular events connected with the book: a couple of positive reviews appeared, some giggling and mockery as always, but generally, as at peaks, there is silence. I would like to believe that this silence is associated with some kind of creative process of 'taming' performance studies and the inspirations that have resulted from it, and that the process of assimilating performance studies - of which I am an ardent supporter, as of the whole project - is still ongoing. During the Wrocław discussion, Alan Read stated that what performance studies will become in Poland depends on what we, the Poles, do with it. And it might be worth starting from this point, that is, from a question: if, and for what, Poles might make use of performance studies, what possibilities and opportunities does this proposition create, which potential dangers do we perceive in this project, and what is the root of the symptoms marked by the resistance that performance studies has encountered?

**Ratajczakowa:** So, what is performance studies? Schechner in his book defines it as 'an academic discipline designed to answer the need to deal with the changing circumstances of the "glocal"- the powerful combination of the local and the global.' (2006: 26). He also speaks about synthesis, but I think that we can perceive it as something more: the act of melting disciplines. We treat performance studies as a classical discipline. But classical academic disciplines are constructed in a different way. This is not such a discipline.

Performance studies is an answer to a performative world because, according to Zygmunt Bauman's writings, 'the spirit of modernity' melts everything that is solid, or too static, and grinds it down over time. This process started from the melting of traditions, violation of what was held sacred, of principles of loyalty, habitual laws and commitments. Initiative was freed from ethical doctrine, family ties were loosened or broken, and at this moment nothing retained its shape for any length of time. And performance studies is a response to this inability to 'retain shape over time'.

Naturally, given such a direction of activity, performance studies changes the situation of other disciplines. It is a 'light discipline', which has a 'light' subject of research. Light in the sense that it is so vast that it cannot be fully determined. According to Schechner, performance studies does not investigate an object as an object, it concentrates on the elements of a constant, continuous interplay of relationships and relations, thus investigating the practice of events and behaviours that are repeatable and at the same time ephemeral, elusive. Hence, there is no solid, constant 'subject', divided between disciplines that encompass it from different points of view, as is customary. After all, performance studies investigates 'restored behaviours', re-enacted and presented. It absorbs everything – art, observation, knowledge and practical activity. It integrates and joins.

So what can be done with it, why does it cause resistance, what perspectives does it open? Other than his very apt notion of the 'risk society', two useful terms appear in Ulrich Beck's book on theory (Beck 1992). Bauman also cites them: 'zombie categories' and 'zombie institutions'. So these are things that appear to be alive, but which in fact are already dead. I think about whether our theatre might be such a 'zombie institution', which continues to exist only by its own momentum, the power of certain conventions, of its rootedness in society. And about whether theatre criticism and theatre studies might behave in a similar way. Disciplines are subject to transformations, the lines between them become blurred, methods become outdated, whole areas of research are formulated anew, parts of the former roots of academic study die out and new ones are shaped. What emerges from these ruins is already different, and this is the way things must be. But performance studies seems as if it does not have to be rooted. It is similar to hydroponics, it can grow and bloom everywhere, in different fields of life and art. It is the product of a fluid reality – non-systemic, unregulated, extremely flexible in comparison to classical disciplines, which always looked for a secure anchor.

To what extent might today's theatre, not the whole thing but this kind of theatre that attempts to 'freeze time', be a 'zombie institution' (particularly when it comes to its 'system', to its structure), and theatricality, in its traditional sense, a 'zombie category'? Shouldn't we also look at our subject of research through the lens of performance studies? To loosen the corset of performance? To enter into broader, more fluid areas of research? What is wrong with having various aspects to a discipline? Or with drawing inspiration from performance studies? After all, in simultaneity appears non-simultaneity, a time is always constituted by numerous times, and colourful scholarship is far more interesting than that which is devoid of shades. Sometimes we speak [in Debord's phrase, ed.] of modern societies as 'societies of the spectacle'. Isn't it also that these societies are societies of performance? Alongside the ongoing processes of individualization, alongside the changes taking root within individuals – not in systems – performance studies captures the essence of what we are dealing with today, what we have to confront. We have entered the territory of the 'risk societies' (but also, increasingly, of 'risk academia') and there is no way out. I think that if we are going to talk about the 'society of performance', performance studies will have a good chance to show what it can do. And theatre – it may still last, even partly as a zombie institution, partly as a quasi-place, of which Bauman writes: a kind of place which no longer belongs to us. It becomes a peculiar transitory place, which establishes only superficial communities of those who buy a performance, and which vanish immediately after coming into being, like the superficial communities of a shopping mall.

**Dudzik:** I would like to refer to what performance studies is – not so much for us as in general. The difficulty lies in the fact that, from Schechner's point of view, it wants to be everything. I will put it in the form of an anecdote. When, quite recently, I was ordering new doors for my house, the contractor offered three locks, with one key that would work for all of them. I have the impression that Schechner wants to give me such a key, to all locks – which may be very attractive, but which brings about the danger that Dobrochna Ratajczakowa was talking about in other terms, using the word 'melting'. In this way, the tool becomes something in between a key and a lockpick.

I have doubts as to whether performance

studies might be called an academic discipline. That is why - with all due respect to the work of the translator of this book - I keep a certain distance from the notion of *performatyka* itself. I am not surprised that Schechner, who doesn't know Polish and its systems, very eagerly picked up on this neologism; it suits his vision of performance studies as a universal discipline. But can we agree to this without offering any criticism?

What is the first law of performance studies? What is the definition of performance studies? Certainly such definitions appear, but these are exclusively prospective definitions, that's why I would deem Schechner's proposition - which is, in part, close to what I do myself, that is, the anthropology of performances - a project, a perspective showing different possibilities and presenting us with different tools for the performative analysis of human activity, but not only one universal tool! As a matter of fact, when we look through this book and at the various biographical notes, lists and long quotations that appear on almost every page, this way of understanding performance studies imposes itself on us all the more clearly. It is not an independent discipline but a perspective, a potential, one of the possible ways of understanding human beings, based on multiple foundations. It is a toolbox for an expert.

Similar doubts are raised by Schechner's statement that every human action can be a performance, starting from his example of when one exhibits oneself, alone, in a mirror. Well, no, it seems to me that this is precisely the limit. Let us recall Witold Gombrowicz, who was the first in Poland to 'do performance studies' - as Schechner would put it. As he begins his journal, he writes: 'Monday - me, Tuesday - me' and so on; at this point nothing is happening yet. Even Gombrowicz doesn't exist! There is only his opinion of himself. On Friday, as we remember, Józefa Radzymińska visits him, and it is only she who confirms that Gombrowicz in fact exists, that is, he exists in the eyes of another person. As a result of the interaction between them, thanks to dialogue, thanks to the - conscious and unconscious - triggering of particular impressions, and also thanks to a copy of the newspaper *Wiadomości*, which Radzymińska brought with her for the writer, communication begins. Only here is there a space for a performance. A performance can only be this, what falls into the field of communication. If we recall other founders of performance studies and of the anthropology of performance - here I think above all of Erving Goffman and Victor Turner, to whom Schechner refers - we can see that their points of departure were in fact interactive, communicational performances. An excessively broad perspective on performance makes using this term more difficult. Culture is also an unusually broad field, but it still does not encompass everything. It can be defined, because we are able to indicate what is not culture. But I would like to state clearly that my wariness about these two key notions, and particularly about the two Polish neologisms that stand for them, is not a disquiet about the subject and its perspectives.

**Leyko:** From the start I would like to avoid a confrontational approach to Schechner's book. I think that the four-month silence following the conference in Wrocław was due to the fact that we were all very pleased with the appearance of *Performatyka*. We accepted it as a particular academic perspective, or perspective on research. However, we do not have the possibility of broadening this view by referring to other publications within this field, so all the time we refer to Schechner, certain of whose premises are confrontational towards theatre studies, and which basically impose such a confrontation. But we still don't have Marvin Carlson's book.[1] We don't have McKenzie. So we don't have the possibility of a broader frame of reference. Our only dialogue is with Schechner's basic premises. The solitude of this book restricts us to constant and, as people would have it, unfulfilled or dissatisfied discussions. If we were to take into consideration not only Schechner's position but a broader perspective, and, for example, what was

[1] Marvin Carlson's second edition of *Performance: A Critical Introduction* (2004) has since been translated into Polish by Edyta Kubikowska (2007) *Performans*, ed Tomasz Kubikowski, Warsaw: Wydawnictwo Naukowe PWN.

appropriated from performance studies by German theatre researchers, or by Patrice Pavis in France, then I think only then would we gain a proper indication of the possibilities for employing a performance-studies perspective in our own situation.

**Ratajczakowa:** Does this mean that you are suggesting two things? Firstly, to wait and organize another such discussion when further books appear. Secondly, to do what German theatre academics did and treat performance studies as it treats other disciplines, to melt it - to take out what is needed and to introduce it to our discipline?

**Leyko:** Yes, because I am afraid of the kind of thinking that appears to be suggested in Schechner's book - isolated from the broader field of research - which implies that performance studies will replace theatre studies. This voice is not representative of the whole field of performance studies since, for example, Marvin Carlson thinks that performance studies prevents the 'closure' of theatre studies, and Janelle Reinelt is quite simply opposed to the globalization of performance studies as a discipline, supporting aspirations to make it international and plurivocal. So this is exactly the same approach to application that we can observe in Germany or in France.

**Kubikowski:** I fully share Małgorzata Leyko's discomfort. First of all, one has to treat seriously what Schechner himself declares in the preface: this book is very authorial, it is charged throughout with his biography, with his origins and formation. I have been following the development of performance studies for a long time with great interest, and I am sure that one would have to read many books that were written more or less independently from one another over at least the last seventeen years - in order to shape one's own, informed opinion on this subject. Especially because all of the books that aim to be comprehensive are attempts to describe

an element that constantly escapes us. The so-called theoretical explosion, which was noted and named in 1992, is still difficult to grasp.

The first such attempt, very valuable at the time, was Carlson's book from 1996 which, let's hope, will appear in Polish this year. It remains a good introductory guide. The list of authors that are worth engaging with should be extended though, because I cannot imagine reflecting on performance studies without some familiarity with the thought of McKenzie, Auslander, Roach, Blau, Phelan and many others from the USA, where the discipline came into being, not to mention from its subsequent expansion.

When we look at this theoretical explosion at the end of the 1980s and the beginning of the 1990s, it seems that performance studies became an excellent way of breaking a certain deadlock in which, in the area of thinking about theatre and similar things, the dominant critical approaches - semiotics, anthropology and sociology (three of the roots of performance studies) - found themselves at that time. In this moment, when these three kinds of reflection began to go around in circles, a very useful category of 'performance' crystallized, which allowed the possibility of finding common ground for certain things, of gluing them together, naming them and giving them a new critical impetus.

I deliberately chose the term *performatyka*. I will not insist that this is the most graceful way of translating 'performance studies' into Polish, but I think that the ongoing use of the English term is a certain, maybe unconscious, attempt at the stigmatization of the phenomenon, of recognizing it as something strictly American. Like McDonald's. I don't think that this area of thought is in such an unfavourable position that it doesn't have its own field of study, as argued by Wojciech Dudzik. It is in the same situation as semiotics was in the moment of its conception, one hundred years ago, or as sociology was in the nineteenth century. Actually, the name *semiotyka* (semiotics) crossed my mind when I was thinking about how to translate 'performance studies' into Polish. Before, I was using the literal translation *studia performatywne*. A hundred years ago, a couple of people, independently from one another, from within different theoretical traditions, became aware that there is something like a structure of signs. This was also still very broad; it was defined in various ways. Even now, after a hundred years, all of these traditions do not fit together completely. We cannot put Peirce and de Saussure in one line, because they are not compatible. We have semiotics, semiology, at the moment even semasiology, and so on. There has not been less theoretical confusion there than in performance studies.

Later, as a matter of fact in the field of logical semiotics, a conception of performativity came into being, and this went on … I would like to indicate one further, important thing: that reflection on performance goes deeper than its simply having roots in cultural studies, that a perspective adopted from cultural studies or from anthropology allows us to deal with only part of the phenomenon. Let us not forget about the work of Searle, one of the most important philosophers of our time, after John Austin the principal architect of performative theory and simultaneously one of the leading theorists of consciousness. The functioning of performative mechanisms can be found in the sphere beyond culture, or in the pre-cultural sphere, on the biological level, or maybe within informatics - which is something that in my own work interests me greatly. It extends to numerous, different disciplines.

Performance became, for a moment, the key to all locks - I agree. Partly because this is like the normal teething troubles of a new discipline, which pass, and partly because this is a totally healthy way of trying out a tool - how else can we check which locks the key fits and which it does not? Here again, it would be very useful to compare it with semiotics, because we have lots of research, for example under the name 'semiotics of culture', in which it can be seen that semiotic tools are simply an inspiration for further work. Let's consider the whole Russian school. I once got to thinking about whether Lotman would have written such brilliant books if the semiotic tools he used had not previously been developed. It is very probable that he would have, but that something else would have inspired him. In any case, a huge wave of fascination in the 'performative key' arose in the 1990s - right now it has cooled somewhat.

Professor Ratajczakowa's description of a 'light discipline' is very accurate. This discipline has the character of a butterfly net, with which truly elusive phenomena can be captured. A certain part of performance studies' teething troubles - its rather ostentatious rebelliousness towards structures, with which we dealt in the 1990s in particular - was based precisely on the fear of overloading this net. And here there is the next paradox, because Schechner's book marks another phase: it is an attempt to place performance studies into an academic routine. After all, it is a handbook.

**Dudzik:** Can a performance be treated in the same way as a sign in semiotics?

**Kubikowski:** It depends on which kind of semiotics we are talking about. After a hundred years there are still many. In any case, discussing a performance does not entail a more tolerant attitude towards possible inaccuracies on our part than when discussing a sign in semiotics. And obviously it is not a synonym for the performative.

**Dudzik:** But still, I would be opposed to talking about performance studies as an academic discipline. Let us remind ourselves of what kinds of doubts were raised - not so long ago - about theatre studies, of how long the debate continued and whether it was possible to talk about it as an academic discipline, or simply as 'knowledge about theatre'. Ten years ago, we established our own faculty within the Institute of Polish Culture at the University of Warsaw, and this is why we named it 'knowledge about culture'. I don't think

I have to recall the arguments on this matter.

**Ratajczakowa:** There is no one structuralism, just as there is no one semiotics. And no one performance studies. They are many, and this multiplicity is a consequence of our whole reality, which, after all, is also a mosaic. Clearly delimited, restricted points of view - solely structuralist, solely performative or solely semiotic - build a certain, limited unity. I think that performance studies will not behave in this way. Since it projects multiple possibilities, we will be able to confront them with one another. New volumes will appear, but Schechner's work already takes account of the multiplicity of performance studies, and this is its normal course. Secondly, if we recognize that we live in an extremely individualized world, we will consequently not be surprised at the diversification of performative perspectives. It is something that seems normal to me, but we still haven't become used to such a situation. Going back to what Wojciech Dudzik said about Gombrowicz and the mirror, it is also some sort of communication after all, because it is about what I do with myself in this mirror, what Gombrowicz does. Let's think about these reflections in the eyes of others. I would not be so eager to throw this mirror away ...

**Leyko:** The possibilities of applying performance studies are best illustrated in the German and French experiences that we have already mentioned, and I think that there is no point in arguing about the possibility of any kind of unification or systematization, because this is not inscribed anywhere in performance studies, which in the American perspective only responds to the problems of modernity and thus escapes any kind of canonization. If we take a look at what European theatre academics do with performance studies, maybe we could free ourselves from the compulsion to treat things systematically. Patrice Pavis, for example, proposes to introduce a notion 'mise-en-performance', suggesting that theatre in the 1980s, under the influence of non-literary and non-European elements, found itself between mise-en-scène and performance. He even speaks about a paradigm shift in theatre itself. Christopher Balme, on the other hand, stresses the interculturalism and intermediality of contemporary theatre and indicates, using the example of the Rimini Protokoll how inadequate a theatre-studies perspective is for understanding this phenomenon. Erika Fischer-Lichte, using the example of theatre and performance art, attempts to create a performative aesthetics that can be referred, not only to other fields of the arts but also to other areas of social and political life, and so on. Today it is still difficult to establish whether this is useful and valid within the frame of performance studies in its existing sociological, ethnological and anthropological orientation. Undoubtedly though, it provides new research tools for theatre studies, whose traditional methods have coped with difficulty when faced with processual phenomena in the history of theatre or with capturing the specifics of postdramatic performances.

**Kosiński:** How might performance studies be most usefully engaged in Poland? I think that Polish theatre studies needs to endure these teething troubles of performance studies, because our attachment to the category of theatre, with its conviction that we know what theatre is, is merely a pretence at knowledge. In reality, we know that the category of theatre is not clearly defined at all but that at the same time it is being defended more and more often.

**Kubikowski:** Again, a paradox. On one hand, people constantly spoke about what exceeds theatre, an 'other' theatre or something beyond theatre, subconsciously evaluating it in a positive way - this is the legacy of the neo-avant-garde, which is very alive here, even on the popular level. Let's have a look at the press reviews. It is very amusing that the critics, when they want to give the highest evaluation of a performance, usually write that it 'went beyond the limits of theatre'. And yet, on the other hand, we are holding on to this theatre. The attempts to find other reference points, of which the most lasting in the twentieth century appeared to be ritualism, associated with a longing for the sacred - these are also exhausted. The category of performance might be extremely useful here because it is emotionally quite neutral, even like some sort of abstract number that is worth being brought into our calculations, because it provides us with different points of view.

**Dudzik**: I think that there are others who are able to make better use of this than theatre academics. Performance studies may only cause theatre researchers to broaden their field of interest, enabling them to perceive what they were looking at before without understanding - looking without seeing. But could it also be used in order to investigate a theatrical work as it is? I am not sure.

**Ratajczakowa**: If we take a closer look at the process through which theatre studies was created, it becomes clear that its conception emerged under the weight of scientism. It attempted to manage this situation, ignoring the fact that it is actually directed towards something 'non-existent' - that is to say, performance. A performance is a very light subject of research, as is the work of the theatre arts. In the past a disastrous thing occurred in Polish theatre studies: we neglected phenomenology, which would have opened various doors - to structuralism, semiotics, communication theory. That is why we should not reject performance studies, because it may constitute a real opportunity for our research. Through it, we can examine a work in another way, and with a different perspective there is always an extensive, hidden potential.

**Leyko**: The problem with accepting performance studies is due to the history of Polish theatre studies, which has not passed through certain currents of research. Today's situation is like a fast track. Suddenly we reach for something that has already taken shape, that is mature, except it does not have any roots here or an essential foundation. Maybe our reluctance and the threat that we perceive from performance studies are due to this. On the other hand, how can we do without it in the interpretation of modern theatre? If we were to view Marek Fiedor's *Baal* only from the perspective of traditional notions of theatre studies and theatre criticism, we would have to reject this performance because it would not fit with the existing canon of theatre aesthetics. There are the same concerns with Anna Augustynowicz's *Measure for Measure*. We would be in trouble as well, we would be on shaky ground if we wanted to perceive only a 'character' or a 'part' in these performances.

**Kubikowski**: It is true that we are on a fast track and that we are still trying to make contact with the outside world after the catastrophic 1980s. For Polish theatrical awareness, these years were a catastrophe, maybe even more than in other areas of life. Firstly, due to a very alive and important theatrical movement, we found ourselves at the centre of events: thanks to Grotowski, to Kantor, to the whole wave of 'off-' theatres that accompanied them. Then later, the doors were shut in the aftermath of martial law and for ten years we became totally cut off from how these developments were discussed, digested and contested elsewhere. At the same time, a different cultural situation emerged, in whose beginnings we did not participate. And later, taken out of the freezer after ten years, we emerged with the sudden realization of a queen who has been dethroned: on the one hand feeling that what occurred beyond our reach was somehow less 'worthy' than what happened here; on the other hand, incapable of understanding this other and the situation in which it came into being - and even its points of reference. Again, almost twenty years have passed and it is still visible: we constantly try to build bridges, to find ourselves - sometimes a little farcically - but somehow this process develops nonetheless.

Performance studies may well become useful beyond theatre. For me - in basic considerations of consciousness and of being in the world. There is a famous and brilliant book by Jon McKenzie in which he argues that, just as it has been since the mid-twentieth century, performance will be for the twenty-first century what discipline was in the two previous centuries (McKenzie 2001). It is as if McKenzie added another chapter to the thought of Michel Foucault. Anyway, this raises basic questions about the extent to which performance studies is a way of describing a certain culture, and the extent to which it is a symptom of this culture. And also to what extent we in Poland participate in this culture. Well, we participate to an increasingly large extent - and this produces somewhat ambivalent feelings within us.

**Dudzik**: Performance studies, as I have already said, is needed by theatre academics in order to broaden their field of interest. But this performative toolbox should serve in the first place to investigate culture, social life, the place of human beings within culture, communication. Researchers into culture may benefit to an even greater degree here, and theatre researchers may at least stop looking at theatre in isolation - which is worth demanding. A dozen or so years ago, along with Leszek Kolankiewicz, I proposed the heading 'Teatr w kulturze' ('Theatre in Culture') - this was the title of the coursebook that we edited - and this slogan somehow took hold and functions, but still too rarely is it reflected in research. And without taking into consideration the contexts, interactions, relations and all the communicative aspects of theatre, there is no chance of encompassing the whole entity. Furthermore, theatre is an exceptional case of a kind of immediate, elusive communication, which establishes an equally elusive work of art. Looking at all of the branches that run from, and into it, accessing the sources should now be easier thanks to these new tools. Theatre is not an objective for performance studies, it is one of the possibilities of its application, but all these perspectives are far more useful in the anthropology of culture, in order to extend our knowledge of the human being as a creator of culture, to describe the dramaturgical sphere of human activity.

**Kosiński**: The dramaturgical sphere of human activity - is this a field that we, theatre academics, should leave to researchers of culture? Isn't it us who have the tools at our disposal that might be applied to such an open field?

**Ratajczakowa**: Yes, certainly. But let's see what performance studies proposes to us. Maybe it will offer us the perfect alibi for some sort of poaching of different fields. For a long time I have had the feeling that, by looking at theatrical performance mainly as an aesthetic object, we cut many of its cultural 'strings', we cut it off from reality. We narrow our field of experience, and as a consequence we lose sight of the aims and functions of the theatre. Once, I faced the objection that I am neither a semiotician, nor a structuralist, nor a phenomenologist. I replied that I am all of these, as they are all necessary for the theatre and because it is not afraid of anything, because it reaches for all areas of life, art, practice and academia. Why do we reach so infrequently for cultural studies, anthropological studies, theories of social communication and all sorts of others, and never treat them as frameworks for interpretation?

**Dudzik**: Cultural studies, as an academic discipline, has only existed in Poland for three years. Such a pathway has obviously existed for a long time, but the discipline has only just been acknowledged. At the University of Warsaw, the first doctorate in the field of cultural studies has just been awarded. This shows how much time is needed to consolidate an apparently self-evident discipline.

**Leyko**: I don't know whether other disciplines,

such as sociology or ethnology, are as interested in performance studies as is theatre studies. If we don't reach for these tools, we will - like Polish theatre as a zombie institution - be doomed to encounter zombie performances, in which something will escape us because we will treat them as dead. They are alive, just using a different language.

**Kubikowski:** If we were to accept McKenzie's position, certainly we theatre researchers should make use of management theories and business literature.

**Ratajczakowa:** The entire art of management is a wonderful performance.

**Kosiński:** Isn't it that, in the society of 'Embodied Spectacle' (to use Krzysztof Rutkowski's term) theatre cannot fill the role of a place that is 'not ours'? Isn't it that theatre escapes from it so as not to become a zombie? Theatre artists react much faster to change and to the developments that are happening right in front of us with theatrical performances, which are becoming more and more like 'events', and should be described as such. The changes that Gardzienice's *Metamorphosis* has gone through - no one described this because *Metamorphosis*, treated as an abstraction, which doesn't really exist but which we consider as a certain sum, cannot be described.

**Leyko:** From this inertia, theatre escapes as an art but not as an institution. The theatre critics, who are not connected with academic theatre studies and who accept this new perspective in an unconscious way, react to it equally quickly. When we read the latest reviews, what is striking is that in describing what we used to call 'character' or 'role', the critics refer to the actor more and more often using their name. Erika Fischer-Lichte suggests that a role becomes transparent. We used to try to remain on the surface, and in doing so it seemed to us that we perceived a character. In the meantime, all performative experiences perceived from this attempt at aesthetics show that these roles are transparent. The performance studies perspective emerged from within completely different conditions of theatrical organization. Performance studies was born from America's protest against the institutionalization of European theatre, which was foreign to its cultural tradition. America created its own form of theatre - performance - and it used new tools to describe and to teach it, including within the university system. We are confused as to why we have 'theatre as a zombie institution', theatre studies, which tries to counter this inertia, and theatre as art, which more and more often breaks through this crust.

**Kubikowski:** When we touch on the question of the life and death of the theatre, and also of escaping from life, and death, I cannot help but recall Edward Gordon Craig who, in the face of continuous appeals to life, said that one should not be afraid of stillness in the theatre and should not be afraid of death, because death is perfect. Craig's theatre was dead. Dead by design. In this stillness lay its richness. The fact is that theatre tries to escape from stillness, sometimes in a panic, sometimes chaotically, sometimes too slowly. At the same time, there is something in it that means that whenever you intend to go somewhere, you reach the opposite place. Kafka's parable: leopards enter a temple and drink the contents of the sacrificial chalices. This happens again and again, and in the end it is included in the ceremony. Every transgression becomes part of a rite. Each of them becomes fixed. And vice versa, something that is dead is eventually discovered as a carrier of untold value.

**Leyko:** With stillness and death it is like with truth: for as long as the theatre has existed it has aimed at truth and nature, only it defines them in a different way each time. What Craig opposed was also a dead theatre.

**Ratajczakowa:** With such a high degree of

mediatization in our lives, theatre appears, to a large extent, to be a communicational backwater. It seems to be such an antiquated means of communication that in fact it should not even exist. But fortunately it does still exist, because we are still meeting face to face with one another. It is the only immediate art that is still capable of being reborn, although not completely and not in all circumstances.

**Kosiński:** What possibilities do you see for changing this situation, for enforcing this escape from the zombie-ism of theatre studies by possibly drawing inspiration from performance studies for our teaching practice?

**Leyko:** In cultural studies, as a faculty, even the ministerial educational standards allow for such an area within compulsory classes, which are not determined by the name of the subject but whose thematic scope is signalled by the heading 'Theatre and cultural performances'.

**Dudzik:** In our teaching practice at the Institute of Polish Culture, this perspective has existed for over ten years, although not under this name. Our first coursebook was entitled *Theatre in Culture* - I have spoken about this already. We started work on *Antropologia widowisk* ['The Anthropology of Performances'] - a handbook, thus named after the work of Victor Turner - long before the appearance of the American edition of *Performance Studies: An Introduction*, which is the book that we have been talking about. So we now have another handbook.

**Kubikowski:** At the faculty where I work, some sentiments and aspirations that we have been speaking about today appeared at the moment of its founding. It was a faculty which, from the very beginning, was called 'Knowledge about Theatre', as suggested by Bohdan Korzeniewski. Also from the start, theatre was considered here to be some sort of social event, whose existence refers to various domains of culture, but not only of culture.

The relation between performance and *widowisko* ('spectacle') - what in the translations of works by Milton Singer we name *widowisko kulturowe* ('cultural spectacle') is in fact *performans kulturowy* ('cultural performance'). It is also like this in Turner. The mutual relation between these two notions is very interesting. Zbigniew Raszewski employed the category of *widowisko*, which is identical to one of the early definitions of performance given by Schechner. These categories are somehow complementary. The question of Embodied Spectacle and the question of the optional presence of an audience, however, make performance a richer category.

**Ratajczakowa:** To conclude, the threads of performance studies are, in one way or another, already in existence in Poland, not only from today or from the moment when Schechner's book appeared. So I wouldn't complain too much. I would accept this proposition instead. A different point of view, fresh air of this kind will do us no harm at all.

Translated by Adela Karsznia and Duncan Jamieson

This is an edited version of the conversation first published in Polish in a special section of (2007) 'Performatyka' ['Performatics'] in Krakowska, Joanna (ed) *Dialog* 7/8, Warsaw, pp. 140-50.

REFERENCES

Beck, Ulrich (1992) *Risk Society: Towards a New Modernity*, London: Sage.

Debord, Guy (1992) *Society of the Spectacle*, trans. Ken Knabb, Rebel Press.

McKenzie, Jon (2001) *Perform or Else*, London and New York: Routledge.

Schechner, Richard (2006) *Performance Studies: An Introduction*, 2d revised edition, London and New York: Routledge.

---

[1] We have translated *nauka* as 'discipline' here, as 'science' has more precise connotations in English than *nauka* does in Polish and is not generally used to designate most academic disciplines. (Trans.)

# The Street is the State · Rangoon/Yangon, September 2007

Performance entails doubling, sharing, plenitude; like this sentence, it is cumulative, viral, fecund. Performance begets performance, and while Janelle Reinelt may correctly state that the charge of imperialism in performance studies 'appears not to hold up to scrutiny of its history' (2007: 13), there is nevertheless a tendency in the discipline to reproduce the expansionist impulse of its object. Richard Schechner provides a somewhat ironic demonstration of this when he writes in his *Performance Studies* textbook: 'Any behavior, event, action, or thing can be studied "as" performance. Take maps, for example' (2006: 40). He goes on to explain how maps and mapmakers have always performed an interpretation of the world, often in the service of imperial power. Moreover: 'It's not just maps. Everything and anything can be studied "as" any discipline of study' (42). But if Schechner's argument about the significance of maps 'as' performance is to hold, there's surely no 'just' about them – maps are not an 'example', they are *exemplary*: even as they provide an opportunity to flaunt performance studies' anti-imperialist credentials, they facilitate the resource-hungry march of the discipline. Sometimes, the map really is the territory.

There is a terminological problem here. 'Performance', 'performativity' and 'performance studies' are simply too thick with each other. They form a tight-bound hermeneutic knot that cannot be undone by the interjection of mere prepositions like 'as'. Might 'performatics' help? There are reasons for skepticism. New terminologies usually augur a disciplinary land-grab, especially when they entail a noun with such a prestigious suffix: '-ics' combines the accepted form for 'names of sciences' and for 'matters of practice' (OED). In this light, Jarosław Fret's and Grzegorz Ziółkowski's assertion that 'the real potential of the phenomenon [of performatics] can be tested by its possibility of projection' (in Gough 2007), suggests a pre-emptive critical strike on future objects of study. But here, now, while the meaning of 'performatics' is itself still up for grabs, the opportunity exists to harness it as a means of moderating, rather than exacerbating, performance studies' rate of interpretive inflation.

Take Burma/Myanmar, for example. In September 2007 Buddhist monks and ordinary citizens launched protests against the oppressive rule of the military junta, which responded with a violent crackdown. Many of the events of that period came to the attention of the outside world through a series of acts that ostensibly fall within the ambit of contemporary performance studies. And yet:

1) Although the monks initiated the protests by marching in the street, the maximum they could do without provoking retaliation was the minimum possible – walking swiftly and silently in a loose formation. Sympathetic onlookers responded in kind, with furtive applause.

2) Although Burma/Myanmar became the object of intense international attention, almost everything of diplomatic significance was stated either behind the scenes or (as in the case of China's comments and the junta's response before the UN) so implicitly as to bear little direct relation to the words being publicly uttered.

3) Although a reasonably steady stream of media footage depicted events on the ground, most was shot clandestinely, from the hip, or from obscure angles on the tops of buildings. It was grainy, shaky, out of focus; it lacked the clarity lent by the more conventional contiguity between camera and eye, and none of it achieved the combination of formal, symbolic and journalistic qualities that make for an iconic image. Perhaps the most-reproduced piece of footage, the shooting of Japanese video-journalist Kenji Nagai, was striking not for its visual impact but for the offhandedness of the brutality and the sickening bounce of his body after hitting the road.

4) Although there were large-scale pro-junta counter-demonstrations, participants almost certainly acted under duress. Meanwhile, the official *New Light of Myanmar* newspaper explained local dissent away by claiming that 'stooges of foreign countries, neglecting the national prestige and integrity, put on a play written by their foreign masters' (2007).

5) Although Burma/Myanmar briefly

[1] The exception that proved the rule was provided by the Association of Southeast Asian Nations (ASEAN), whose softly-softly approach to the junta since admitting Burma/Myanmar in 1997 has been a conspicuous failure. Publicly expressing 'revulsion' at the junta's actions - an uncharacteristically forthright term - was the only way to maintain international credibility.

experienced, to borrow Peggy Phelan's characterization of live performance, a 'plunge into visibility' (1993: 148), this was countermanded by the silence of the Generals, bunkered down in the remote new capital of Naypyidaw, and the uncountable disappearances of protesters in the weeks following the uprising. Meanwhile, less than a month after the crackdown, then Acting Prime Minister Thein Sein was able to open the 15th Myanmar Traditional Cultural Performing Arts Competition by exhorting performers to 'be vigilant with national awareness against various forms of psychological warfare and cultural influence delicately penetrating into the nation through the cultural and economic fields' (Thein Sein 2007).

Political demonstrations hold a privileged place in the foundational texts of performance studies. In particular, the anti-Vietnam war activism of the 1960s and 1970s provided an influential aesthetic and a political bridge between theatre and the world. During such times, Schechner has argued, 'the street is the stage' (1993: 45–93). He is not wrong. Yet, in the events listed above, performance was an identifiable but marginal component: subordinate to basic human needs, state power and realpolitik. Sometimes the street is only minimally the stage, and perhaps 'performatics' was made to teach us that. If we take its pseudo-scientific airs seriously – more seriously, perhaps, than was intended of it – then we are compelled to deflate our rhetoric, and ask instead: what's the least we can do, and still be performing? How does that relate to everything else we're also doing? And aren't there more important things to worry about?

REFERENCES

Gough, Richard (2007) 'Invitation to submit a short 'definition/provocation' on/about: *Performatyka – Performatics*', personal correspondence, 17 September, no page numbers.

*New Light of Myanmar* (2007) 'Forthcoming constitution vests national races with better rights on the basis of the prevailing conditions of the nation,' 11 October, <http://www.myanmar.com/newspaper/nlm/index.html>.

Phelan, Peggy (1993) *Unmarked: The Politics of Performance*, London and New York: Routledge.

Reinelt, Janelle (2007) 'Is Performance Studies Imperialist? Part 2' in *The Drama Review* 51(3): 7–16.

Schechner, Richard (2006) *Performance Studies: An Introduction*, 2nd edn, London and New York: Routledge.

Schechner, Richard (1993) 'The Street is the Stage' *The Future of Ritual: Writings on Culture and Performance*, London and New York: Routledge, pp. 45–93.

Thein Sein (2007) 'It is the duty of all to collectively strive for further glorifying, flourishing and developing in accord with the time the cultural structure in the hearts of Myanmar people', in *New Light of Myanmar*, 17 October, <http://www.myanmar.com/newspaper/nlm/index.html>.

PAUL RAE

# Back of Beyond

RICHARD GOUGH

*This is an edited version of a performative lecture given at the Grotowski Centre, Wrocław, Poland, 8 December 2006. Certain sections of this talk were previously delivered in Singapore, Shanghai and California earlier in 2006.*

First of all, I should like to thank Jarosław Fret and Grzegorz Ziółkowski of the Grotowski Centre and Tomasz Kubikowski from Warsaw Theatre Academy, for this opportunity to revisit Wrocław.

Poland feels like a spiritual home for me. Since 1974 it has influenced significantly the origins and development of Cardiff Laboratory Theatre and Centre for Performance Research (CPR). So many colleagues, travels, collaborations, trials and tribulations, encountered, forged and found in Poland, with numerous theatre companies and many individuals, scholars and practitioners, a lacework of friendships and professional allegiances that continue to this day. These individuals, these companies and this work have challenged, informed and inspired me and many of my colleagues in Wales.

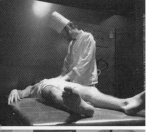

I say this at the outset because I have been asked to speak about how Performance Research and Performance Studies have emerged in Wales. It is by mistake, by a series of chance encounters, serendipity and coincidence, in defiance of cultural policy, through adaptation and mutation, through contamination and perseverance, through blood, sweat and tears and through a specific set of located practices, and yet in thinking about formations, a circularity of reflection operates here that leads me back to Poland and our origins as an experimental theatre group (Cardiff Laboratory Theatre), inspired to a large degree by Grotowski and subsequent collaborations with artists in Poland.

This is a book, and this is a chain.

I want to start with books and end with chains, the distinction between the two is perhaps clear to most people but at this moment in my life I am perplexed about the difference – both positively challenged and deeply troubled.

For someone who proclaimed in his youth to be illiterate on purpose, it is disturbing for me to realize that I am spending (and have spent) a great deal of my time on building a series of libraries; one of cookery books, one on world music, one on bees and apiculture and the one on theatre and performance. It was curious to me that we began the conference last night with a series of slides of our collective publications – an introduction through a roll-call of book covers. The night before I had spent part of the evening with Jarosław Fret, and I realized afterwards we had spent the whole time talking about books; our joint venture to publish a series of Polish theatre scholarship in English, the immanent arrival of Richard Schechner's *Performance Studies: An Introduction* in Polish, the difficulties of realizing a Polish edition of Grotowski's *Towards a Poor Theatre*, the recent publication of CPR's *Performance Cosmology*. We are theatre directors, but we talked about books, passionately, fervently, almost with a sense of the erotic.

And so I immediately return to chains; this is the chained library in Hereford Cathedral. I used to hide in this place, avoiding rugby, cricket and other compulsory games while at the Cathedral School (an English 'public' boarding school). I even spent all-night vigils spooked-out by the silence, the pitch darkness and the haunting presence of velum; these illuminated manuscripts offered me no light or solace.

'*I want to share with you a few samples from my collection,*' he says in a slightly menacing and truly deranged manner. The act of curation here is simple: the smallest, the largest, the oldest, the newest, a significance here and a significance there.

Back of Beyond

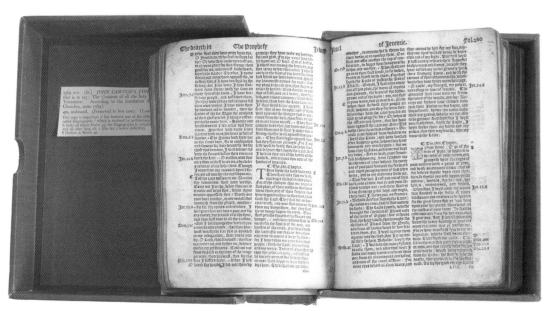

This is my oldest book: a bible of 1598. It could have been from the chained library, I promise you it is not, but it belongs there; it is of the same vintage.

I have spent a great deal of time over the last year discussing with an irascible and highly opinionated yet sharp and perceptive octogenarian the possible gift of one of the world's largest private collection of theatre books to CPR and Aberystwyth University. Last month he signed the deeds; tens of thousands of books are now arriving in Aberystwyth, about twice the number of people who live there.

In applying for Arts and Humanities Research Council funding I was asked to describe the proposed research in simple terms and in a way that could be publicized to and understood by a general audience. This part of what I wrote:

Performance (as aesthetic practice) and Performance Studies (as academic discipline) together with Performance Research (as practice-informed theoretical enquiry) are burgeoning areas of development (research, practice and teaching) within the UK. Most drama and theatre studies departments now have performance or/and performance studies courses within their curricula, some have distinct and distinctive programmes and many have chairs and named professors in Performance and Theatre or Performance Studies, together with research projects and research centres, pursuing both theoretical investigation and practice-led enquiries that further develop and expand the field.

And yet most archives, collections and resources in relation to theatre in the UK remain true to the 1950s/60s formulation of the discipline Drama, and its (1970s/80s) expansion into Theatre Studies, emphasizing the literary aspect of drama and the dramatic text (and predominantly Western traditions of drama) and the interpretive nature of theatre production (design not scenography, directing not devising, acting not performing, the producer not the auteur). As excellent as those archives and collections remain – rigorous in their curation and much needed by both the academy and the profession – there is an urgent need for resources to support the growth and development in Performance (Performance Studies and Performance Research) and expanded notions of Theatre Studies, resources and archives that will promote a dynamic interchange between scholarship and practice in the expanding field of performance, that will, in their curation, be interdisciplinary in vision and international in scope and that will emphasize contemporary performance within changing cultural contexts and explore the relationship of innovation to tradition by maintaining collections on both world theatre traditions and contemporary experiment.

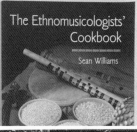

125

We did not secure a grant, but despite that and the sheer size, weight and volume of this project, I am excited and challenged about the possibility of realizing a library and archive that supports, invigorates and propels Performance Research and Performance Studies.

I realize that what I value most about Performance Studies is that it promotes a broad spectrum approach to the appreciation and understanding of human endeavour - culture in the broadest sense. It is an optic, a way of looking at the world and a way of constructing alternative views (proposing 'new' realities, different options, making the familiar unfamiliar, opening perceptions). It is inclusive, intercultural, interdisciplinary and integrating. It allows for new formulations and emphasizes process rather than product.

It does not enshrine cultural values and pronounce upon them with certainty; rather it contests them and offers a space/site for dynamic negotiation. It includes uncertainty and diffidence, promotes experiment, nurtures a sense of becoming and evolving and encourages reflection. It emphasizes the provisional, action with contingency, mutability - culture in a subjunctive mode.

It does not oppose, replace or deny the European tradition of theatre (its canon and practice), rather it promotes this as one hue among many in the spectrum and then positively embraces the performative traditions of other cultures, hybrid forms and innovative fusion.

It encourages an understanding and appreciation of the methods, techniques and aesthetic concepts of other cultures and societies both from around the world and within our own nation.

And so now to a restaurant.

I first went to Das Sreedharan's Southern Indian vegetarian restaurant *Rasa* in Stoke Newington, London, in 1995. *Rasa*, as many of you will know means, flavour and is a complex concept in Indian aesthetics to describe the quality of dance and the emotions it gives rise to in both the watcher and the watched. Such has been the success of Das Sreedharan's food that there are now several Rasa restaurants in London including one in Mayfair.

Here are some of the delights of Das's food, for the eye only. Pure vegetarian, stunningly fresh and light with the power to transport you, where? To Kerala, I imagine.

As with many successful chefs, Das has published a book. But Das's success has been achieved through the realization of a paradox familiar to theatre and the acting profession: to achieve the best possible public presentations he has delved into the most private resources; to realize extraordinary restaurant food he has developed skills and recipes from home cooking. Das now sends his chefs home to Kerala to spend time with his mother in her family kitchen. They work alongside her and learn from her.

Mastering methods and techniques of simplicity, directness and immediacy, learning an art of food-preparation nurtured over generations. The chefs return to take up their posts in London, and now in a canny twist of intercultural transaction the Keralan government sends officials from the tourist office over to London to understand better how Kerala can be promoted as a distinct and distinctive Indian state, with *Rasa* as a shining example.

In Shanghai last month I gave a non-existing slide show to structure a talk about training. One image was of Richard Schechner standing outside the *Kerala Kalamandalam* Kathakali School. I don't know if such a picture exists, but if I had it I would have liked to cross fade it, so we could see Eugenio Barba, and Jerzy Grotowski before him, and then Peter Brook and Phillip Zarrilli and numerous other luminaries of late-twentieth-century Western theatre afterwards.

The *Kerala Kalamandalam*, located in Cheruthuruthy, Kerala, South India, has been a place of pilgrimage for Western theatre practitioners over the last forty years, a place, a school that has had a formative influence on many contemporary 'masters' of Western physical, experimental and innovative theatre, where the connections between dance/theatre and the martial arts, combats of play and display, and the transpositions and hybrid forms merge into an extraordinary practice.

What did they witness there? They saw a radical re-formation of the performer's body, a training through inculcation and exactitude. Sometimes ancient knowledge is embedded in a training to do with breath and posture, balance and mental states. This can be encrypted and not articulated, the origins perhaps even forgotten, the reasons lost – tacit knowledge. In part it took Grotowski's understanding and insightfulness to illuminate the lessons of the training and knowledge it conveyed, transforming it himself into another body of incorporated practice – a translation of a tradition, a restoration, a re-formation.

What is fascinating to me is how the school, founded by Vallathol Narayana Menon, is modeled on an English public school, with a strict regime and separation of practices, an invention of the 1930s, an intercultural transaction that was to have formidable repercussions and influence on the development of European and North American theatre forty years later. In talking about performance mastery, practice and tradition, it is not always possible to trace roots and origins. Transformation and transmutation happen in unforeseen ways, whether in the kalari in Kerala or the kitchens of Rasa.

This is the first book on theatre that I bought, at the age of fifteen – *The Seven Ages of Theatre.* It was in here that I first encountered Kathakali and a whole range of world theatre traditions. It's a fabulous and simple general history of theatre emphasizing the development of the art through different phases/ages and acknowledging their parallel and at times simultaneous emergence, destabilizing any notion of higher evolution. Richard Southern (whom I like to refer to as RS # 1) wrote in the introduction in 1961:

If you *do* something or *perform* something – speak, move, play an instrument – you can embody in that action whatever you have to say. But it is important to emphasize at the beginning that the secret of the theatre does not lie in the thing done but rather in something that arises from the manner of doing. Drama may be *the thing done*, but theatre is *doing*. Theatre is an act.   (Southern 1962)

But how is an early interest in theatre and performance formed?

Growing up in North Wales in the late 1950s and 60s, I do not recall going to the cinema as a family except on

- **Mappa Mundi**
© The Hereford Mappa Mundi Trust.

one particular Saturday when, for some peculiar reason, we went twice: it was as if the afternoon sojourn did not satisfy some paternal yearning or sense of duty, for, on return home in the afternoon, we were out again within the hour. It was an expedition that was confusing and exciting in the first place, and then, doubly so. In the Odeon we saw the adventures of Fu Manchu, an outrageous construction of China and the Chinese, and in the evening we went to see *The King and I*. The experience of these two films marked me deeply, and my mother can still not offer me an explanation as to why this was the only time we went to the cinema, and why we went twice in the same day. A combination of seeing both Fu Manchu and *The King and I* was, however, powerfully intoxicating. Notions of Siam and China entered my childhood games and formed a parallel reality. Yul Brynner was my hero.

'Shall we Dance All Night' joined the songs from *My Fair Lady* that filled the house on Sunday afternoons: my father would retire to the front room, his records playing loud would drift through the house, co-mingling with and supporting the scenarios that were being enacted in my bedroom, live, no spectators required, adding sound tracks to non-verbal enactment in intriguing and unpredictable ways. Is it possible to trace one's preferences in theatre and performance – in my case juxtaposition, rupture, coincidence – to particular occurrences and events. Could so much be formed in one weekend?

In my own work and my early attempts to determine an aesthetic, I was drawn to objects. Objects that seemed to emerge into daylight from dusty attics, mouldy sheds, damp garages and, most of all, the junk shops. I liked the patina, the sense of use and purpose, the scars and markings of an object well-used, of functionality and distress; objects abandoned, discarded, rejected and forlorn. Struggling to assimilate Grotowski, Artaud and Brook, the writings and work of Duchamp, Breton and Magritte perhaps held greater force. I liked to find objects, I liked found objects, I liked to find the action that went with the object and defined the found; I was inspired to liberate them from their moribund existence.

They were numerous, an ensemble that included the broken coffee grinder, the old tricycle, the washboard, the bird cage, the antique child's pram, the box cameras, the magic lantern projectors, the distressed umbrella, the cobbler's shoe stretchers. They were legion, they were loyal, they were ever so compliant, always ready to work, uncomplaining, delighted with this second life, this second order, this second being within a third theatre without a fourth wall, a sort of fifth column of radical objects with a sixth sense, in a seventh heaven, reborn on the eighth day.

But how is a world view of theatre and performance nurtured and encouraged? As a child in Prestatyn I used to collect stamps. Outings to Chester and Liverpool enabled small packages to return home, there to be sorted, organized and arranged in a reverse taxonomy guided by atlas globe and Stanley Gibbons catalogue. I reconstructed the world geographically and historically and became acquainted with its outer reaches. As the philatelist drive became more serious, so the need to specialize became apparent. Not content with the still far too broad fields of British Commonwealth, the Reign of Elizabeth II, Australia and New Zealand, I focused more sharply. I chose Nyasaland. First British Central Africa, then Nyasaland Protectorate, then just plain Nyasaland, Nyasaland and Rhodesia, even Northern Rhodesia and simply Rhodesia.

It is curious to me that I should have had the wisdom to specialize at such an early age and to discover the virtue and wonder of restricting one's field of study. Later, Peter Brook's advice to encourage discipline and structure in order to allow creativity in theatre would have great resonance and nostalgia for me. Now a confirmed and incorrigible generalist, I envy the discipline of my earlier calling. This decision with regard to collection pursued to the limits had two effects. One, collecting now had a diminishing return. With only several hundred stamps to assemble the end was always in sight and rapidly advancing with every new acquisition. Two, I became rather more playful with the

stamps, countries and cultures that were no longer in my field of vision, that were no longer valuable or collectable. I began to construct new commonwealths, new continents and new colonies; I even began to graft stamps together in a project of hybridization born from reading H. G. Wells's *The Island of Dr Moreau*.

It was only recently that I came across the work of Donald Evans, the American artist who painted stamps of non-existent countries, a fabulous project of imagining, speculation and provocation, wryly commenting on colonialism, imperialism and nationalism.

It would seem to me that there are still wide avenues for experiment and research to explore through performance, notions of nationality and identity. Guillermo Gómez-Peña and Coco Fusco, among others, have pointed the way with humour and insight; to rephrase Raymond Williams - every time I hear the phrase national culture, I reach for my fancy dress. Perhaps that reach can be extended, perhaps there are very positive aspects to confusion, in the way that there also are with regard to insecurity.

My own secure grasp on the world was certainly shaken by the *Mappa Mundi* in Hereford Cathedral. As a schoolboy at Hereford, I had to walk past it everyday for seven years. This is a most extraordinary complete world map, made in 1242, which follows the medieval and classical construction of maps with a division of the world into Asia, Africa, and Europe, with Jerusalem in the centre. But by a terrible mistake at the end of the entire process the cartographer misnamed the central sections. The east section (Africa) appears as Europe and the west section (Europe) as Africa. It contains extraordinary depictions of places and ideas through the elaboration of a bestiary and a set of ideograms, so when you find Crete, for example, you also see the labyrinth. I often loitered staring transfixed at this fabulous map, an exercise in fantasy and magic realism that I was only really to understand later when I read Jorge Luis Borges and Gabriel García Márques and saw the boxes and miniature installations of Joseph Cornell.

This the smallest book in my collection, part of a set twenty-four. The complete works of Shakespeare. This is *A Midsummer Night's Dream*.

Following a standard British education at Hereford, the values of English drama and the dominance of the play and the playwright were drummed into me. I still love Shakespeare and going to see a great production of Shakespeare (not usually British!), but equally I reject or rather contest all that education taught me about privilege, Euro-centricity and the supremacy of English dramatists. It still astonishes me how few Drama or Theatre departments in the UK embrace a world view of theatre and performance, and I know this also true for the United States and the rest of Europe. As if my position were not already marginal enough, a few years ago at a gathering of UK. drama, theatre and performance studies lecturers and professors, and as part of a much longer keynote paper, I set them a test, a quiz to challenge their Western theatre bias. It went like this:

1. Other than Chikamatsu, name a Japanese playwright who wrote for the Bunraku and Kabuki stage.
2. What are the roots of *Candomble*?
3. Which came first, *Kun Ju* or *Jing Ju*?
4. Name an Islamic playwright.
5. Who wrote the *Nātyaśāstra* (and this is a trick question)?
6. What is the sung, epic, narrative form of traditional Korean theatre called?
7. In what part of Africa is the Yoruba found, and can you name a Yoruban playwright?
8. Name three Noh plays.
9. What is the difference between *Lokadharmi* and *Natyadharmi*?
10. Name three contemporary Australian theatre companies.

Or just as an example, to reverse the questioning and evoke the standard British reference points:

The answer is Shakespeare, the play *A Midsummer Night's Dream.*
(The question would have been: Who was a contemporary of Chinese playwright Tang Xianzu, and which play was possibly written in the same year as *Peony Pavilion*?)

This is a first edition of the 1965 publication of *TDR* – the *Tulane Drama Review*, as it was then – the 'Polish Lab' issue. A remarkable convergence of four major figures of twentieth-century theatre: Eugenio Barba and Ludwik Flaszen writing the first articles on the work of Jerzy Grotowski and published by the editor of *TDR*, Richard Schechner. Subsequently all of these men were to visit Cardiff and to work in our studio; Barba and Schechner several times, Ludwik Flaszen twice, Grotowski sadly only once.

I bought this copy of *TDR* along with fifty-two others in Hay-on-Wye in 1975 and have been building a theatre library ever since. Frustrated by not being able to find information on the sort of theatre that Cardiff Laboratory was making and that we as a group were increasingly encountering, I became determined to construct an alternative library that placed a greater emphasis on the physical and visual aspects of theatre. In 1976, aged twenty and not having gone to university, I was to set myself a task, an autodidactic programme of theatre education: the compulsory reading of an entire set of *TDR/Tulane Drama Review* was a severe but rewarding assignment.

Not found in the 'Polish Lab' issue but in a later edition was this piece of ephemera: the programme to *The Constant Prince*, together with the letter from Grotowski (written to accompany the programme of *Apocalypsis cum Figuris* that appealed for an understanding that the work was a

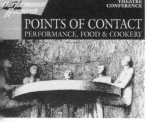

collective creation. This began another collection – *Texte Trouve* – found ephemera inserted like 'dangerous supplements' in other unrelated books. In one I found a crumpled sheet with instructions from the past; delicate handwriting forming a calligraphic text whose title was 'How to Act Responsibly'.

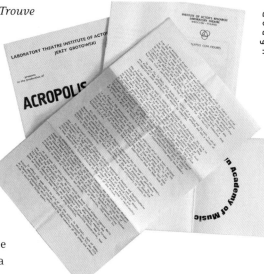

But what does it mean to 'act responsibly'? As theatre-makers we know how to construct beginnings, middles and endings, we know how to create narratives, how to re-present/represent reality, restore behaviour, embody meanings, illustrate history and social situations and illuminate a peoples' aspiration. But do we know well enough how to open up the process of theatre, to create holes in the text, to rupture the spectacle, score, tear and puncture narratives, to arrest the action in time, to allow space for alternative endings and a return to the beginnings?

Shakespeare said that theatre holds up a mirror to nature, and Brook said let the mirror be concave to focus reality, scrutinize it and allow truth to emerge. Perhaps what I have in mind here is a hall of distorting mirrors where reality bends and cracks and different versions of the 'truth' appear. That truth (whose truth?) that can be held up to power. In those mirrors the body, the situation, the community is distorted playfully; through laughter and tears it is also possible to see the whole picture turned upside-down.

But how does one know another culture?

Is to dance the dance, the form, of another tradition an indication that knowing, feeling, embracing another culture and understanding is any closer, nearer or more possible – in this day and age?

I began to collect recordings of music from around the world in the mid 1970s, my interest was mainly in the human voice and its extraordinary range of possibilities, solo and choral, *a cappella* and accompanied. From the hunting calls of the Baku Pygmy to the song games of the Inuit of Greenland and Canada, from the Wayang Operas of Java to the waulking songs of Scotland, from the mouth music of Tuva to the yodelling of the Solomon Isles, I avidly collected not as a musician or as an ethnomusicologist but simply as an enthusiast curious to hear the whole wide world and the worlds of song within it; their differences and similarities. The collection is now vast, but within the first fifty vinyl discs, bought somewhere around 1977, was an extraordinary recording of Georgian polyphony, the first playing of which I still recall as a moment suspended in time.

In an opening address to one of CPR's *Giving Voice* conferences, *An Archaeology of the Voice*, I asked if we could imagine the vocal folds of a nation, the vocal folds that form and help define a culture. I had in mind this early encounter with Georgian polyphony, where the sounds not only enthrall and excite but function as a sort of aural epiphany, an illumination through sound – a sonic/acoustic immersion of harmonies and dissonance – to an ancient world of unbroken tradition, where the vocal folds unfold and wrap around you – a polyphonic embrace!

Of the many strands of the Centre for Performance Research programme *Points of Contact* is a continuing series of international conferences that aims to generate investigation, critical debate and cross-disciplinary approaches to performance studies through contact and confrontation with other disciplines. For *Points of Contact: Performance Food and Cookery* we decided to stage a full Georgian Feast with fifteen courses, a *Tamada* (toast master) and a song to accompany each toast.

The conference/festival was to explore themes that are reflected in the overlap between performance food and cookery, theses included: food in performance and food as performing art; the performative in cookery, its staging in the kitchen and at the table; the processes in cooking and performance-making, exploring piquant analogies and correlations; the theatricality of food, the table as stage and food as a model for theatre, multisensory, processual and communal. We wanted to bring together artists, chefs and scholars from several cultures in an interdisciplinary collaboration. And we promised that participants would enjoy an immersion experience at the intersection of food and performance, theory and practice. The conference programme was to include: cooking demonstrations; workshops and performances that involve food, cooking and eating; scholarly papers (which ranged from the staging of Napoleon's Banquets to The Divine Role of Fasting to the Aesthetics of Taste), films and illustrated talks and participation in traditional banquets, unusual feasts and provocative food events.

To stage a complete Georgian Feast among the thirty other projects and performances we were producing offered a great challenge. Why not just approximate, translate or mutate, why not create some hybrid or fusion food? But would we do that with the music? Such adaptation and approximation would traduce the enterprise and render it meaningless. It seemed to me that it was within the challenge to reproduce the unfamiliar - the polyphonies, their harmonies and dissonance and the taste, textures and aromas of the food - that the lessons of understanding were to be learned. How do we begin to understand the complexities of another culture and the ancient knowledge imbedded deep in their structure? To adapt and mutate, worse still to approximate, seems like an act of arrogance, a strategy of assimilation. To respect otherness and difference and then struggle to attain without compromise the difficulties, in this case of musical structure and cuisine, seems more like a constructive encounter.

In terms of contemporary theatre practice the 'innovative' is often what CPR champions and promotes in Wales. We pioneer and create the opportunities for the new, the unpredictable and the unforeseen. But we have always said that we are interested in the relationship between innovation and tradition. Often we encourage translation, mutation and betrayal with regard to methods of and approaches to performance-making. But the Georgian Feast project was an exercise in authenticity, in the struggle and stretch to reach the unattainable, for we were clear that it was always to function as an homage and as evocation. To sing another culture's songs is to begin to understand a little of that culture, this strikes a cord, a harmonic accord perhaps, with that other figure, alongside Jerzy Grotowski, who appears to be among us in these proceedings, the anthropologist Victor Turner (who said, 'Through their dances shall we know them').

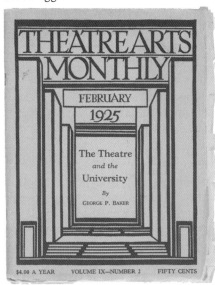

Another journal that I have avidly collected. *Theatre Arts* is remarkable in that during the editorship of Edith Issacs and across the whole period from 1918 through to around 1936 it took a world view of theatre. In its approach - inclusive and embracing (because it also included articles on rituals, folk traditions and customs and incredibly insightful and substantial documentation of world theatre traditions, even a whole issue on Balinese Dance, for example) - it precedes Performance Studies in terms of its optic, its object of study. This issue contains a focus on Mei Lanfang.

In 1986 and 1987 we brought to Wales and then the rest of the UK entire troupes of *Kun Ju* and *Jing Ju* – Chinese Opera – in addition to staging exhibitions and Summer Schools. The Chinese authorities were very curious about why we wanted to bring over opera teachers. What could they possibly teach in four weeks, did we not know that the training programme took seven years? Of the many things we have introduced and promoted, this has always remained a very interesting issue. I remember reading Mei Lanfang's *My Life on the Stage*.

In the winter I remember fighting and pacing around on ice while still wearing short stilts. At first I slipped easily, but once I became accustomed to walking on stilts over the ice, it was effortless to go through the same motions on stage without stilts. Whatever you do, if you go through a difficult stage before reaching the easy ones, you'll find that the sweetness is well worth the bitter trouble. (Mei: 1961)

Zhen Cheng Zhao, a living national treasure, when teaching on one of the CPR Summer Schools could actually demonstrate a summersault done perfectly – realized with skill and precision – and one done with 'virtuosity' (a term he used through translation). The difference was stunning, defying logic and understanding; the one seeming elegant and athletic, the other an action of gravity and grace; the first like a printed text or equation, the other like a signature in calligraphy.

A definition of the virtuoso is: a person who has a masterly or dazzling skill or technique in any field or activity. But what is skill? Skill is special ability acquired by training or technique requiring special training or manual proficiency. However, an archaic use of the word is 'understanding', from a root word from Old Norse for 'distinction', also related to 'difference'. Technique is practical method, proficiency in a practical or mechanical skill, a special facility, and the knack.

While the contemporary use and definition of the words emphasize the practical and the manual, ability and dexterity, the roots lie in notions of understanding, both mental and physical. And in relation to distinction and difference, what marks one from another, what allows us to recognize a difference and what draws attention and is thus distinctive?

It is these techniques of the 'extra-daily', to borrow Eugenio Barba's term, techniques that require a training, that are learned and developed through a daily practice and that demand specific release and application of energy.

Virtuosity is also a surpassing of technique, the attainment of skills and then the surpassing of those skills, a curious act of devotion and denial, but I am also interested in the passing of technique (before the surpassing), the transmission of performance knowledge and the transformation of performance knowledge.

But how do we trace the migration of techniques and compositional methods? How could a theatre history be written about the transmigration of skills and methods? A ripple effect of one innovative and creative strategy/training across cultures, from one individual to another, in unforeseen and unpredictable ways, serendipitous, subversive and subterranean: the transmission of performance knowledge, the chain of participants, the necklace of technique, the impact that sustained, highly-perfected and detailed training has on the world, the world of theatre, and the world. Avoiding dogma, bridging the present – one foot in the past, one in the future.

Part of my largest book; a four volume elephant-sized folio with inserts, maps, charts, schema, DVD and web links. These charts outline methods, techniques, theories and a philosophy for the creation of the most extraordinary, truly fabulous cuisine.

Ferran Adrià's creativity in the kitchen, staging in the restaurant, choreography and dramaturgy and his engagement with the diners' imaginations, playing games with expectation, memory and the senses inspire me. This, together with the fact that he closes his restaurant for six months to work in his laboratory developing new techniques, new methods of food preparation and theories, offers a shining example to theatre and performance practice.

134

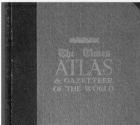

In theatre I hope for a return to performance practice that encourages the inventor, the innovator, the *bricoleur* and the experimentalist in each of us; that nurtures intuition; that, once again, generates courage to realize the fruits of inventive curiosity.

I should like to see a greater integration of theory and practice, training that develops body and mind, creativity in the full sense, nurturing practitioners who do not feel threatened or impoverished by theory, and theorists who do not feel soiled or distracted by practice, or envious or jealous. I want practitioners to embrace theory as practice, to work with it, along side it, above it, beneath it, within it.

I want practice embodied, ennobled, made more vigorous through such incorporations - stretched, challenged, revitalized. Look at any of the great traditions of theatre and dance around the world, such a separation does not exist, is inconceivable. A physical training is a mental training, and compositional strategies, aesthetic concepts are nurtured and developed, even inculcated from the outset, reinforced and made manifest through this training. But here I am not only wishing for incorporation, embodied theory, I am also very practically wishing for more training that develops the performer's mind and creativity. I want to see a training that develops the performer's observational skills, looking and listening, seeing and hearing. I want to see a training of the intellect not divorced from the body, that enables courage - courage to create, courage to take a risk, courage to try again, to fail better. A training of the mind and body, that enables not only the unimaginable to be imagined but an incorporation to realize it, make manifest, produce action on stage, idea and image synthesized. Training for the performer's imagination, led and supported by a training of the body; an imagination whose visions are compelled by curiosity, an open, naïve, incorrigible inquisitiveness.

For a while I want to set aside performance theory and escape the vortex of super-saturated, over-theorized reiteration, where a recycling of ideas seems to be bringing about a feeding frenzy of cannibalism. I want to return to practical experiment to make an intervention and an addition: I want to propose a Performance Laboratory, a space within Higher Education that interfaces with the profession, a place for performance research and performance practice that embraces Performance Studies and Practice as Research and that re-emphasizes experiment and risk-taking. A site, a utopian zone, a foundry where new theories, methods and strategies for and of performance emerge through trial and error, forged through an empirical approach, integrating theory and practice and

exploring the relationship between innovation and tradition. A Laboratory that will enable articulate practitioners who can interrogate their own compositional processes and theorists who are informed by performance mastery and who remain engaged in the process (transitional and conditional) avoiding fundamentalism and the ossification of insight into rules and regulations. A braiding of performance practice with academic enquiry, an interlacing of a performer's know-how with a scholars knowledge; a small room where great reckonings might take place.

How to become an Institution without becoming institutionalized? The question is as much to me as it is to the Grotowski Centre and Performance Studies. As we celebrate at this conference the transformation of the Centre into the Grotowski Institute and witness the publication of a foundational textbook for the discipline, I can't help but feel a longing (perhaps nostalgically) for the Laboratory, an era of experimentation and a time before the canonization of the field.

I am from Wales, England's first colony. Wales, a Land of Sheep, with a woolly-back population three times greater than people. When Grace Looi arrived from Kuala Lumpur to begin an internship at our centre she was horrified. She got off the train having observed several thousand sheep and said, 'What happened, who vandalized the sheep, why are they all spray-painted with graffiti?' It is a form of branding, of course, a tradition, the way the farmers mark their flock, to keep tabs on animals prone to wander, indeed better for being left to roam – 'mountain lambs taste sweeter', as the billboard pronounces as you drive across from Devil's Bridge.

I hope performance studies, performance research and even *performatics* might remain unbranded (and taste sweeter), unmarked and unsettled – literally, remain maverick. Working at the back of beyond in the middle of nowhere *and* also right here, right now.

REFERENCES

Mei, Lanfang *My Life on Stage* privately published (1986) for Eugenio Barba's fiftieth birthday by the 'équipe italiana' of ISTA, first published in *Chinese Literature Monthly* 11 (1961), Peking: Foreign Language Press.

Southern, Richard (1962) *The Seven Ages of the Theatre*, London: Faber and Faber.

ACKNOWLEDGMENTS

Thanks to the Hereford Mappa Mundi Trust and the Cathedral Library in Hereford for permission to reproduce images of the Chained Library and the Mappa Mundi - All production images courtesy of the CPR Archive. Thanks to Keith Morris for images of Wales and books - © Keith Morris / www.artswebwales.com

# Installing *Performatics* : Terms and Conditions

*[To be signed by both parties in the drafty auditorium of a closed-down theatre, with Bauhaus's 'Party of the First Part' playing on a loop in the background.]*

CAVEAT
All words are in asymptotic relation to the 'thing' they stand for. Words and deeds are as fated as like poles to always remain apart, repelling each other.

1. The party of the *first part* (critics, theorists, philosophers, academics) agrees to install and use *Performatics* with the party of the *second part* (performers, actors, directors, practitioners).

2. In installing *Performatics* both parties agree that this shall not become the pretext for issues of ownership, whereby one party claims the rights exclusively. *Performatics* is an operating system that works *between* things not on things.
   a. Nomenklatura appear everywhere.
   b. *Performatics* rejects their attempts at appropriation from every sphere.

3. *Performatics* does not echo *pragmatics* unnecessarily. The complexities of the generation of meaning inherent in performance (of all kinds) require that the specific context of the performance be articulated. *Performatics* would be the process through which such articulation is possible, not the lens – or study – by which such a process is then analysed.
   a. In this context *Performatics* does not efface other terms to which it may be related (Theatre, Performance Studies, Drama, Event, Action).
   b. Rather, it puts the thinking of them into play.

INTERLUDE
Assistant: *[Timidly]* What about a little ... a little ... gag?
Director: For God's sake! This craze for explicitation! Every i dotted to death!
Little gag! For God's sake!
       Samuel Beckett, Catastrophe

4. There is an inherent pomposity in Neologism. This cannot be helped. Neither party in this contract can determine where *Performatics* may lead. It is a dead end or a new horizon.

5. The privileges associated with the institutions of the party of the *first part* shall be shared with the party of the *second part*, as have the works of the party of the *second part* been, for too long, the succour of the party of the *first part*.

6. These terms and conditions (more to follow, no doubt) shall apply as directly to the party of the *first part* as they shall to the party of the *second part*. But sign quickly. Time is always running out.
*[Nomenklatura emerge from behind the auditorium seating and take up their seats]*. As the Director in Beckett's *Catastrophe* states, 'Step on it, I have a caucus.'

Party of the First Part:

_____

Party of the Second Part:

_____

**DAN WATT**
October 2007

## To the editors

Dear Sirs,

I'm seventeen years old. I'm studying Grotowski for my A-level exam, together with many others of my age in this country. You might be a little surprised by this – how is it possible, and why so many – but it is true. And if you look on the Internet you can find out what the examiners expect by way of answers. Here are just some of the words they expect to find: the play as a 'poetic paraphrase' of reality; the role of the actor within a 'Total Act' of theatre; the actor's focus on achieving 'communion' with the spectator; an actor's act of 'self-penetration', using the role to 'dissect' himself; the work of the 'holy' actor; the 'conquest' of space by the actor; the achievement of the impossible. Now, I love Grotowski's work and for me perhaps the best things he ever did were the early works – the acting in 'Apocalypsis cum figuris' – even though I have only seen it on film. It's what they are doing that's important for me. I've been told that the word 'drama' comes from the Greek word *dromenon*, which means 'a thing being done.' I like that. I like to look at these words carefully, one by one, beginning with 'a thing', so that I can get a real feel of what they mean. They are ordinary words, which have gathered their meanings over years. (And there's also a verb in there – doing something!) The words in exams that I have to use seem so far removed from the experience, almost like the mind wants some kind of revenge over experience. I think perhaps they're what my grandmother meant when she said something was 'breathless talk'. So I am wondering why we need a new word. Every time I try to say it, it comes out different. It probably sounds much better in Polish. My teacher told me once about the word 'illusion', how it means that something isn't real. But he also said that really it comes from the Latin *in ludus*, which he said meant 'in play', which is something else entirely, and that the word changed its meaning for theatre quite naturally sometime after Shakespeare. I like that. If it were me, I would just leave words alone to get along by themselves.

Yours faithfully,
**PETER HULTON**

# Raft and Mooring

DARIUSZ KOSIŃSKI

Review of Richard Schechner's *Performatyka: wstęp*, translated by Tomasz Kubikowski (Wrocław: Ośrodek Badań Twórczości Jerzego Grotowskiego i Poszukiwań Teatralno-Kulturowych, 2006), and of the conference *Performatyka: perspektywy rozwojowe* / Performance Studies: and Beyond (Wrocław: Ośrodek Badań Twórczości Jerzego Grotowskiego i Poszukiwań Teatralno-Kulturowych, 7-10 December 2006)

The Centre for Study of Jerzy Grotowski's Work and for Cultural and Theatrical Research in Wrocław, which became the Grotowski Institute on 28 December 2006, completed its programme of activities under its previous name with a double event of significant importance, which is (as I understand it) the preview to a further widening of its already broad field of interest. This event was the session *Performatyka: perspektywy rozwojowe* (a title which is better rendered in English: 'Performance Studies: and Beyond'), and the duality I mentioned was due to the fact that the occasion of its organization was the publication of Tomasz Kubikowski's Polish translation of Richard Schechner's *Performance Studies: An Introduction* (this translation, entitled *Performatyka: wstęp*, is obviously published by the Grotowski Centre).

This is not the first book discussed within these pages to which we might refer as a 'keystone', although on this occasion, because the format of the volume is A4, with some 402 pages of greater than usual thickness, it bears more similarity to a paving stone of quite considerable size than to a brick. Fortunately, in this case, the physical weight reflects both the intellectual weight and the weight of the subject. Schechner's book, published for the first time in 2002, has already created a stir around the world, and the concepts of performance and performance studies presented within it constitute probably the most important proposition to have appeared in the area of performance research during the last few decades. Obviously, some of the ideas presented here are already known (also to Polish readers) from the previous books of the author of *The Future of Ritual*, but here they are collected and arranged in the form of a handbook, equipped with bibliography, 'homework' and questions to consider.

*Performatyka: wstęp* is divided into eight large chapters, each of which discusses the problems that map out - according to the author - the most important areas of the field presented within it (or rather, established by it). The first chapter is dedicated to the presentation of the new discipline: its character, the history of how it came into being and its expansion, which are closely tied to Schechner's academic biography. The second chapter - already partly known from its publication in Polish, in abridged form, in the journal *Dialog* - attempts to respond to the question 'what is performance?', at the same time detailing the project of performance studies with a description of its basic concepts ('restored behaviour') and points of departure (the distinction between 'is' performance and 'as' performance). The two subsequent chapters are dedicated to two poles of performance, which are at the same time its two most basic and often interwoven aspects: ritual and play (many arguments that will already be familiar from *The Future of Ritual* are presented in this section). The fifth chapter, entitled 'Performativity', is a journey through linguistics (Austin and Searle), poststructuralism (Derrida, Foucault, Baudrillard) and gender studies (Butler) in order to show how different ideas of performance interconnect and transform various fields of modern, humanistic thought (this chapter is also known from an abridged version published in *Dialog*). The subsequent section, in the Polish translation rendered unfortunately as *Performanse* (in the original – 'Performing', which perhaps, to be consistent in translation, might be better conveyed as *Performowanie*), is dedicated to the presentation of what might be described as 'performative acting' (incidentally, the term 'acting' was retained in the titles of several of the sub-sections). The seventh chapter describes – using methods already familiar from Schechner's previous work – performative processes, and the last chapter is filled with considerations of perhaps the most current topic: 'Global and intercultural performances'.

The book is constructed in such a way that the author's argument – Richard Schechner's voice, which at the beginning very clearly presents him as a historically, culturally and biologically specific subject – is accompanied by a multiplicity of voices, of dozens of authors cited at length in boxes integrated into the text. These two streams are interwoven by yet another – that of the significant and pertinent illustrations, the majority of which are suitable for further analysis and reflection. As a result, *Performatyka* is a book of multiple uses and applications. It can be read in a traditional way, following the voice of the author, or one might interrupt him, listening to the voices of others; one can read it in fragments, by subject, or one can 'simply' browse through it, benefiting from and enjoying each of these ways of reading. So as far as composition and organization are concerned, the publication is truly performative, even like a 'happening' in itself, consciously playful but at the same time a serious challenge for its readers, not to mention its publishers.

Glancing through and reading the Polish edition, it is hard not to express admiration and respect for those involved in the editing process: Marcin Rochowski (translation editor), Monika Blige (volume editor), Grzegorz Ziółkowski and Iwona Gutowska (who added photographs) and Barbara Kaczmarek (graphic and cover design). I mention these contributors – who are normally omitted in reviews – because in the case of *Performatyka*, their work must have been unusually difficult, and the results are simply excellent.

What is immediately clear is the way in which the book was brought closer to the Polish reader – or even located – by the addition of a set of illustrations and photographs different from the original volume, selected by the Polish publishers. And it is not only about substituting the selection of 'everyday' photographs with examples closer to our experience (a whole gallery of very personal pictures) or about using examples of performances taken from Polish ritual and theatrical traditions. In the choice of illustrations one can see a conscious tendency to broaden the area of investigation to include the specific experiences of Eastern Europe (for example, photographs from the 'Orange Revolution' in Ukraine) and a concern for balancing the number of 'foreign' examples, which otherwise might lead to performance studies being transformed into a strange, exotic creation from which it would be easy to distance oneself. Even in the choice of photographs itself, performance studies appears to be something that concerns us as well, something which is our affair.

This is very important in the face of the unusual difficulties that result from the task of translating into Polish a project that is rooted in a foreign term, and one so specific as 'performance'. This English term carries meanings that cannot be conveyed by any Polish word that translators have previously used (among them *występ*, *wykonanie*, *odegranie*) or by any considered to be – especially in a theatrical context – rough equivalents. Neither *zachowanie* ('behaviour'), in which Tomasz Kubikowski discovered similar tensions between different meanings (Kubikowski 2000: 34-7), nor *przedstawienie* ('performance'), which I have tried and am trying to present as a polysemic term that can open up wider perspectives than those of theatre, nor *widowisko* ('performance'/'spectacle') reflect the full range of meanings of the notion of performance (Kosiński 2005: 9-15). In this situation, the translator took the risky decision to translate English names into Polish and to write about *performans* and *performatyka*. This decision obviously has its flaws, among which the most important is the strangeness of the terms. At least for some time, these new words will have to be explained on each occasion, and language purists will still frown upon this 'Americanization'. The benefits outweigh the costs, in my opinion. Because *performans* and *performatyka* are strange they are not obvious, and they therefore do not impose limitations on thought from the very beginning. To a certain extent they come near to the 'no name' that I have already outlined in my recent review of *Theatre Histories* (Kosiński 2006). Simultaneously, by its novelty and its dissimilarity from the original term (after all *performatyka* is not the same as *studia performatywne* - performance studies, or *studia nad performansem* - studying performance, since the latter would limit the area to exploring different types of performances), the name of the field introduced by Kubikowski poses a challenge for us, which was formulated by Alan Read during the conference promoting the book: what *performatyka* will become in Poland depends on what Poles will do with it. It is our usage of Schechner's categories and conceptions that will or will not give meaning to this still strange-sounding name.

Obviously, the translator's troubles did not end with the title. I suspect that Tomasz Kubikowski spent a great number of hours resolving doubts concerning the best way to convey the linguistic innovation of the original and the multiple wordplays that Schechner likes so much. Some of Kubikowski's decisions do not necessarily seem fortunate to me, but faced with the huge density of the text and the complex material, picking up on details would be pedantic. If I were to have any reservations, they would be about not marking those places where the Polish language had to give up and where the original made use of a particularly refined and multi-levelled wordplay. A good example here is the categorization of performances into types - 'make-belief' and 'make-believe' - which in the translation are inevitably simplified, and conveyed by *naprawdę* and *na niby*. In these situations, it would perhaps be useful to give the original terms in brackets, signalling their complexity to the readers. But, I repeat, these are minor issues and in no way do they change my high estimation of the work of the creators of the Polish edition.

It must be noted that the Polish translation of Schechner's book is a translation of the second, revised edition, which appeared in 2006. This makes up, in a way, for the brief delay since the publication of the first edition, and thanks to this - this is worth stressing - we receive an up-to-date book, immersed in today's reality, its finger on the pulse of our contemporary experience. This contemporaneousness is due in the first place to the changes made by the author. Most of them appear in chapter 8, where the sub-sections 'Is globalization good or bad?' and 'Jihad/terrorism as performance' have been significantly extended and updated (the latter section was also recomposed and moved to a different location within the book). Many changes also appeared in chapter 1 (here numerous points of information were added, testifying to the development of performance studies throughout the world), chapter 5 (an extensive chapter on reality TV; significantly expanded, with very interesting passages on the practical weaknesses of leftist performative discourse) and chapter 7 (added to the sub-section on the 'Performance Quadrilogue' (Schechner 2006: 250-4) are examples originating - characteristically - from beyond the dramatic theatre). There are many minor additions - new frames and illustrations, sentences added to particular paragraphs etc. As a whole, though, the project of performance studies retains the basic premises outlined in the 2002 edition.

The book states its aspiration to give intellectual responses to changes occurring in the world, meaning that it becomes less 'like a book' and more like a series of actions taken according to specific and, at the same time, changing patterns, in order to influence observers or participants. To put it simply, it is increasingly evident that the world is becoming a performative series and, in order to keep up with the changes within it, it is necessary to elaborate not only new tools but also new ways of seeing things. Traditional European terms like 'theatre' or '*widowisko*' ('performance'/'spectacle') are insufficient here because, although they were applied in social research, they inevitably led to an excessive schematization and division of what in reality is dynamic and changeable. The best example of the inadequacy, even outright harmfulness of the 'theatrical metaphor' is its application to politics. If it is said that politics is like theatre and politicians are like actors, it is automatically assumed that all the rest are spectators, who - even according to the most common conventions - do not have the right to speak. This kind of thinking not only does not reflect the reality but also enforces social passivity, allowing hacks of the worst sort to perform on the political stage, about whom the audience only moan in the hall.

Performance studies is, then, an attempt to create a new paradigm of intellectual reflection about human life, or - more precisely - some of its aspects. Maybe the most accurate definition, of those of which I am aware, is that formulated by Schechner at the beginning of his book. The Polish translation '*co ludzie robią, kiedy to właśnie robią*' does not reflect the full connotations of 'what people do in the activity of their doing it', but it indicates the fundamental feature of performance studies, which is its focus on action and on the multiple aspects of action. Concentrating on actions - their course, structure, context and effects - performance studies does not 'read' them but analyses them as ways of behaving, and only from this analysis does it draw conclusions regarding their effects, their practical results. The point of departure for performance studies is a kind of reduction - one does not assume *a priori* that one knows what will be the subject of research; one does not accept without criticism the interpretations and names proposed by authors or participants. Starting from this reductive approach and the analysis of behaviour, one has the opportunity to give a truly critical interpretation of events, to reveal hidden or unconscious meanings and consequences. This obviously opens up the possibility of using performance studies as an ideological tool. However, its originators openly acknowledge that their task is not the (in any case impossible) objective description of reality but its transformation through the promotion and dissemination of a certain critical attitude. Performance studies - with its emphasis on practice and active observation - indicates one of the possible ways of crossing the border between the increasingly pathetic scene of public life and the increasingly irritated audience. It is no accident that the first illustration in the Polish edition of Schechner's book is a photograph of Tadeusz Kantor climbing onto the stage of the Słowacki Theatre in Kraków …

The key issue here is the openness of the discipline, which is founded on the openness of the source term. Accepting the cultural relativity of performance and limiting ourselves to the definition which tells us that performance is what, in a given context, is marked and distinguished as performance, allows us at the same time to keep the variety and the cultural autonomy of particular types and genres. The phrase 'this is performance' does not explain the phenomenon in itself but only opens a way to describe and analyse the performative genre with which we are dealing. It absolves us from the need to demonstrate in the first instance that we have the right to research the processes of action that interest us. Thus it has a different function from the term 'theatre', which from the very beginning causes serious problems in our manner of perceiving things. Anyone who has ever struggled to qualify phenomena that take place beyond the obvious limits of theatre as a Western institution can at last breathe a sigh of relief. Instead of wasting energy deciding whether African masquerades or Pomarańczowa Alternatywa (Orange Alternative)[1] actions are theatre or not, they will be able to direct this energy towards the description and analysis of these very ways of 'doing what people do'.

Schechner - who strongly stresses this openness of performance studies in the sub-section 'Caution! Beware of generalizations' - at the same time does not content himself with this and - courageously and at the same time impudently - suggests that everything might be considered 'as' performance (2006: 36-8). This means that phenomena that are neither distinguished nor denoted as performances by a particular culture might be treated 'as if' they were. This magic 'if' opens yet another level of functionality of performance studies as a tool of critical analysis. Obviously it is a very risky operation, because behind it stands a paradoxical 'vote of no confidence' in the cultural context, which, in the case of 'is' performance, has been given the power to decide. In this strategy, I perceive a double level of security: trust in the culture creating the 'performance' being researched, which allows us to break our dependency on Euro-American schema that divide the world of human activity into inviolable categories (play, ritual, theatre, everyday life, politics etc.), and at the same time distrust, which, within this 'as if', breaks our dependence on the subjects being researched and is a cunning ruse, an evasion, an escape from the name, that - contrary to Shakespeare - changes the fragrance of the rose. The kinds of results this escape gives are best depicted in the chapter entitled 'Jihad/terrorism as performance', which, thanks to performative analysis of the phenomenon, reveals important aspects that escape the attention of European commentators, indignant at suggestions that the attacks of 11 September 2001 could be treated as some kind of work of art or *widowisko* ('performance'/ 'spectacle'). Their outrage is understandable, but at the same time it is based on a misunderstanding caused by the words themselves. Comparatively the most transparent term, *performans* ('performance') prevents such misconceptions, opening previously closed but important possibilities of understanding the world in which we all participate.

Personally, I welcome Schechner's proposition with enthusiasm, which to some might seem the enthusiasm of a neophyte. I would like to be well understood: I do not treat *Performatyka: wstęp* as a 'bible', not only because this would be against its nature as a book that poses more questions than it gives answers. I do not agree with many of its more detailed propositions; in many places I perceive a lack of depth due to the specificity of the American experience (for example, the typology of acting is exceptionally 'lacking', with almost the entire European history of this art excluded). But treated as a whole project, performance studies seems to be a discipline that creates extensive opportunities to move beyond a number of increasingly sterile theatrical discussions (for example, the never-ending debates on 'theatre and ritual'). Furthermore, it provides a chance to perceive as yet unknown areas lying very close to us, as well as different, more accurate perspectives on already-familiar but distorted subjects.

This last thing seems to me to be particularly important in Poland. Jarosław Fret, in a brilliant summing-up of the Wrocław session, noted that thanks to Schechner's performance studies, we will be able to perceive something that has been present for a long time in Poland but that we covered with the inadequate term 'theatre'. I think that this will develop, that it is already happening, among other things thanks to Leszek Kolankiewicz, who applied similar analytic methods, although from within a different orientation, in order to uncover hidden sources of what he called '*polskie widowiska*' (Polish performances/spectacles). Yes - as long as we investigate our native tradition, starting from Adam Mickiewicz, we will have to struggle with its 'unsuitability for the stage' and its

[1] Orange Alternative was an underground protest group that organized absurd and nonsensical happenings in Poland from the mid-1980s, mocking the communist regime at its demise.

'betweenness'. Considered as a certain form of activity, it not only has an opportunity to show its breadth, which crosses borders, but also its connection with traditions that were normally described by ethnologists.

Many other examples might be found, but only by elaborating and researching these by means of performance studies will we see evidence of the usefulness that I perceive in this approach. This is precisely the way to domesticate and adapt this American concept, and sooner or later - I presume - a significant group of researchers will move in this direction.

Impetus to follow this path, and at the same time the first step towards the domestication of performance studies, was provided by the conference 'Performance Studies: and Beyond', organized in conjunction with the publication of the translation of Schechner's book. It took place in (what was at that time still) the Grotowski Centre from 7-10 December 2006, and its main organizer, apart from the Centre, was Tomasz Kubikowski. The sessions gathered a truly excellent group of academics representing performance studies or - to a greater or lesser degree - associated with it. Present in Wrocław were (naming them in alphabetical order): Christopher Balme, Marvin Carlson, Richard Gough, Heiner Goebbels, John McKenzie, Patrice Pavis, Alan Read, Janelle Reinelt and - obviously - Richard Schechner. Phillip Zarrilli had to cancel for ill health but sent a speech recorded on video; at the last minute, also due to ill health, Marco De Marinis cancelled his visit. The Polish perspective was represented by - apart from Tomasz Kubikowski and the directors of the Centre, Jarosław Fret and Grzegorz Ziółkowski - Małgorzata Leyko and Dobrochna Ratajczakowa, whose principal contribution occurred during the 'round table of Polish academics'. Particularly striking was the absence of Leszek Kolankiewicz or one of his colleagues from the Instytut Kultury Polskiej (Institute of Polish Culture), which, after all, is the only centre in Poland that can boast its own 'answer to performance studies'. Although Małgorzata Leyko recounted the achievements of the 'Warsaw school of the anthropology of performances' at length in her presentation, the lack of the true voice of the IKP in the discussions during the conference was felt particularly strongly at times.

There is not space here to give detailed accounts of particular papers, almost all of which would deserve extensive summary, sometimes exegesis, sometimes polemics, sometimes 'performative' description. Instead, I will allow myself to indicate two general thematic lines that stood out during the sessions. The first thread was the problem signalled by the title of the conference, that of the development of performance studies, at this very moment, in which the new discipline has already gone through (in the West) a wave of initial enthusiasm and has come to be subject to critical evaluation because of its excessive ambitions (the papers of Carlson and Reinelt) and on the other hand because of its negligence towards and restriction of new possibilities (the papers of McKenzie, Read and Kubikowski). Whereas Carlson's and Reinelt's papers seemed to suggest that performance studies should aim to consolidate and to be more precise in its details, to draw its limits, the papers of the second group indicated the areas neglected - performance studies was criticized as too strict (especially by McKenzie) - due to its close connection with the theatre. Their authors indicated areas that were not yet covered by performance studies research, such as management or technology (McKenzie), architecture and urban studies (Read) and research into consciousness (Kubikowski, who presented the main arguments of his book *Reguła Nibelunga* ['Nibelung's principle']), which, by the way, could be a candidate for the title of the most important, misunderstood and neglected book of the decade in Poland).

The second thread (Zarrilli, Gough, Balme and Goebbels) was more associated with the practical, applied aspects of performance studies, which influence ways of thinking and the artistic work. What is interesting is that the researchers and artists who represented this perspective, whose work is extremely diverse, did not have any problems with the reconciliation of performance studies and theatre studies. What is more, they showed best – because in a practical way – how both of these disciplines might collaborate with each other, without colliding, and avoid open conflict.

It was impossible to restrain this conflict completely during the conference. It appeared already in the papers of Carlson and Reinelt, who (especially Reinelt) assessed the 'younger colleague' from a theatre studies perspective. The conflict appeared again in the presentations delivered by Małgorzata Leyko and Dobrochna Ratajczakowa, who summarized the whole session, and who misunderstood the conventions of performance research by never taking the floor throughout the rest of the conference. Both Polish researchers remained silent in the face of open challenges and Schechner's questions, which were aimed directly towards them. This silence was apparently linked to their assumption that 'we are summing up everything at the end'. This assumption, which may have derived from the best of intentions, effectively gave the impression of a certain superiority and of having isolated themselves from the rest.

Addressing the question 'why does this happen?' would take us not only deep into the world-view and psychology of particular researchers and schools but also behind the scenes of Polish academic life. This scene, rather shameful and hence eagerly passed over, rose to the surface during the discussions on the last day of the conference when Marta Steiner from Wrocław University, responding to one of her students, listed the institutional-administrative reasons why she could not change the name of her course to *Performatyka* ('Performance Studies'). Grzegorz Ziółkowski, commenting on her answer, pointed directly to the reason behind all these difficulties. It is the unreformed, centrally-run, unresponsive system of higher education in Poland, which helps to maintain once-gained privileges and positions and effectively discourages new initiatives. It is not entirely true that nothing can be changed (Kraków's drama studies department recently provided proof that this is possible, that it can be done – and even quite extensively), but the fact remains that Polish academic life, at its essential and intellectual surface level, is very much influenced by deeper financial, institutional and unspoken agreements, of which – as wiser heads suggest – it is better not to speak at all. Throughout years of efforts and struggles, theatre studies has managed to grow into this multi-levelled and complex construction. Perhaps performance studies, rebellious and chaotic by design, will be able to do so as well. We can only hope that this will not mean that it loses its uncompromising, critical approach to reality. That performance studies, instead of closing in on what it knows and values, will keep following this approach, the crucial aspect of which lies in a fluctuating, always changing, and diverse current of life.

Translated by Adela Karsznia and Duncan Jamieson
This text was first published in Polish in *Didaskalia* (2007) 77, pp. 121-124

REFERENCES

Kosiński, Dariusz (2005) 'Co to jest teatr?' ['What is Theatre?'], in D. Kosiński, A. Wypych-Gawrońska, A. Stafiej, A. Marszałek, M. Sugiera and J. Leśnierowska (eds) *Słownik wiedzy o teatrze*, Bielsko-Biała: Park, pp. 9-15.

Kosiński, Dariusz (2006) 'No name', *Didaskalia* 76, pp. 105-8. Review of Zarrilli, Phillip B., McConachie, Bruce, Williams, Gary Jay, Fisher and Sorgenfrei Carol (2006) *Theatre Histories: an Introduction*, New York and London: Routledge.

Kubikowski, Tomasz (2000) 'Zachowanie (się)' ['Behaving (oneself)'], *Opcje* 4, pp. 34-7.

Schechner, Richard (2006) *Performance Studies: An Introduction*, 2nd revised edition, London and New York: Routledge, pp. 250-54.

# Performatics : Inscribing the Blur at the Place of Difference

Performance, performative, performing, dynamic semiotics, acting technique, interaction between the digital and the art (of performance), performance studies – all of these concepts are in certain cases signified by the notion *performatics*. Often wrongly.

For example, when Judith Butler talks about performativity of gender, she speaks about *performative (utterance)*, the concept derived from the philosophy of language by John Austin. When this aspect is signified by the term *performatics*, the signification indicates performing in general, which erases the references/differences crucial for this theorization (see, for instance, Basu 2004). When it signifies *interaction between the digital and the art* (Fabián Wagmister), the term *performatics* leaves the digital aside. When *performatics* signifies *dynamic semiotics* (Lothar Köster), the *performative* stands for movable, while the suffix *-(t)ics* stands for *semiotics* as if it were characteristic just for the semiotics as science. Partly in this line of misusage, *performatics* was recently introduced to alter performance studies (beginning with the translation of Schechner's *Performance Studies* by Tomasz Kubikowski [2006]). Performatics here covers both the performance and its theorization, without specifying a relation between them.

Maybe a short etymology of the term *performatics* will help. The term consists of the noun *performance* plus the suffix *-tics*. *Performance* comes from Anglo-French word *(parfornir→performen→) performer*, which consists of the Latin prefix *per-* plus the verb *fournir*, to furnish. In artistic sense it was in use from the seventeenth century. The suffix *-(t)ics* comes from Greek and is derived from *techne*, and is usually used to construct names of sciences, arts and techniques: mathematics, music, electronics …

Taking into consideration that the suffix is used both for sciences and arts, the term *performatics* potentially signifies both *the art of performing* and *the science about the art of performing*. When it addresses the field of research, the term is in fact conservative. In the Serbian (and eastern European) cultural and academic context, the predominant theoretical field in the performing arts is *theatrology*, which comes from German cultural tradition (*Theaterwissenschaft*). Its suffix *-logy* comes from Greek *logos* and directly indicates science as a secondary/meta discourse 'about' certain phenomenon.

In the local context, the most important shift toward legitimization of critical theoretical practices in this part of the humanities is rendered by the recent introduction of the concept of *studies*: theatre and performance studies (as a course at the University of Arts in Belgrade and an academic book *Introduction to Performance Studies* [Jović evič and Vujanović 2007]). It signifies the theoretical discourse whose imperative is not a neutral, positivist approach to the objects of research. The concept legitimizes a research that is not necessarily scientific but whose methodologies become the problems of the very research. In that sense, the term *performatics* appears here as equivalent of the term *performatology* – which, in spite of introducing new phenomenon, maintains the epistemological continuity with *theatrology*, i.e., with a science about performance as cultural and artistic practice.

That is why I would emphasize that affirmation of performatics as a new alternative to performance studies is actually a step backward, a step towards 'return to the order' in the humanities. Postmodernism should already be a lesson that widening does not always mean opening and often hides in itself a trap of conservativism, which hates one thing above all: a request for a clear and precise discursive articulation.

REFERENCES

Basu, Biman (2004) 'The Genuflected Body of the Masochist in Richard Wright', *Public Culture* 16(2): 239–63.

Jović evič, Aleksandra and Vujanović, Ana (2007) *Uvod u studije performansa*, Belgrade: Fabrika knjiga.

Schechner, Richard (2006 [2002]) *Performatyka: wstęp (Performance Studies: An Introduction*, 2nd edn.), trans. Tomasz Kubikowski, Ośrodek Grotowskiego, Wrocław.

**ANA VUJANOVIĆ**

# Performatics: Against Definition

How, I have been asked, would I define the word 'performatics'? But perhaps the more pressing question is, how would I even *pronounce* it? The model for this neologism is presumably 'informatics,' which according to the OED came into English via Russian—perhaps a point in favour of adopting the similarly Slavic *performatyka*. The stress on the first and third syllables of in*for*ma*tics* is consistent both with the stresses in the existing English word 'information', and with the existing English suffix 'atic'—as it appears in words such as dramatic, operatic, bureaucratic. These suffixes observe an English language convention known as 'antepenultimate primary stress,' and while people in Performance Studies pride themselves on their unconventionality, I suspect that mauling the language is not an objective of the current proposal. Let us assume, therefore, that we are to pronounce this new word as '*per*for*mat*ics' – taking in*for*ma*tics* as the model. And yet ... this emphasis sounds bizarre and counter-intuitive because it loses the standard stress on the second syllable of 'per*form*.' We could perhaps get away with this if the word is to be used primarily as an adjective and we allow the major stress to fall on a subsequent noun – as in 'bureaucratic nightmare' or, perhaps, 'performatic gesture' – but that would simply function to pull focus away from the very word being proposed. So that leaves us with the alternative of stressing the second and fourth syllables of the new word: per*for*mat*ics*. Yet this option seems equally unappealing because we lose our antepenultimate primary stress, and our familiar 'atic' suffix. We end up, instead, with something that sounds very much like 'performer ticks'— the very thing that avant-gardists since Gordon Craig have been trying to stamp out.

It's worth noting that the Polish word *Performatyka* does not suffer from the same problem, because its fifth syllable makes the '*tyk*' sound antepenultimate. So if push came to shove and this coining were being forced on us, I would opt to retain the Polish original rather than the awkward English de-translation. Thankfully, however, we are not yet living in a thought-policed state, so instead I propose to reject the proposition outright, with loud raspberries. The real reason I object to it, moreover, is less the issue of linguistics than of principle.

According to the call for responses to which this is a response, the term 'performatics' is being proposed on the grounds that it might

> have the potential to function universally and denote a field of study that might otherwise be difficult to capture by the Anglo-American definition of Performance Studies with its specific terms of reference (a term which is often lost in translation, diffused and confused even as it strives for global recognition).

First of all, why do we need a term 'to function universally'? If poststructuralist theory has taught us anything, it is surely that we ought to be suspicious of such universalizing moves, both because of the signification slippages to which they are inevitably prey and because of the imperialist power politics that are so often implicit in them. Who is it, exactly, that wants the 'field of study' currently denoted by 'the Anglo-American definition of Performance Studies' to achieve 'global recognition'? And why? And what kinds of avoidance are entailed in that phrase 'as it strives for global recognition'—as if Performance Studies were itself an active agent, rather than a banner held up by the scholars who promote it?

I have to say, moreover, that it is news to me that 'the Anglo-American definition of Performance Studies' has 'specific terms of reference.' Where can I find them please? I was under the impression that Performance Studies prided itself on being an 'anti-discipline,' all subversion and 'challenge' (viz. McKenzie's 'liminal norm') rather than a monolithic entity – PERFORMATICS! – seeking to encompass the globe. Of course, an anti-discipline might find such global recognition difficult to achieve, if nobody could agree on what it was, so maybe somebody somewhere has agreed on terms of reference and just not told me. Maybe the terms of reference are the ones in Richard Schechner's *Performance Studies: An Introduction*, now translated into Polish as *Performatyka*. In which case we are now talking about the specifically Schechnerian, NYU brand of Performance Studies as the global

DEFINITION . DEFINICJA

market leader. Certainly, the proposal that we adopt the term 'Performatics' strikes me first and foremost as a branding exercise, straight out of Naomi Klein's logo-centric nightmares. This gnomic but vaguely sexy sounding term could indeed be an international brand, if only we could only agree how to pronounce it. Better still, it helpfully denudes 'Performance Studies' of its decidedly unsexy associations with the concept of actually 'studying' something.

If we were to return, however, to our merely Anglo-American context and consider what it is that those of still studying actually study, we might well find that it is—for most—still that specifically aesthetic form of performance that might, elsewhere on the globe, still be conceived of under (translations of) the word 'theatre.' This assumes, of course (returning to the question of definition), that we adopt the inclusive, Cageian definition of theatre as that which occurs at the conjunction of visual and time-based art forms, rather than the wilfully narrowed-down definition which recognizes theatre only as the presentation of dramatic literature (not that there's anything wrong with drama).

To be sure, we have all had our horizons expanded by the excursions into other disciplinary areas opened up by the expansionary vision inherent in (Schechnerian) Performance Studies. But in the end, in my experience, most of us in this field are still preoccupied with the art of performance, and its socio-cultural ramifications. Bearing this in mind, we might well find that translation beyond English is much easier than we imagine if we forget performatics and once again allow the word 'theatre' its full breadth of reference. It is worth noting, moreover, that the word 'theatrics' – unlike 'performatics' – has no difficulty with its antepenultimate primary stress.

**STEPHEN BOTTOMS**

148

# Performance Research: On Performatics
Notes on Contributors

## ISSUE CO-EDITORS

**Richard Gough** is general editor of *Performance Research*, a Professor at Aberystwyth University, Wales, and Artistic Director for the Centre for Performance Research (CPR). He has curated and organized numerous conference and workshop events over the last 30 years as well directing and lecturing internationally.

**Grzegorz Ziółkowski** is a lecturer at the Adam Mickiewicz University in Poznań and the author of *Teatr Bezpośredni Petera Brooka* ['Peter Brook's Immediate Theatre'] (2000) and *Guślarz i eremita. Jerzy Grotowski: od wykładów rzymskich (1982) do paryskich (1997-1998)* ['Sorcerer and Hermit, Jerzy Grotowski: from Rome (1982) to Paris (1997-1998) lectures'] (2007). In 2004 Dr Ziółkowski was appointed Programme Director of the Grotowski Centre. Currently, with Jarosław Fret, he leads the Grotowski Institute.

## CONTRIBUTORS

**Paul Allain** is Professor of Theatre and Performance at the University of Kent, Canterbury. As well as working as a movement practitioner, he has published extensively on Polish theatre and actor training. He is currently researching the legacy of Grotowski's work through the AHRC-funded British Grotowski Project.

**Christopher Balme** holds the chair in theatre studies at the University of Munich. He has published widely on German theatre, intercultural theatre and theatre and other media. He is vice-president of the IFTR and was Senior Editor of *Theatre Research International*. Recent publications include *Decolonizing the Stage: Theatrical Syncretism and Postcolonial Drama* (Oxford 1999); his most recent books are *Pacific Performances: Theatricality and Cross-Cultural Encounter in the South Seas* (Palgrave Macmillan 2007) and *The Cambridge Introduction to Theatre Studies* (2008).

**Johannes Birringer** is an independent choreographer / media artist and artistic director of the Houston-based AlienNation Co. He founded the international Interaktionslabor in Germany (http://interaktionslabor.de) and also directs the DAP-Lab at Brunel University, London, where he is currently Professor of Performance Technologies. His latest book is *Performance, Technology and Science* (2008).

**Stephen Bottoms** is Professor of Drama and Theatre Studies at the University of Leeds. His books include *Playing Undergound: A Critical History of the 1960s Off-Off-Broadway Movement* (2004), *Small Acts of Repair: Performance, Ecology and Goat Island* (co-edited with Matthew Goulish, 2007) and *Performing Masculinity* (co-authored with Diane Torr, forthcoming 2009).

**Enzo Cozzi** is an actor and ritual theatre therapist with a BA in Sociology, an MA in Modern Drama Studies and a PhD in Performance Ecologies. He divides his time between Chile, China and the UK, where he teaches ritual and therapeutic intercultural performance at Royal Holloway, University of London.

**Maria M. Delgado** is Professor of Theatre and Screen Arts at Queen Mary, University of London and co-editor of *Contemporary Theatre Review*. She has published widely in the area of Spanish- and Catalan-language theatres. Her books include *Federico García Lorca* (Routledge 2008), *'Other' Spanish Theatres* (MUP 2003) and six co-edited volumes including two collaborations with Caridad Svich.

**Wojciech Dudzik** is an associate professor at the University of Warsaw, a member of the Committee on Art Studies of the Polish Academy of Science, member of the board at Disk, the Czech journal for the studies of dramatic art, editor of the anthology of contemporary polish theatrical thought *Świadomość teatru* ['Consciousness of Theatre'] (Warsaw 2007) and author of *Karnawały w kulturze* ['Carnivals in Culture'] (Warsaw 2005).

**Florian Feigl** is a performance artist. He has been creating and realizing performance art work since 1997. Besides his solo work he collaborates with various artists and artists' collectives (Wagner-Feigl-Forschung/Festspiele, prodesse&delectare). Feigl teaches performance art workshops and writes about performance art for German and international fanzines and art magazines.

**Karoline Gritzner** is a lecturer in Drama at Aberystwyth University. She is the co-editor (with David Ian Rabey) of *Theatre of Catastrophe: New Essays on Howard Barker* (Oberon Press 2006) and is currently completing a monograph entitled *Adorno and Contemporary British Theatre: The Drama of the Damaged Self in Beckett, Barker, Rudkin and Kane*.

**Peter Hulton** is founder and director of ARTS ARCHIVES (www.arts-archives.org), a Council of Europe-initiated digital moving resource for performance practice research. A documentary film-maker and writer, he has been Head of the Theatre Department and Principal of Dartington College of Arts and is now responsible for Exeter Digital Archives at Exeter University.

**Lynette Hunter** is the Professor of the History of Rhetoric and Performance, University of California, Davis. She researches, among other areas, new democratic rhetorics and collaborative performance structures and is developing the academic recognition of the values and knowledges of performance practice in the United States.

**Leszek Kolankiewicz** is a professor, culturologist and performance anthropologist. He is head of the Institute of Polish Culture at the University of Warsaw, Professor at the Aleksander Zelwerowicz's Theatre Academy in Warsaw and Chairman of the Committee of the Science of Culture of the Polish Academy of Sciences.

**Rudi Laermans** is professor in Sociology at the Catholic University of Leuven, Belgium, and guest teacher in Social Theory at P.A.R.T.S., Brussels. He has recently published several books in Dutch on cultural policy matters and arts participation and is currently doing research on contemporary dance.

**Małgorzata Leyko** is a professor at the University of Łódź where she is head of Department of Drama and Theatre. She is a historian of theatre and theatre theory. Her research interests include German theatre of the nineteenth and twentieth centuries, German and Polish theatrical connections and the history of Jewish theatre.

**Dariusz Kosiński** is the professor at the Drama Department of the Jagiellonian University in Krakow. He was a Polish theatre historian, specializing in the theory and history of nineteenth-century acting (two books published in 2003 and 2005, and the edition of sources in 2008) and in Polish drama of the same period (book of essays published in 2004). In 2007 he published the book *Polski teatr przemiany* ['Polish Theatre of Transformation']. He is also the co-editor of the texts of Juliusz Osterwa and the author of several popular books (mainly dictionaries) on theatre and drama.

**Tomasz Kubikowski** is a professor at the Aleksander Zelwerowicz Theatre Academy in Warsaw and deputy artistic director and dramaturge of the National Theatre, Warsaw. His books on performance theory include *Siedem bytów teatralnych* ['The Seven Theatrical Beings'] (1994) and *Reguła Nibelunga* ['The Principle of the Nibelung'] (2004). He has written the theatre play *Nauka o barwach* ['The Science of Colours'] (1998) as well as numerous reviews, essays and translations.

**Jon McKenzie** is Associate Professor of English at the University of Wisconsin, Madison, where he teaches courses in performance theory and new media. His writings include *Perform or Else: From Discipline to Performance* (2001), 'Democracy's Performance', 'Laurie Anderson for Dummies' and 'Global Feeling: (Almost) All You Need is Love'.

**Paul Rae** teaches on the Theatre Studies Programme at the National University of Singapore. He publishes on cosmopolitanism and contemporary Southeast Asian performance and was the co-editor, with Martin Welton, of *Performance Research 12.2*, 'On the Road'. His short book *Theatre and Human Rights* will be published by Palgrave Macmillan in 2009.

**Dobrochna Ratajczakowa** is Professor and head of the Drama and Theatre Department at the Adam Mickiewicz University in Poznań. She is a theatre, drama and literature specialist. In 2006 her essays were collected in two volumes and published as *W krysztale i w płomieniu* ['In the Crystal and the Flame']. Currently, she edits three theatre series: *Theatroteka*, *Nowoczesna myśl teatralna* ['Contemporary Theatre Thought'] and *Kolekcja Teatralna* ['Theatre Collection'].

**Alan Read** is Professor of Theatre in the Department of English at King's College, London, and director of the Centre for Theatre Research in Europe. He is the author of *Theatre and Everyday Life: An Ethics of Performance* and editor of *The Fact of Blackness: Frantz Fanon and Visual Representation* and *Architecturally Speaking: Practices of Art, Architecture and the Everyday*. He is a founding member of the journal *Performance Research* and was the guest editor of 'On Animals'. He is currently responsible for the five-year Arts and Humanities Research Board project 'Performance Architecture Location'. As part of this work, the international symposium 'Civic Centre: Reclaiming the Right to Performance' took place across London in April 2003.

**Freddie Rokem** teaches in the Department of Theatre Studies at Tel Aviv University, where he served as the Dean of the Yolanda and David Katz Faculty of the Arts (2002-6). His *Performing History: Theatrical Representations of the Past in Contemporary Theatre* (2000) received the ATHE Prize for best theatre-studies book in 2001. His forthcoming book is titled *Philosophers and Thespians*.

**Włodzimierz Staniewski** formally founded his theatre in 1977 under the name Centre for Theatre Practices 'Gardzienice'. Today this centre is world famous, and Staniewski's method of acting is known as 'the ecology of theatre', which was first formulated in 1977. Staniewski has toured his performances successfully all around the world. As a director and writer he runs masterclasses and gives lectures in most prestigious theatres and drama schools. His work and practice have been described in a number of books, including *Twentieth Century Actor Training* edited by Alison Hodge (2000) and *Gardzienice: Polish Theatre in Transition* by Paul Allain (1997). Together with Alison Hodge he has also published *Hidden Territories: The Theatre of Gardzienice* (2004). The latest work of Staniewski is Euripides' *Iphigenia at Aulis*.

**Caridad Svich** is an award-winning US Latina playwright and translator. She is alumna playwright of New Dramatists in New York City, founder of theatre alliance and press NoPassport, contributing editor of *TheatreForum* and associate editor of *Contemporary Theatre Review*. Her works are published by TCG, Manchester University Press, Smith and Kraus, Playscripts and others.

**Ana Vujanović** is a freelance worker (theoretician, lecturer, organizer, writer, dramaturge …) in the fields of contemporary performing arts and culture. Her PhD in Theatre studies is from the FDA in Belgrade. She is permanent collaborator of TkH platform for performing arts theory and practice <www.tkh-generator.net>.

**Daniel Watt** is a lecturer in English and Drama at Loughborough University. Dr Watt's research interests include fragmentary writing, ethics and literature and philosophical and literary influences on theatre and performance in the twentieth century.